THE

Sunday Brunch

COOKBOOK

Over 300 Modern Classics
to Share with Family and Friends

The Sunday Brunch Cookbook

Over 300 Modern American Classics to Share with Family and Friends

CIDER MILL PRESS

BOOK PUBLISHERS

KENNEBUNKPORT, MAINE

The Sunday Brunch Cookbook

13-Digit ISBN: 978-1-60433-837-9
10-Digit ISBN: 1-60433-837-7

This book may be ordered by mail from the publisher.
Please include $5.99 for postage and handling. Please support your local bookseller first!

Books published by Cider Mill Press Book Publishers are available at special discounts for bulk purchases in the United States by corporations, institutions, and other organizations. For more information, please contact the publisher.

Cider Mill Press Book Publishers
"Where good books are ready for press"
PO Box 454
12 Spring Street
Kennebunkport, Maine 04046
Visit us online!
www.cidermillpress.com

Typography: Archer, Hoefler Text, Garden Grown, Minion Pro
Image Credits: Pages 43, 55, 67, 73, 99, 106, 133, 153, 198, 210, 246, 254, 266, 278, 291, 308, 317, 326, 333, 350, 364, 371, and 389 courtesy of Derek Bissonnette. Pages 49, 57, 62, 66, 74, 80, 87, 88, 93, 166, 171, 188, 217, 231, 248, 252, 283, 339, 377, 383, 384, 395, 414, 419, 424, and 430 courtesy of Shane Hetherington. Page 90 courtesy of Appleseed Press Book Publishers. Pages 108, 170, and 274 courtesy of Amy Hunter. Page 202 courtesy of Rustic Bakery. Page 357 courtesy of OTTO Pizza. All other images are used under official license from Shutterstock.com.

Printed in China
2 3 4 5 6 7 8 9 0

Dedicated to the family cooks and chefs,
who are keeping Sunday traditions alive.

Sunday brunch is an

time with loved ones and savor

Sunday has always been a day to focus on the things you value. Whether it's family, religion, community, hobbies, or food, we all tend to make sure the first day of the week (and final day of the weekend) is grounded in something important.

Of late, a new ritual has taken hold on Sundays: brunch. An opportunity to catch up with

friends and family and unwind with a few drinks and delicious food, it has become something of a sanctuary in a world that moves increasingly fast. Effortlessly bridging the gap between breakfast and lunch (and increasingly dinner), brunch is able to accommodate myriad individual tastes, both for food and how the vitally important last day of the weekend should unfold.

While the variety and experience available in an ideal brunch is tough to beat, it is frequently a nightmare in practice. The number of people who have made it a staple of their Sunday routine ensures long waits and high prices at any decent restaurant, and, as legendary culinary figure Anthony Bourdain once pointed out, those restaurants may not necessarily be putting their best

opportunity to spend

the good things in this world.

foot forward after the whirlwind of the weekend.

But once you separate brunch from all of the complications and compromises that typically attend it, the revival available in the combination of good drinks, good food, and good people comes to the fore. With little more than a pot of coffee, a delicious cocktail, a few comforting classics, and an inventive dish or two, you can make each and every Sunday one to remember.

To do this, it's important to choose a balance of sweet and savory preparations that are tasty enough to be enjoyed at any time of day. Doing this allows a gathering to acquire a feel that is both relaxed and freewheeling, establishing a pace that is perfect for either the end of a long night or the beginning of a relaxed day.

Featuring menus tailored to every season and the holidays that frame our experiences of them, *The Sunday Brunch Cookbook* provides you with everything you need to establish your home as the hub of a brand-new Sunday tradition.

Kitchen Essentials

A cook could go crazy in a kitchen supply store. This checklist of kitchen essentials is by no means exhaustive, but a kitchen provisioned with these items should have no problem preparing any of the recipes included here.

Cookware

Cast-iron skillet
Dutch oven
Large nonstick frying pan
Small 2- to 3-quart saucepan with lid
Large 4-quart saucepan with lid
10- to 14-inch sauté pan with lid
Steamer basket

Bakeware

9- to 10-inch round cake pan
Cheesecake pan
Cooling racks
5 x 9–inch loaf pan
Muffin tin
9- to 10-inch pie plate
9 x 13–inch rectangular baking pan
8- to 9-inch square baking pan
Sheet pans

Measuring

Dry ingredient measuring cups
4-cup liquid measuring cup
Measuring spoons
Kitchen scale
Kitchen timer
Instant-read thermometer
Oven thermometer

Bowls and Containers

Nest of mixing bowls
Large colander
Strainers

Utensils

Bread knife
Chef's knife
Garlic press
Paring knife
Serrated carving knife
Vegetable peeler
Mandoline
Box grater
Microplane
Large wooden cutting board
Small plastic cutting board
Can opener
Corkscrew
Ladle
Locking metal tongs
Oven mitts
Potato masher
Rolling pin
Rubber spatulas
Slotted spoon
Whisks
Wooden spoons

Small Kitchen Appliances

Blender
Food processor
Hand mixer
Standing mixer
Slow cooker
Salad spinner
Toaster
Waffle iron

How to Care for Your Kitchen Tools

We invest a great deal in our kitchens. Cookware, knives, and the like do not come cheaply, and to keep these tools working well for the long haul, it's best to clean and maintain your kitchen tools after every use.

Common sense is key when cleaning your kitchen tools. Be sure to follow the manufacturer's instructions and, when in doubt, wash by hand. Most kitchen tools can be easily cleaned with just soap and water and dried with a clean cloth. When cleaning small appliances like a blender or food processor, take the pieces apart and clean them separately. Always make sure that any electrical appliances, such as slow cookers, are unplugged and that they have cooled before washing.

Pots and Pans

When using a nonstick pan, avoid metal utensils that can damage the nonstick finish. Instead, use wood, plastic, or silicone utensils.

Once your pots and pans have cooled after use, be sure to clean them in a timely manner. Avoid leaving them soiled or soaking them overnight, which can damage the finish and/or cause rust. While many pots and pans claim to be dishwasher-safe, handwashing and drying are better options if you want to extend the life of your cookware.

For both stainless steel and nonstick pans, never use abrasive cleaners or a scouring pad, which will scratch surfaces and ruin nonstick coatings. Instead, use a nylon net pad or sponge. Copper-bottom pots and pans should be cleaned with a copper cleaner after every use.

To avoid rusting or pitting, be sure your cookware is completely dry before storing, and avoid stacking your cookware if space allows for it.

Knives

First, make sure you use the right knife for the right job. Using a knife as intended will extend its life.

Knives are at their best and last longer when sharpened. Before each use, hone your blade by using the steel included with your knife set, and have your knives sharpened by a professional once or twice a year. Local sharpeners can be found online or at many local farmers markets, and the cost is inexpensive, particularly compared to the cost of a new, high-quality knife.

After you've used the knife, clean and dry it by hand. Never leave knives soaking, which can warp the wooden handle. Likewise, never wash knives in the dishwasher, as they can be damaged. Any rust can be removed with scouring powder and a gentle scrubbing.

Make sure your knives are completely dry before you store them, as this will keep them free from rust. Store your knives in a wooden knife block or sheathed in a drawer. These precautions will keep your knife from coming into contact with anything that can damage the blade.

Wooden Items

Never soak wooden items like cutting boards or wooden spoons, and never wash them in a dishwasher, as the heat will cause the wood to swell and crack. Instead, wash with mild dish detergent and hand-dry them immediately.

Keep in mind that wood is prone to bacteria growth, so wash immediately after use, and rub with a lemon before using to help fight the spread of bacteria.

Wooden cutting boards and spoons need to be oiled every few months to prevent them from drying and cracking. Use a cloth to coat your wooden items with mineral oil or walnut oil, allow the oil to soak in, and wipe away any excess oil after 30 minutes.

Plastic and Rubber Items

Most plastic and rubber cutting boards, spatulas, and measuring cups are generally dishwasher-safe, but some cheaper plastic utensils may melt or crack with excessive heat. Be cautious when using plastic in the dishwasher; handwashing and hand-drying your plastic and rubber items will ensure that they last as long as possible.

Coffeemakers

Coffeemakers can be cleaned using equal parts white vinegar and water. Fill the coffeemaker with the mixture, and run halfway through a cycle. Turn the machine off and let sit for 1 hour. Then turn the machine on and complete the cycle. Next, rinse the filter chamber and the pot to eliminate the vinegar odor, and run a final cycle with only fresh water. Repeat as necessary.

Cast-Iron Cookware

Seasoning a New Skillet

If you go shopping for a new cast-iron skillet, you'll come across Lodge pans—a company that has been making cast-iron skillets since the late 1800s. They brand themselves as "America's Original Cookware," but Lodge isn't resting on its laurels. Instead, it has recently developed a method to season its cookware so that it will last as it always has but with minimal (consistent) care. What Lodge does is coat the pan with vegetable oil and bake it in at very high heat, which is just what you need to do to an unseasoned cast-iron pan. With a new Lodge seasoned piece, you can begin cooking with it almost immediately.

But let's start at the beginning, with an unseasoned skillet. Here's the procedure to bring it into use:

Wash with hot, soapy water.

Rinse and dry thoroughly.

If there's any rust on the pan, sand it lightly with fine-grained sandpaper. Apply Coca-Cola to the rust spots and let it sit for 10 to 15 minutes. Wash again with soapy water, rinse, dry, and put the skillet on a burner over low heat to dry any excess moisture.

If there's no rust, after drying the cookware all over, apply a light layer of cooking oil (vegetable oil, NOT olive oil, butter, or margarine!) all over the pan with a paper towel, rubbing even the handle. The pan should have a light sheen to it.

Place the skillet upside down on the middle rack of the oven and preheat the oven to 400°F with the pan inside. Put a piece of foil or a baking dish on the lower rack to catch any oil that may drip. Let the pan cook in the oven for about 2 hours.

Turn the oven off and let the pan cool (upside down) in the oven.

When the pan is cool, take it out, wipe it down with a clean paper towel, and it's good to go.

If your pan has taken on a slightly brown color, you can repeat the process, which will further season the pan and darken its color, improving its appearance. This will also happen naturally over time.

Caring for Your Cast-Iron

Rule #1: Never wash your seasoned pan with soapy water.

Rule #2: Never put a cast-iron pan in the dishwasher.

Why? Soap breaks down the protective seasoning, and you have to season the pan all over again. Leaving any kind of water on the pan will lead to rusting, which will demand reseasoning from the beginning. It seems counterintuitive, especially when you're used to thinking "it's not clean unless it's been washed in (really) hot, soapy water," but this is actually a great thing about cast-iron.

After you've cooked in your skillet, clean it with hot water (no soap) and a plastic, rough-surfaced scrub brush. Dry the cookware completely (all over) after washing. Put a teaspoon of vegetable oil in the pan and, with a paper towel, rub it in all over the pan until it has a nice sheen.

Rule #3: Never use steel wool.

Cast-iron is a softer material than steel. Using an abrasive sponge on your cast-iron has the potential to scratch the surface enamel or otherwise strip your pan's seasoning.

If there's a mess that water and a brush cannot handle, you can create a scrubbing paste by adding coarse kosher salt to your hot water before using your scrub brush to loosen the food. Stubborn residues may also be loosened from your cast-iron by soaking very briefly in water, but do not leave your pan submerged in water. You can also simmer the mess over medium-low heat to aid in loosening up extreme instances of grime.

Never clean your pan by burning it in a fire. The rapid overheating of the metal can cause warps, cracks, red patchy scales, and/or brittleness that compromises the structure of your pan and can occasionally prevent it from being able to hold its protective seasoning.

Again, once free of leftovers, dry your cast-iron extremely well and rejuvenate the lovely sheen by rubbing in the vegetable oil, wiping excess off with a clean paper towel.

Rule #4: Store your cast-iron in a dry place.

Good air circulation and a moisture-free environment will ensure that your pan stays rust-free and clean until the next time you wish to use it. If you need to stack it with other pans in your pantry or cupboard, put paper towels between the cookware to prevent scratches or other damage. Dutch ovens should be stored with their lids off, so that no moisture is trapped within.

Storing cast-iron within your oven is also a popular option, so that it is nearby and ready for use whenever you're cooking. Just be sure to remove any pans before preheating your oven! Or you can leave it on your stovetop if you can't seem to cook a meal without it. An overhead rack is also a good option, but if you have multiple cast-iron skillets, make sure that your cookware rack is well secured and can handle the weight. Both of these options display your rustic, heirloom cookware proudly, and make a beautiful aesthetic statement for your kitchen.

Give It a Lot of Love

The best thing to do with your cast-iron skillet is use it. When you start using it for all the different things it can do (as evidenced by its numerous appearances in this book), you'll probably find that the skillet lives on your stovetop, waiting for its next assignment. The more you use it, the better it gets. Nothing will stick to its surface. You can go from the frying pan to the fire, as it were, starting a dish on the stove and finishing it in the oven. You can use your skillet over very high heat (and even put it in the campfire), and it'll always help you put your best foot forward.

In short, with regular use, the cast-iron skillet is like a fine wine, getting better and better with age.

Here's why: flavor. And, yes, the overall look of the meal served in cast-iron. There's something very elemental about it.

Slow Cookers

Slow cookers are inexpensive to operate; they use about as much electricity as a 60-watt bulb. They are also as easy to operate as flipping on a light switch. By using indirect heat, low temperatures, and extended cook times, they are able to preserve and enhance a dish's flavor.

You can purchase a slow cooker for as little as $20 at a discount store, while the top-of-the-line ones sell for more than $200. No matter how much you spend, they all function in the same simple way; what increases the cost is how many, or how few, bells and whistles a model comes with.

All slow cookers have low and high settings, and most also have a warm option. Some new machines have a programmable option that enables you to start cooking on high and automatically reduce the heat to low after a programmed amount of time.

Slow Cooker Tips

Slow cookers can be perplexing if you're not accustomed to using one. Here are some general tips to help you master a few common conundrums:

- Remember that cooking times are wide approximations —within hours rather than minutes! That's because the age or power of a slow cooker as well as the temperature of ingredients must be taken into account. Check the food at the conclusion of the stated cooking time, gauge if it needs more time, and, if so, how much. If carrots or cubes of potato are still rock-hard, for example, turn the heat to high if cooking on low, and realize that you're looking at another hour or so.

- Foods cook faster on the bottom of a slow cooker than at the top because there are more heat coils there, and they are totally immersed in the simmering liquid.

- Appliance manufacturers say that slow cookers can be left on either high or low unattended, but use your own judgment. If you're going to be out of the house all day, it's advisable to cook food on low. If, on the other hand, you're going to be gone for just a few hours, the food will be safe on high.

- Use whole versions of dried herbs such as thyme and rosemary rather than ground versions. Ground herbs tend to lose potency after many hours in a slow cooker.

- Don't add dairy products until the end of the cooking time. They can curdle if cooked for too long.

- Season the dishes with pepper or crushed red pepper flakes at the end of cooking time, because these ingredients can become harsh after spending considerable time in the pot.

If you want a sauce to have a more intense flavor, you can reduce the liquid in two ways. If cooking on low, raise the heat to high, and remove the lid for the last hour of cooking. You can also remove the liquid with a bulb baster or strain the liquid from the solids and reduce it in a saucepan on the stove.

Slow Cooker Cautions

Slow cookers are benign, but they are electrical appliances with all the concomitant hazards of any machine plugged into a live wire. Be careful that the cord is not frayed in any way and plug the slow cooker into an outlet that is not near the sink. Here are some tips on how to handle them:

- Never leave a slow cooker plugged in when not in use. It's too easy to accidentally turn it on and not notice until the crockery insert cracks from becoming overheated with nothing in it.

- Conversely, do not preheat the empty insert while you're preparing the food because the insert could crack when you add the cold food.

- Never submerge the metal casing in water or fill it with water. While the inside of the casing does occasionally get dirty, you can clean it quite well with an abrasive cleaner and wipe it with a damp cloth or paper towel. While it's not aesthetically pleasing to see dirty metal, do remember that food never touches it, so if there are a few drips here and there it's not really important.

- Always remember that the insert is fragile, so don't drop it. Also, don't put a hot insert on a cold surface; that could cause it to break. The reverse is also true. While you can use the insert as a casserole in a conventional oven (assuming the lid is glass and not plastic), it cannot be put into a preheated oven if chilled.

- Resist the temptation to look and stir. Every time you take the lid off the slow cooker you need to add 10 minutes of cooking time if cooking on high and 20 minutes if cooking on low to compensate for the heat that was lost.

- Don't add more liquid to a slow cooker recipe than what is specified in the recipe. Even if the food is not submerged in liquid when you start, meats and vegetables give off liquid as they cook; in the slow cooker, that additional liquid does not evaporate.

- Modern slow cookers run slightly hotter than those made 30 years ago; the low setting on a slow cooker is about 200°F while the high setting is close to 300°F. If you have a vintage appliance, it's a good idea to test it to make sure it still has the power to heat food sufficiently. Leave 2 quarts water at room temperature overnight, and then pour the water into the slow cooker in the morning. Heat it on low for 8 hours. If the temperature is not at least 185°F, any food you cook in this slow cooker might not pass through the danger zone rapidly enough.

High-Altitude Adjustment

Rules for slow cooking, along with all other modes of cooking, change when the slow cooker is more than 3,000 feet above sea level. At high altitudes the air is thinner, so water boils at a lower temperature and comes to a boil more quickly. The rule is to always cook on high when above 3,000 feet; use the low setting to keep dishes warm. Other compensations are to reduce the liquid in a recipe by a few tablespoons, and add about 5% to 10% more cooking time. The liquid may be bubbling, but it's not 212°F for a little bit longer.

The Best Kitchen Secrets

While most of us like tinkering in the kitchen, not all of us have the skill set of a professional chef. If you find yourself looking through these recipes and asking, "What does this mean?" here's some basic terminology and techniques that will help you navigate these menus with a minimum of difficulty.

Whisking: Used to combine ingredients, it's best to put your mixing bowl at an angle and utilize a side-to-side motion with your wrist, as opposed to stirring or beating (see "Beating Eggs" and "Beating Egg Whites" below).

Folding: Combines ingredients without removing air from the mixture. Use a rubber spatula, add the lighter mixture (eggs, etc.) to the heavier mixture (e.g., chocolate), run the spatula along the side of the bowl, and "fold" the mixture on top of itself.

Separating an Egg: Yes, it seems basic, but some amateur chefs are uncertain how to get just an egg white or just a yolk. If that's you, get a clean bowl and crack an egg in half over it. Separate the two halves of shell and pass the yolk back and forth between the two halves, allowing the egg white to drip into the bowl below. Eventually all the white will be in the bowl, and the yolk will be in one of the pieces of shell.

Beating Eggs: Using a fork or whisk, first break the yolks, then combine the yolks and the white by mixing in a rapid, circular motion.

Beating Egg Whites: Use fresh eggs at room temperature, and make sure that your bowl is totally clean. When using a hand mixer, it's best to start on a slow setting and increase the speed, taking care not to overbeat, as overbeaten eggs will liquefy. When you have removed the beaters, "soft peaks" will curl down, and "stiff peaks" will stand straight. Use beaten egg whites right away.

Tempering Eggs: This is adding a hot mixture to room-temperature eggs, or vice versa. While whisking, slowly pour the one mixture into the other, gradually bringing the eggs up to temperature without overcooking and creating scrambled eggs.

Creaming Butter and Sugar: Use butter that's been softened; butter that's too firm won't incorporate the sugar as well and the mixture will be lumpy. Beat the butter and sugar together until the mixture is fluffy with peaks.

Clarifying Butter: Butter is clarified by removing the water and milk fats, leaving only the butterfat that stands up to high temperatures. To make clarified butter, melt and then simmer unsalted butter in a saucepan. The milk fat will gather on top. Remove the butter from the heat and skim off the milk fats. Then pour through a cheesecloth to remove any remaining or browned milk fats.

Whipping Cream: A fairly easy process; simply add sugar and flavoring to heavy cream and whisk until there are stiff peaks. However, don't overbeat or you'll end up with something that tastes like butter.

Proofing Yeast: Proofing helps ensure you'll get the rise you want out of your baked goods. Proof your yeast by adding it to the water called for in the recipe, plus a pinch of sugar. Stir gently and let stand for 10 minutes. The yeast will react with the sugar, and the resulting foam is "proof" that the yeast is alive.

Crimping a Piecrust: Crimping creates a defined and decorative edge for your piecrust. Place one hand on the inside edge of your crust, and the other on the outside of your pie plate. Working your way around the pie plate, carefully press the edge of the dough together, creating a scalloped pattern, about an inch apart.

Zesting Citrus: Zest is finely grated citrus peel used to flavor. Using a microplane, gently grate the exterior peel of the fruit, but only as far as the pith (the bitter, white membrane between the peel and the pulp). Zest from end to end and rotate as necessary.

Dicing an Onion: Here's a helpful hint to dice an onion easily. After removing the skin, cut your onion in half lengthwise (from "pole to pole"). Lay the onion on its side, and cut off the end where the stalk has grown, so the nub end still holds the onion layers together. Next, cut thin layers lengthwise with your knife parallel to the cutting board, stopping just before the nub. Finally, use your hand to hold the onion steady, and slice across the onion to dice.

Mincing Garlic: Similar to dicing an onion (above), thinly cut a peeled garlic clove lengthwise. Then turn and cut crosswise.

Grating Ginger: Ginger is easiest to work with when frozen, as it is easier to peel. A microplane works well if you don't have a ginger grater.

Pitting an Avocado: Cut the avocado in half lengthwise, carefully rotating the blade around the large pit. Use your hands to slowly twist the two halves apart. Finally, use a chef's knife and carefully slap the blade into the avocado pit. Twist the knife to pull the pit out of the avocado.

Cutting a Mango: Mango is difficult to work with because it has a long, thin seed in the middle. To overcome this difficulty, hold the mango and envision a centerline. Cut about a ¼ inch on either side of this centerline to avoid the seed in the center.

Pumpkin Puree: While you can buy pumpkin puree at your grocery store, it's easy to make at home. Just cut a sugar pumpkin in half and remove the seeds and pulp. Place the pumpkin halves facedown on a baking sheet and roast for an hour at 325°F. Scoop the pumpkin meat from the shell and puree in a food processor.

Tomato Concasse: A number of recipes call for you to remove the skin and seeds from a tomato, as they can be bitter. To do this easily, boil enough water for a tomato to be submerged and add a pinch of salt. Prepare an ice bath and score the top of the tomato with a paring knife. Place the tomato in the boiling water for 30 seconds, carefully remove it, and place it in the ice bath. Once the tomato is cool, remove from ice bath and peel with the paring knife. Cut into quarters and remove the seeds.

Sautéing: Frying your ingredient with a small amount of butter or fat in a shallow pan over high heat. Sauté is French for "jump," and the trick is to keep the food moving so it doesn't stick to the pan and burn.

Basting: Cooking meat in its own juices to add flavor and moisture. Basting in these recipes refers to capturing the meat's juices from the pan and pouring it over the meat to keep it moist. This can be done with a baster or a large spoon.

Deveining Shrimp: Once you've peeled your shrimp, it's best to remove the dark, unsightly digestive tract on their back. Simply use a paring knife and make a shallow cut down the length of the shrimp. Use the tip of your knife to scrape out the vein. With practice, you will be able to remove the vein as one continuous piece.

Cleaning and Filleting Fish: It's certainly easier to buy your fish cleaned and filleted, but it's not difficult to do at home. First, remove the head just behind the gills, then cut off the tail at its most narrow part. Next make a horizontal cut along the body, running the blade along the ridge of the backbone, and separate the meat from the ribs. This may require a number of steady, small cuts. Once one side is done, repeat the process on the other side. Now remove the smaller pin bones with tweezers. Pin bones are smaller, delicate bones, some just slightly thicker than a hair. If needed, turn the fillet over and remove the skin. This can be done with a knife, and sometimes simply by pulling the skin off carefully by hand.

How to Cook Eggs

If you're going to be regularly hosting brunch, you're going to want to get your egg-making game in order. Not every menu features them, but a number feature preparations that fried, poached, scrambled, hard-boiled, or soft-boiled eggs will provide a perfect complement to.

Just remember that it's best to bring your eggs to room temperature before cooking, as this helps maintain even heating of the yolk. And be sure to wash your eggs before cooking, particularly if they've come fresh from the farm.

Frying Eggs

Once you get this method down, you'll never overcook (or undercook) an egg again.

1. Heat 2 teaspoons of butter in a nonstick skillet over medium-high heat.

2. When the butter is melted, slip the eggs into the pan one at a time and immediately reduce heat to low.

3. Cook until the whites are set and the yolks begin to thicken. Carefully flip the eggs over and cook to desired texture. Season with salt and pepper before serving.

Scrambling Eggs

The lighter and fluffier your scrambled eggs are, the better. Feel free to add herbs in addition to salt and pepper. But don't overcook them or they'll get hard and rubbery.

1. Beat eggs with a splash of milk and a dash of salt and pepper. Milk will help make the eggs fluffier, but too much will make the eggs watery.

2. Melt a teaspoon of butter in a nonstick pan over medium heat and pour in the egg mixture.

3. As the eggs begin to set, use a spatula to pull the eggs away from the side of the pan, lifting and folding the eggs as they continue to thicken. Reduce the heat as the eggs near completion to prevent any burning. Cook until the eggs are fluffy and all the liquid has evaporated.

Poaching Eggs

While poaching an egg seems difficult, it's quite simple if you make a point to use fresh eggs.

1. Bring a saucepan of water to a boil. Once the water is boiling, reduce to a simmer and add a splash of white vinegar to aid in thickening the egg white.

2. Crack an egg into a small bowl or measuring cup. Gently place the egg in the water and cook for about 4 minutes, or until the whites have solidified. Slowly stir the water with a spoon, creating a small whirlpool that will keep the egg contained.

3. Use a slotted spoon to remove the egg from the water and dry quickly on a folded paper towel. Season with salt and pepper and serve immediately.

Hard-Boiling Eggs

Follow this method to eliminate any chance of overcooking an egg, which will result in a tough, greenish yolk.

1. Place eggs in a saucepan in a single layer. Cover by 1 inch with cold water and bring to a boil over high heat.

2. Remove the saucepan from heat, cover, and let stand for 12 minutes (slightly less if using smaller eggs and slightly more if using extra large eggs or cooking at high altitudes).

3. Drain the saucepan and run cold water over the eggs. Any uneaten eggs will keep in the refrigerator for 1 week.

Soft-Boiling Eggs

Soft-boiling eggs requires a bit more finesse than hard-boiling, but it's still relatively simple.

1. Bring a saucepan of water to boil and then reduce to a simmer.

2. Carefully place your eggs in the saucepan, one at a time. Cook no more than four eggs at once.

3. Boil for 5 minutes (or slightly longer for a less runny yolk).

4. Use a slotted spoon to remove the egg and run under cold water for 30 seconds. Use a sharp knife to cut the top off and serve immediately in an egg cup.

Essential Recipes

CHICKEN STOCK

Makes 6 Quarts   Active Time: 20 Minutes   Total Time: 5 Hours and 20 Minutes

When cooking stocks, the more time, the merrier. Use your palate to judge what the stock needs, and if you're unsure whether it's ready, it's probably not.

10 pounds chicken carcasses and/or stewing chicken pieces

½ cup vegetable oil

1 leek, trimmed and carefully washed, cut into 1-inch pieces

1 large yellow onion, unpeeled, root cleaned, cut into 1-inch pieces

2 large carrots, peeled and cut into 1-inch pieces

1 celery stalk with leaves, cut into 1-inch pieces

10 quarts water

1 teaspoon salt

8 sprigs of parsley

5 sprigs of thyme

2 bay leaves

1 teaspoon peppercorns

1. Preheat oven to 350°F. Lay the chicken carcasses and/or stewing chicken pieces on a flat baking tray, place in oven, and cook for 30 to 45 minutes until they are golden brown. Remove and set aside.

2. Meanwhile, in a large stockpot, add the vegetable oil and warm over low heat. Add the vegetables and cook until the moisture has evaporated. This allows the flavor of the vegetables to become concentrated.

3. Add the water and the salt to the stockpot. Add the chicken carcasses and/or stewing pieces and the aromatics to the stockpot, raise heat to high, and bring to a boil.

4. Reduce heat so that the stock simmers and cook for a minimum of 2 hours. Skim fat and impurities from the top as the stock cooks. As for when to stop cooking the stock, let the flavor be your guide. A stock will typically be ready after cooking for 4 to 5 hours.

5. When the stock is finished cooking, strain through a fine sieve or cheesecloth. Place stock in refrigerator to chill. Once cool, skim the fat layer from the top and discard. Use immediately, refrigerate, or freeze.

BEEF, LAMB, OR VEAL STOCK

Makes 6 Quarts   Active Time: 20 Minutes   Total Time: 5 Hours and 20 Minutes

Veal bones will give your stock a smoother taste and better sheen than beef. That said, beef bones are much cheaper and more accessible.

10 pounds veal, beef, or lamb bones

½ cup vegetable oil

1 leek, trimmed, and carefully washed, cut into 1-inch pieces

1 large yellow onion, unpeeled, root cleaned, cut into 1-inch pieces

2 large carrots, peeled and cut into 1-inch pieces

1 celery stalk with leaves, cut into 1-inch pieces

10 quarts water

1 teaspoon salt

8 sprigs of parsley

5 sprigs of thyme

2 bay leaves

1 teaspoon peppercorns

1 cup tomato paste

1. Preheat oven to 350°F. Lay the bones on a baking tray, place in oven, and cook for 30 to 45 minutes, until they are golden brown. Remove and set aside.

2. Meanwhile, in a large stockpot, add the vegetable oil and warm over low heat. Add the vegetables and cook until the moisture has evaporated. This allows the flavor of the vegetables to become concentrated.

3. Add the water, salt, bones, aromatics, and tomato paste to the stockpot, raise heat to high, and bring to a boil.

4. Reduce heat so that the stock simmers and cook for a minimum of 2 hours. Skim fat and impurities from the top as the stock cooks. As for when to stop cooking the stock, let the flavor be your guide.

5. When the stock is finished cooking, strain through a fine sieve or cheesecloth. Place stock in refrigerator to chill. Once cool, skim the fat layer from the top and discard. Use immediately, refrigerate, or freeze.

Tips:

- *If you're going to use lamb bones, use half lamb and half veal or beef bones. The strong flavor of the lamb bones can easily overwhelm a soup if you are not careful.*

- *Stocks will keep in the freezer for up to six months.*

- *These are large recipes, which can easily be reduced to half or one-quarter the amount. However, as the same amount of time is required, we always recommend making a larger quantity and saving some for the future.*

VEGETABLE STOCK

Makes 6 Cups   Active Time: 20 Minutes   Total Time: 2 Hours and 20 Minutes

This stock can be used to replace the meat stock in a majority of the recipes in this book, and it's a great way to make use of your vegetable trimmings. Just avoid starchy vegetables such as potatoes, as they will make the stock cloudy.

2 tablespoons vegetable oil

2 large leeks, trimmed and carefully washed

2 large carrots, peeled and sliced

2 celery stalks, sliced

2 large onions, sliced

3 garlic cloves, unpeeled but smashed

2 sprigs of parsley

2 sprigs of thyme

1 bay leaf

8 cups water

½ teaspoon black peppercorns

Salt, to taste

1. In a large stockpot, add the vegetable oil and the vegetables and cook over low heat until the moisture has evaporated. This will allow the flavor of the vegetables to become concentrated.

2. Add the aromatics, water, and salt. Raise heat to high and bring to a boil. Reduce heat so that the soup simmers and cook for 2 hours. Skim impurities from the top as the stock cooks.

3. When the stock is finished cooking, strain through a fine sieve or cheesecloth. Place stock in refrigerator to chill. Once cool, skim the fat layer from the top and discard. Use immediately, refrigerate, or freeze.

BAKED CRUST

Makes 1 12-Inch Crust   Active Time: 20 Minutes
Total Time: 2 Hours

This simple baked crust is fast, easy to put together, and will work for a number of the preparations in this cookbook.

1¼ cups flour, plus more for dusting

¼ teaspoon salt

½ cup (1 stick) unsalted butter, chilled and cut into small pieces, plus 1 tablespoon

4 to 6 tablespoons cold water

Rice, for baking

1. In a large bowl, combine the flour and salt. Add the ½ cup butter and work it into the flour mixture with a pastry blender or 2 knives until the dough resembles coarse meal. Add 3 tablespoons cold water to start, and use your hands or a fork to work the dough, adding tablespoons of water as needed until the dough just holds together when you gather it in your hands.

2. Working on a lightly floured surface, gather the dough and form it into a solid ball or disk. Wrap tightly in plastic wrap and refrigerate for about 1 hour. The dough can be refrigerated for a couple of days or frozen for a couple of months.

3. Preheat the oven to 450°F. Take the dough out of the refrigerator and allow it to warm up a bit. Put the dough on a lightly floured surface and use a lightly dusted rolling pin to flatten the dough into a circle, working both sides to extend it to a 10- to 12-inch round.

4. Grease a cast-iron skillet or a pie plate with the remaining butter. Carefully position the crust so it is evenly distributed, pressing it in lightly. Crimp the edges and use a fork to prick the crust on the bottom and sides. Line with foil or parchment paper, and fill with uncooked rice as a weight.

5. Bake for 10 to 12 minutes until lightly browned. Transfer to a wire rack to cool before filling.

FLAKY PASTRY CRUST

Makes 2 9- to 12-Inch Crusts   Active Time: 30 Minutes   Total Time: 2 to 3 Hours

While it's tempting to take a shortcut and use a mix or even a pre-made crust, there truly is nothing as delicious as a crust made from scratch.

2½ cups flour, plus more
for dusting

1 teaspoon salt

¼ cup vegetable shortening

½ cup (1 stick) butter, chilled
and cut into small pieces,
plus 1 tablespoon

6 to 8 tablespoons cold water

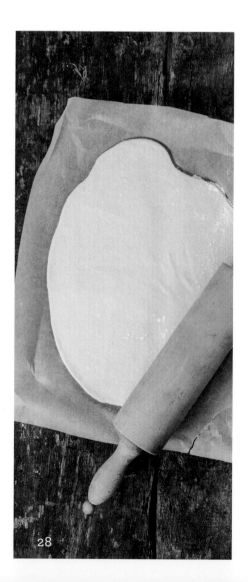

1. In a large bowl, combine the flour and salt. Add the shortening and use a fork to work it in until the mixture forms a very coarse meal. Add the ½ cup butter and work it into the dough with a pastry blender or your fingers until the dough is just holding together. Don't overwork the dough; there can still be chunks of butter in it. Add 4 tablespoons cold water to start and use your hands or a fork to work the dough, adding tablespoons of water as necessary, until the dough just holds together when you gather it in your hands.

2. Working on a lightly floured surface, gather the dough and form it into a solid ball. Separate into equal parts and form into disks. Wrap each tightly in plastic wrap and refrigerate for 30 to 60 minutes. The dough can be refrigerated for a couple of days or frozen for a couple of months.

3. Take the dough out of the refrigerator to allow it to warm up a bit. Put the dough on a lightly floured surface and use a lightly dusted rolling pin to flatten the dough into 2 circles, working both sides to extend each into a 9- to 12-inch round.

4. Grease a pie plate or a cast-iron skillet with the remaining butter. Carefully position the crust so it is evenly distributed, gently pressing it in and allowing the dough to extend over the side. If making a single-crust pie, crimp the edges as desired. If filling and adding a top crust, leave the extra dough so it can be crimped with the top crust. Fill the pie as directed, and then roll out the top crust so it is just bigger than the top of the skillet or pie plate. For an extra flaky pastry crust, refrigerate the assembled pie for about 30 minutes before baking.

Tip: If using unsalted butter, increase salt to 1¼ teaspoons.

GRAHAM CRACKER CRUST

Makes 1 10-Inch Crust   Active Time: 20 Minutes   Total Time: 45 Minutes

We recommend crushing actual graham crackers to make this crust, but you can also purchase graham cracker crumbs in the baked goods aisle of your grocery store.

1½ cups graham cracker crumbs

2 tablespoons sugar

1 tablespoon maple syrup

5 tablespoons unsalted butter, melted, plus 1 tablespoon

Rice, for baking

1. Preheat the oven to 375°F. In a large bowl, add the graham cracker crumbs and sugar and stir to combine. Add maple syrup and melted butter and stir to thoroughly combine.

2. Liberally grease a cast-iron skillet or pie plate with the remaining butter. Pour the dough into the chosen container and lightly press into shape. Line with aluminum foil and fill with uncooked rice. Bake for 10 to 12 minutes until golden.

3. Allow to cool on a wire rack before filling.

GLUTEN-FREE CRUST

Makes 1 10-Inch Crust   Active Time: 20 Minutes   Total Time: 1½ Hours

Approximating the flakiness of a homemade piecrust is the goal with a gluten-free crust.
This comes very close, and it's delicious, too.

1¼ cups gluten-free multipurpose flour blend

1 tablespoon sugar

½ teaspoon xanthan gum

½ teaspoon salt

6 tablespoons unsalted butter, chilled and cut into small pieces, plus 1 tablespoon

1 large egg

2 teaspoons fresh lemon juice

1 to 2 tablespoons cold water

1. In a large bowl, combine the flour blend, sugar, xanthan gum, and salt. Add the 6 tablespoons of butter and work it into the flour mixture with a pastry blender or your fingers to form a coarse meal that includes whole bits of butter.

2. In a small bowl, whisk the egg and lemon juice together briskly until the mixture is very foamy. Add to the dry ingredients and stir until the dough holds together. If dough isn't quite holding, add cold water in 1-tablespoon increments until it does. Shape into a disk, wrap tightly in plastic wrap, and refrigerate for 30 minutes or overnight.

3. When ready to make the pie, take dough out of the refrigerator and allow to rest at room temperature for about 10 minutes before rolling. Working on a flat surface dusted with gluten-free flour, roll the dough into a 10-inch disk.

4. Grease a cast-iron skillet or a pie plate with the remaining butter. Carefully position the crust so it is evenly distributed, gently pressing it in and crimping the edges. Fill and bake as directed.

BASIL PESTO

Makes 1 Cup   Active Time: 25 Minutes   Total Time: 25 Minutes

This simple pesto is always great to have on hand, as it will give you options in a number of preparations.

¼ cup walnuts

2 large garlic cloves, peeled

Sea salt and freshly ground black pepper, to taste

2 cups basil leaves, tightly packed

½ cup extra virgin olive oil

¼ cup Parmesan cheese, grated

¼ cup Pecorino Sardo, grated

1. Heat a small skillet over low heat for a minute. Add the walnuts and cook while stirring until they begin to give off a toasty fragrance, about 2 to 3 minutes. Transfer to a plate and let cool completely.

2. Place the garlic, salt, and walnuts in a food processor or blender and pulse until the mixture is a coarse meal. Add the basil and pulse until finely minced. Transfer the basil mixture to a medium bowl and add the oil in a thin stream as you quickly whisk it in. Do not mix oils in your food processor or blender, as it makes them bitter.

3. Add the cheeses and thoroughly mix with a spoon. Use or store in an airtight container in the refrigerator for up to 4 days or the freezer for up to 3 months.

SIMPLE SYRUP

Makes 1½ Cups   Active Time: 5 Minutes   Total Time: 40 Minutes

---

Being able to make this in your sleep is an absolute must if you're going to be regularly whipping up drinks for guests.

1 cup water

1 cup sugar

1. Combine the water and sugar in a small saucepan and cook, while stirring, over medium heat until sugar is dissolved. Remove from heat and allow syrup to cool slightly.

2. Transfer to a jar and refrigerate for at least 30 minutes before using. The syrup will keep in the refrigerator, tightly sealed, for up to 2 weeks.

SACHET D'EPICES

Makes 1 Sachet   Active Time: 1 Minute   Total Time: 1 Minute

---

This handy bundle will save you a bunch of time and is a great way to add flavor to soups and stews.

3 parsley stems

¼ teaspoon thyme

½ bay leaf

¼ teaspoon cracked black peppercorns

½ garlic clove, minced

1. Place all ingredients in the middle of a 4-inch square of cheesecloth and lift each corner to create a purse.

2. Tie one side of a 12-inch piece of kitchen twine around the corners and make a knot. Tie the other side of the twine to the handle of your pot and then toss the sachet in.

WHIPPED HERB BUTTER

Makes ½ Cup   Active Time: 10 Minutes
Total Time: 10 Minutes

If you're running a little bit behind in your preparations, toss a dish of this delicious butter out with some warm bread. No one will even notice your absence.

1 tablespoon extra virgin olive oil

1 garlic clove, minced

1 tablespoon thyme, chopped

1 tablespoon basil, chopped

½ cup (1 stick) butter

1. Place the olive oil, garlic, thyme, and basil in a medium bowl and stir to combine.

2. Using the whisk attachment on your hand mixer, place the butter in the work bowl and whip at medium speed until it softens and lightens in color, about 5 minutes.

3. Add the herb oil to the butter and beat for 1 minute, or until combined. Remove butter and place in the refrigerator until ready to serve.

Menus

Winter

There are times when the bitter winds, lack of plant life, and rapidly disappearing daylight begin to wear a person down. It can seem like there's little to look forward to, which puts everyone on edge.

Winter is a season where the need for warmth, comfort, and fun is at its highest. When the need for all those things arises, the best antidote is food, drink, friends, and family, a combination that brunch just happens to be the perfect package for. Hosting a weekly brunch will wash away the blues everyone's built up over the seemingly endless stretch of bleak days, and set their sights on the good the world contains.

Yes, it's cold outside and everything's a little tougher. But we believe that if you can turn that inclination to stay inside into an opportunity to gather your loved ones, whatever's outside will be a world away from your mind.

New Year's Day

You want to make sure you put your best foot forward when you and your loved ones turn toward the New Year, as striking the perfect note can make all the difference in how someone feels when confronting this new beginning. The best way to do this is a menu that strikes a balance between comfort and elegance, and light and rich offerings. Such an array gives people an opportunity to feel inspired and hopeful, and leaves space for those who just want to take it easy after a trying holiday season. The Carolina Crab Cakes with Remoulade Sauce, Swedish Meatballs, and Rocky Mountain Chili do just that, freighting your table with a variety of flavorful foods and ensuring that everyone gives whatever resolutions they've made a few more days to take hold.

French 75

Prosecco Soup

Virgin Mary

Carolina Crab Cakes
with Remoulade Sauce

Swedish Meatballs

Rocky Mountain Chili

Pear Clafoutis

Cheesecake

FRENCH 75

1 sugar cube

Juice of 1 lemon wedge

1 part gin

2 parts Champagne

1 lemon twist, for garnish

1 cherry, skewered, for garnish

1. Add a sugar cube to a champagne flute and then add the lemon juice.

2. Pour in the gin and top with Champagne.

3. Garnish with the lemon twist and place the skewered cherry over the mouth of the champagne flute.

PROSECCO SOUP

4 parts dry Prosecco

1 part Sprite

1 part triple sec

Splash of Simple Syrup (see page 32)

1. Pour all of the ingredients into a punch bowl filled with ice.

2. Stir until thoroughly combined and then ladle into champagne flutes.

VIRGIN MARY

1 cup tomato juice

Dash of Worcestershire sauce

Dash of lemon juice

Dash of black pepper

Garnish with anything your heart desires

1. Add tomato juice to a pint glass filled with ice.

2. Add the Worcestershire sauce, lemon juice, and black pepper and stir thoroughly.

3. Garnish with anything your heart desires.

Variation:

This is just the base for a successful Virgin Mary. If you'd like to add other common ingredients (like horseradish or salt, for example) that you happen to have lying around, you can easily build off this recipe.

CAROLINA CRAB CAKES
WITH REMOULADE SAUCE

Makes 6 Cakes   Active Time: 1 Hour   Total Time: 1½ Hours

For the Remoulade Sauce

1 cup mayonnaise

2 tablespoons mustard (preferably Creole, otherwise Dijon will do)

1 teaspoon Cajun seasoning

1 tablespoon sweet paprika

1 tablespoon pickle juice or fresh lemon juice

1 tablespoon hot sauce, plus more to taste

1½ teaspoons garlic, minced

2 tablespoons fresh parsley, finely chopped (optional)

Salt and freshly ground black pepper, to taste

For the Crab Cakes

1 pound lump crab meat (preferably blue crab)

¼ cup onion, minced

½ cup bread crumbs

1 teaspoon Worcestershire sauce

1 teaspoon Old Bay seasoning

2 tablespoons hot sauce

1 teaspoon dried parsley flakes

1 tablespoon mayonnaise, plus more as needed

1 tablespoon milk

1 large egg, lightly beaten

Salt and freshly ground black pepper, to taste

¼ cup oil (preferably peanut, but olive is fine)

Lemon wedges, for serving

1. In a medium bowl, combine the ingredients for the Remoulade Sauce and stir until thoroughly combined. Cover and chill in the refrigerator until ready to serve.

2. In a large bowl, combine the crab meat, onion, bread crumbs, Worcestershire sauce, Old Bay seasoning, hot sauce, parsley flakes, and mayonnaise. Whisk the milk into the egg and then add this mixture to the crab mixture, stirring gently until thoroughly combined. Season with salt and pepper and add additional mayonnaise if the mixture seems dry.

3. Heat a cast-iron skillet over medium-high heat. Add the oil and once it is glistening, add 3 or 4 heaping spoonfuls of the crab mixture, pressing down on the tops of each to form a patty. Cook on each side for about 3 minutes, or until they are brown. Try to turn the cakes over just once. If you're worried about them not getting cooked through, put a lid on the skillet for a minute or so after they've browned on each side. Transfer the cakes to a plate and cover with foil to keep them warm while you cook the next batch.

4. Serve with lemon wedges and the Remoulade Sauce.

SWEDISH MEATBALLS

Makes 4 to 6 Servings   Active Time: 20 Minutes   Total Time: 45 Minutes

Vegetable oil spray

4 tablespoons unsalted butter

1 small onion, chopped

¼ cup milk

1 large egg

Yolk from 1 large egg

3 slices of fresh white bread

¼ teaspoon ground allspice

¼ teaspoon nutmeg, grated

Pinch of ground ginger

¾ pound ground pork

½ pound ground beef

Salt and freshly ground black pepper, to taste

¼ cup all-purpose flour

2½ cups Beef Stock (see page 25)

½ cup heavy cream

1. Preheat the broiler, line a rimmed baking sheet with heavy-duty aluminum foil, and spray the foil with vegetable oil spray.

2. Heat 2 tablespoons of the butter in a large skillet over medium-high heat. Add the onion and cook, while stirring frequently, for 3 minutes, or until onion is translucent. Combine milk, egg, and the egg yolk in a mixing bowl and whisk until combined. Break the bread into tiny pieces and add it to the mixing bowl along with the allspice, nutmeg, and ginger. Stir until well combined.

3. Add the pork and beef, season to taste with salt and pepper, and stir to combine. Use your hands to form mixture into balls and arrange the meatballs on the prepared baking sheet. Spray the tops of meatballs with vegetable oil spray.

4. Place the sheet 6 inches under the broiler and cook, turning the meatballs with tongs as they brown. While meatballs are cooking, add the remaining butter to the skillet and heat over low heat. Add the flour and cook for 2 minutes while stirring constantly. Raise the heat to medium-high, add the stock and cream, and bring to a boil over medium-high heat, while whisking constantly.

5. When the meatballs are browned all over, remove them from the baking sheet with a slotted spoon and add to the sauce in the skillet. Bring to a boil, reduce heat to low, cover the pan, and simmer for 15 minutes while stirring occasionally. Season with salt and pepper and serve immediately.

Note: *The meatball mixture can be prepared up to 1 day in advance and refrigerated if it is tightly covered.*

ROCKY MOUNTAIN CHILI

Makes 4 to 6 Servings   Active Time: 30 Minutes   Total Time: 1½ Hours

1 tablespoon vegetable oil

1 onion, chopped

1 pound ground turkey

2 garlic cloves, minced

1 tablespoon chili powder

1 bay leaf

2 sprigs of thyme

2 sprigs of parsley

4 tomatoes, diced

1 (14 oz.) can of tomato sauce

½ cup tomato paste

1 (14 oz.) can of kidney beans

1 (14 oz.) can of white beans

1 (14 oz.) can of black beans

Salt and black pepper, to taste

Cheddar cheese, shredded, for serving

Sour cream, for serving

Corn bread, for serving

Chives, chopped, for serving

1. In a large saucepan, add the vegetable oil and cook over medium-high heat until warm. Add the onion and ground turkey and cook for 5 minutes, or until meat has been browned.

2. Add the garlic and cook for 2 minutes, then add the chili powder, aromatics, tomatoes, tomato sauce, tomato paste, and beans. Bring to a boil, then reduce heat so that the soup simmers and cook for 20 minutes, or until the meat is cooked through.

3. Season with salt and pepper, discard the aromatics, and ladle into warmed bowls. Serve with shredded cheddar cheese, sour cream, corn bread, and chopped chives.

PEAR CLAFOUTIS

Makes 4 to 6 Servings   Active Time: 20 Minutes   Total Time: 45 Minutes

12 tablespoons butter, melted

1 cup sugar, plus 2 teaspoons

⅔ cup flour

½ teaspoon salt

1 teaspoon almond extract

3 eggs

1 cup milk

4 pears, sliced

Whipped cream or confectioners' sugar, for topping (optional)

1. Preheat oven to 400°F. In a large bowl, combine half of the butter, ½ cup of the sugar, flour, salt, almond extract, eggs, and milk until all ingredients are blended and smooth. Set the batter aside.

2. Put 2 tablespoons of the butter in a cast-iron skillet and place it in the oven to heat up.

3. Place another skillet over medium-high heat and add the remaining butter, pears, and ½ cup of sugar. Cook, while stirring, until the pears are just soft and glazed, about 3 minutes.

4. Remove the skillet from the oven and pour in half of the batter. Spoon the cooked pears over the batter, add the remaining batter, and sprinkle with 2 teaspoons of the sugar.

5. Bake in the oven for 25 to 30 minutes until the clafoutis is golden brown and set in the center. Top with whipped cream or confectioners' sugar, if desired.

Note: *Although clafoutis is most delicious served warm, it is plenty tasty served at room temperature or even chilled.*

CHEESECAKE

Makes 8 to 10 Servings   Active Time: 20 Minutes
Total Time: 3 to 4 Hours

---

1 can of sweetened condensed milk

1 teaspoon pure vanilla extract

½ teaspoon nutmeg, grated

2 (8 oz.) packages of cream cheese

¼ cup fresh lemon juice

1 Graham Cracker Crust
(see page 29)

Fresh fruit and powdered sugar, for topping

1. Place the sweetened condensed milk, vanilla, nutmeg, and cream cheese in the bowl of a standing mixer and beat until combined. Add the lemon juice and beat until thoroughly combined.

2. Pour cream cheese mixture into the Graham Cracker Crust and cover with plastic wrap. Place in the refrigerator for a minimum of 3 hours before serving.

Week 1

Need a break after your first week of dieting? You can kick-start your cheat day with a cup of Cuban Coffee. That'll give you more than enough energy to make it through the rich spread of Whole Wheat Cranberry-Pecan Bread, Creamy Sweet Potato Lentils, and Barbequed Chicken Hash. Once you've finished up with a fluffy Dutch Apple Baby, you'll be ready to return to your healthier lifestyle.

Cuban Coffee

Whole Wheat
Cranberry-Pecan Bread

Creamy Sweet Potato Lentils

Barbequed Chicken Hash

Dutch Apple Baby

CUBAN COFFEE

1 part dark rum

3 parts coffee

Spoonful of sugar

Splash of cream liqueur

1. Pour the rum and coffee into a mug and stir.

2. Add the sugar and cream liqueur and stir until thoroughly mixed.

WHOLE WHEAT CRANBERRY-PECAN BREAD

Makes 1 Small, Round Loaf   Active Time: 25 Minutes   Total Time: 3 Hours

¼ teaspoon instant yeast

¼ teaspoon sugar

1½ cups water (110 to 115°F)

1 teaspoon kosher salt

2 cups whole wheat flour

1 cup all-purpose flour, plus more for kneading and dusting

1 cup dried cranberries

1 cup pecans, chopped

1. Place the yeast, sugar, and ½ cup of the warm water in a measuring cup. Cover with plastic wrap and set it aside for about 15 minutes. If the yeast doesn't foam, it is not alive and you'll need to start over.

2. When the yeast is proofed, pour the mixture into a large bowl and add the remaining warm water. Stir gently to combine. Combine the salt and the flours in a separate bowl and then add the resulting mixture to the yeast mixture. Stir with a wooden spoon until combined. The dough should be wet and sticky.

3. Place the dough on a lightly floured surface and knead for 8 to 10 minutes, adding flour as needed. Incorporate the cranberries and pecans as you knead the dough.

4. Place the dough in a large bowl, cover with plastic wrap, and allow to rise untouched for at least 1 hour and up to several hours. Preheat the oven to 450°F. Gently punch down the dough, re-cover with the plastic, and allow to rise for another 30 minutes.

5. Scoop the dough into a parchment-lined Dutch oven. Cover and bake for 15 minutes. Remove the lid and continue to bake for another 15 to 20 minutes, until the top is golden and the loaf sounds hollow when tapped. Remove the pot from the oven and use tea towels to carefully remove the loaf of bread. Allow to cool before slicing.

CREAMY SWEET POTATO LENTILS

Makes 6 Servings   Active Time: 20 Minutes
Total Time: 8½ Hours

1 pound brown lentils, rinsed and drained

3 small sweet potatoes, peeled and diced

¾ cup light cream or half-and-half

3¼ cups unsweetened almond milk

4 cups unsweetened cashew milk

¼ cup maple syrup

1 tablespoon vanilla extract

1 teaspoon allspice

Zest of 1 orange

Pinch of salt

Cashews, crushed, for garnish

Almonds, crushed, for garnish

1. Place all ingredients (except for the garnishes) in a slow cooker and cook on low for 8 hours, or until the lentils and sweet potatoes become smooth.

2. Garnish with cashews and almonds and serve.

BARBEQUED CHICKEN HASH

Makes 4 to 6 Servings   Active Time: 40 Minutes   Total Time: 1½ Hours

2 large russet potatoes, peeled and cubed

1 teaspoon salt, plus more to taste

3 tablespoons butter

1 Vidalia onion, diced

3 garlic cloves, minced

1 small jalapeño pepper, seeded and sliced

1 pound cooked chicken, cut into bite-sized pieces

¼ cup barbeque sauce

Freshly ground black pepper, to taste

Salsa, for serving

Sour cream, for serving

1. Put the potatoes in a saucepan and cover with cold water. Add the 1 teaspoon of salt. Bring to a boil, then lower the heat and cook the potatoes for about 10 minutes. You don't want to cook them until they are tender, as this will cause them to fall apart in the hash. Drain, rinse with cold water, and set aside.

2. Heat the butter in a cast-iron skillet over medium-high heat. Add the onion, garlic, and slices of jalapeño, and cook, while stirring, until the vegetables soften, about 3 minutes.

3. Add the potatoes and press them down into the skillet. Allow them to cook for about 5 minutes, then start turning sections over with a spatula while stirring in the chicken and the barbeque sauce. Continue to cook for about 5 minutes, until the potatoes are browned and the chicken is warmed through. Season with salt and pepper and serve with salsa and sour cream.

DUTCH APPLE BABY

Makes 4 Servings   Active Time: 45 Minutes   Total Time: 1 Hour and 15 Minutes

2 tart apples, cored, peeled, and sliced

4 tablespoons butter

¼ cup sugar, plus 3 tablespoons

1 tablespoon cinnamon

¾ cup flour

¼ teaspoon salt

¾ cup milk

4 eggs

1 teaspoon vanilla or almond extract

Confectioners' sugar, for dusting

1. Preheat the oven to 425°F and position a rack in the center. Heat a cast-iron skillet over medium-high heat. Add the apples and butter and cook, while stirring, until the apples soften, about 3 to 4 minutes. Add the ¼ cup of sugar and the cinnamon and cook for another 3 or 4 minutes. Distribute the apples evenly over the bottom of the skillet and remove from heat.

2. In a large bowl, mix the remaining sugar, flour, and salt together. In a smaller bowl, whisk together the milk, eggs, and vanilla or almond extract. Add the wet mixture to the dry mixture and stir to combine. Pour the resulting batter over the apples.

3. Put the skillet in the oven and bake for 15 to 20 minutes until puffy and browned on the top. Remove the skillet from the oven and let cool for a few minutes. Run a knife along the edge of the skillet to loosen the dessert and then put a plate over the skillet. Using oven mitts or pot holders, flip the skillet over so the dessert transfers to the plate. Dust with confectioners' sugar and serve warm.

Week 2

As the warmth of the holidays dissipates, the harsh reality of winter can begin to take its toll. But when you're sitting in a warm room and looking over a silky Maple Creamer and a stunning Five Spice-Dusted Mussel Cappuccino, even the bleakest day looks a little brighter. The Baked Tomatillo Chicken Casserole will keep you warm all week long, and the Cinnamon Buns—a stone-cold brunch classic—provide a comfortable landing.

Maple Creamer

Virgin Stout 'N' Cider

Five Spice–Dusted Mussel Cappuccino
with Shrimp Crackers

Baked Tomatillo Chicken Casserole

Cinnamon Buns

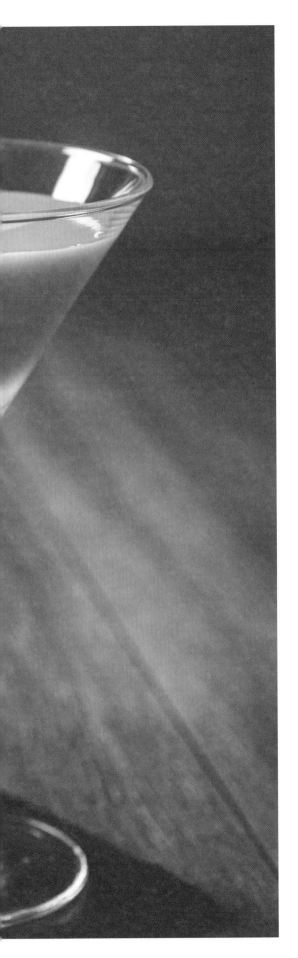

MAPLE CREAMER

1 part maple syrup

2 parts Irish cream

1 part bourbon

1 part milk

1. Add maple syrup, Irish cream, bourbon, and milk to a cocktail shaker filled with ice and shake vigorously.

2. Strain the resulting mixture into a cocktail glass.

VIRGIN STOUT 'N' CIDER

1 part ginger beer

1 part apple cider

Pour the ginger beer into a pint glass and then top with the apple cider.

FIVE SPICE–DUSTED MUSSEL CAPPUCCINO WITH SHRIMP CRACKERS

Makes 4 Servings   Active Time: 15 Minutes   Total Time: 30 Minutes

2 tablespoons butter

2 shallots, chopped

1 garlic clove, minced

½ cup white wine

2 sprigs of cilantro

2 pounds mussels

½ cup heavy cream

1½ cups milk

Salt and black pepper, to taste

Five-spice powder, for dusting

1. In a medium saucepan, add the butter and cook over medium heat until melted. Add the shallots and garlic and cook for 3 minutes, or until soft. Add the white wine and cilantro and bring to a simmer.

2. Add the mussels, cover the pan, and cook for 4 minutes, or until the majority of the mussels have opened. Remove pan from heat, remove mussels with a slotted spoon, and let cool. Once cool, remove the meat. Discard any mussels that do not open.

3. Transfer the contents of the saucepan, the mussel meat, the heavy cream, and ½ cup of the milk to a food processor and puree until smooth. Strain through a fine sieve and transfer to a clean pan. Bring to a simmer and season with salt and pepper.

4. Add the remaining milk, and then use an immersion blender to froth the soup. Ladle into warm cups, top with a spoonful of froth, dust with five-spice powder, and serve with Shrimp Crackers.

Shrimp Crackers

Makes 4 Servings   Active Time: 30 Minutes   Total Time: 16 Hours

4 cups water

8 oz. raw shrimp, shelled and deveined

1 teaspoon salt

1 teaspoon sugar

¼ teaspoon freshly ground black pepper, plus more to taste

½ teaspoon baking powder

2 cups tapioca starch

2 cups vegetable oil

Salt and paprika, to taste

1. In a medium saucepan, add the water and bring it to a simmer. Meanwhile, place the shrimp in a food processor or blender and puree until smooth. Add the salt, sugar, pepper, and baking powder and puree for 2 minutes. Add the tapioca starch and puree until the batter starts to form into a ball.

2. Place the batter on a clean surface and knead until it is a smooth paste, about 5 minutes. Separate into 2 balls and roll each into a 1-inch log. Wrap each log tightly with plastic wrap and tie a knot at each end.

3. Gently place the logs in the simmering water and reduce the heat to the lowest temperature. Cook for 20 minutes, then remove and submerge in ice water until cool.

4. Once the logs have cooled, remove from plastic wrap and place on paper towels to dry. When they are dry, chill in refrigerator overnight.

5. When ready to serve, place the vegetable oil in a Dutch oven and cook over medium-high heat until it is 375°F. Cut the logs into ⅛-inch slices, drop into the hot oil and cook until crispy.

6. Remove with tongs or a slotted spoon and transfer to a paper towel to drain. Season with salt, pepper, and paprika, and serve.

BAKED TOMATILLO CHICKEN CASSEROLE

Makes 6 Servings   Active Time: 15 Minutes   Total Time: 16 Hours

For the Marinade

1 tomatillo, husk removed, rinsed and halved

1 plum tomato, halved

2 garlic cloves

1 shallot, peeled and halved

1 poblano pepper, halved and seeded

¼ cup canola oil (or preferred neutral oil)

1 tablespoon kosher salt

1 tablespoon cumin

For the Salsa Verde

6 tomatillos, husks removed, rinsed

8 to 10 serrano peppers, rinsed and stemmed

½ white onion

2 garlic cloves, minced

Kosher salt, to taste

¼ cup oil

1 bunch of cilantro, chopped, for garnish

For the Casserole

2½ pounds boneless, skinless chicken breasts, sliced thin

2 eggs, beaten

1 (14 oz.) can of fire-roasted tomatoes

Pinch of salt

14 corn tortillas

1 cup Salsa Verde

¼ cup Cotija or feta cheese, crumbled

1. Prepare the marinade. Place all of the ingredients in a blender and blend until smooth. Pour over the chicken breasts and refrigerate overnight.

2. Prepare the Salsa Verde. Place the tomatillos and serrano peppers in a large saucepan and cover with water. Bring to a boil and cook until the tomatillos start to lose their bright green color, about 10 minutes. Drain the water and transfer to a blender. Add the remaining ingredients and puree until smooth. Top with the cilantro and set aside.

3. Preheat the oven to 375°F. Place the chicken and marinade in an 8 x 8–inch baking pan, place it in the oven, and cook until the center of the chicken reaches 165°F. Remove the pan from the oven, remove the chicken, and leave the marinade in the pan. Transfer the chicken to a mixing bowl and shred with a fork. Add the eggs, fire-roasted tomatoes, and salt and stir to combine.

4. Place 4 tortillas in the baking dish. Add ½ of the chicken mixture, top with 4 tortillas, and add the remaining chicken mixture. Top with remaining tortillas, cover with the Salsa Verde, and then place in the oven. Bake for about 30 minutes until the center is hot. Remove, sprinkle the cheese on top, and return to the oven until it is melted. Remove, cut into 6 pieces, and serve.

Tip: *If you don't want the salsa to be too spicy, omit the serranos entirely and replace with 1 poblano pepper.*

CINNAMON BUNS

Makes 6 Servings   Active Time: 1 Hour
Total Time: 1½ Hours

All-purpose flour, for dusting

1 (26.4 oz.) package of frozen biscuits

2 teaspoons cinnamon

¾ cup dark brown sugar, firmly packed

4 tablespoons butter, softened

1 cup confectioners' sugar

3 tablespoons half-and-half

½ teaspoon pure vanilla extract

1. Preheat the oven to 375°F. On a flour-dusted work surface, spread the frozen biscuit dough out in rows of 4 biscuits each. Cover with a clean dishcloth and let sit for about 30 minutes until the dough is thawed but still cool.

2. Combine the cinnamon and brown sugar in a small bowl. When the dough is ready, sprinkle flour over the top and fold it in half, then press it out to form a large rectangle (approximately 10 x 12 inches). Spread the softened butter over the dough, then top with the cinnamon-and-sugar mixture. Roll up the dough, starting with a long side. Cut into 1-inch slices and place them in a lightly greased cake pan.

3. Place in the oven and bake for about 35 minutes, until rolls are cooked through in the center. Remove from the oven and allow to cool slightly.

4. Make the glaze by combining the confectioners' sugar, half-and-half, and vanilla in a small bowl. Drizzle over the warm rolls and serve.

Week 3

This Southwestern-tinged collection of comfort foods will rouse even those who struggle to get their bearings before they've had their coffee. Spicy with a subtle nuttiness, the Fontina Jalapeño Hush Puppies are sure to turn heads. You can toss some tortilla chips beside the Guacamole, but it will also work well smeared over the Huevos Rancheros. Prepare the easy-to-make Nutella Dumplings ahead of time so that you can sit back and bask in the considerable comfort provided by this spread.

Borrowed Thyme

Fontina Jalapeño Hush Puppies

Guacamole

Huevos Rancheros

Nutella Dumplings

BORROWED THYME

1 part vodka

1 part club soda

3 parts grapefruit juice

4 sprigs of thyme

1. Fill a pint glass with ice and then add the vodka, club soda, grapefruit juice, and 3 sprigs of thyme. Stir until thoroughly mixed.

2. Strain the resulting mixture into a glass filled with ice and garnish with the remaining sprig of thyme.

FONTINA JALAPEÑO HUSH PUPPIES

Makes 4 to 6 Servings   Active Time: 15 Minutes   Total Time: 30 Minutes

2 cups vegetable oil

½ cup cornmeal

3 tablespoons all-purpose flour, plus 1½ teaspoons

4½ tablespoons sugar

¾ teaspoon salt

¼ teaspoon baking powder

⅛ teaspoon baking soda

⅛ teaspoon cayenne pepper

¼ cup buttermilk

1 egg, beaten

2 tablespoons jalapeño pepper, seeded and chopped

¾ cup fontina cheese, grated

1. Place oil in a Dutch oven and heat to 320°F. Add the cornmeal, flour, sugar, salt, baking powder, baking soda, and cayenne pepper to a small bowl and whisk until combined.

2. In a separate bowl, combine the buttermilk, egg, and jalapeño. Add to the cornmeal mixture. Add the cheese and stir until combined.

3. Drop spoonfuls of the batter into the hot oil and fry until golden brown. Remove from oil with a slotted spoon and place on paper towels to drain.

GUACAMOLE

Makes 2 to 3 Cups   Active Time: 10 Minutes   Total Time: 10 Minutes

4 avocados

½ red onion, diced

1 jalapeño pepper, seeded and diced

1 bunch of cilantro, chopped, plus more for garnish

1 tablespoon extra virgin olive oil

Juice of 2 limes

1½ teaspoons sea salt

1 teaspoon freshly ground black pepper

1. Scoop out the avocados and place the meat into a mixing bowl. Gently mash the avocados while still leaving large chunks. Add all remaining ingredients and stir until well combined.

2. Transfer to a serving bowl and garnish with the additional cilantro.

HUEVOS RANCHEROS

Makes 6 Servings   Active Time: 10 Minutes   Total Time: 20 Minutes

3 tablespoons cooking oil

1 red bell pepper, seeded and diced

2 Anaheim peppers, seeded and diced

½ cup red onion, diced

1½ cups tomatoes, diced

1½ pounds black beans, cooked

¼ cup cilantro, chopped

1 tablespoon cumin

1 tablespoon kosher salt

1 tablespoon black pepper

12 eggs

Corn tortillas, warmed, for serving

Sliced avocado, for serving

1. Preheat oven to 350°F. Heat the oil in a large cast-iron skillet over medium-high heat. Add the peppers and onion and sauté until softened. Add the tomatoes, cook for 1 minute, and then stir in the cooked black beans, cilantro, and cumin. Add the salt and pepper and cook for 2 minutes.

2. Make 12 small holes in the bean mixture for the eggs. Crack the eggs into the open spots. Put the skillet into the oven and cook until the egg whites are set, about 5 minutes.

3. Serve with warm tortillas and sliced avocado.

Tip: If you don't want to cook the black beans ahead of time, you can use canned. Just make sure to drain the liquid off before adding them to the skillet.

NUTELLA DUMPLINGS

Makes 30 Dumplings   Active Time: 45 Minutes   Total Time: 45 Minutes

2 cups vegetable oil

30 wonton wrappers

30 teaspoons Nutella

Powdered sugar, for dusting

Cinnamon, for dusting

1. Place the vegetable oil in a Dutch oven and heat to 350°F.

2. Lay out the wonton wrappers and place 1 teaspoon of Nutella in each wonton's center. To seal the wonton, dip a finger in water and run along the wonton's outer edge. Pull one side over to form a triangle and seal the wonton.

3. Working in batches of 3 to 4 wontons, place them into the pot and cook for 2 to 3 minutes, until golden brown. Remove cooked wontons from the oil and drain on a paper towel–lined cooling rack. When dry but still warm, sprinkle with a little powdered sugar and cinnamon.

Week 4

Yes, beets are divisive. But after a Mocha Mocha Mocha (or two), we're betting that even the staunchest beet opponent will be blown away by the beauty of the Raw Beet Salad with Blood Orange. Even if you can't win those folks over, the Cheese Gougeres, Potatoes, Peppers, and Eggs, and Lavender Ice Cream give them plenty of places for their stomachs to find solace.

Mocha Mocha Mocha

Virgin Cinnamon Apple

Raw Beet Salad with Blood Orange

Cheese Gougeres

Potatoes, Peppers, and Eggs

Lavender Ice Cream

MOCHA MOCHA MOCHA

1 part vodka

1 part chocolate liqueur

1 part coffee liqueur

2 parts milk

1. Add the vodka, liqueurs, and milk to a cocktail shaker filled with ice and shake vigorously.

2. Strain the resulting mixture into a rocks glass filled with ice.

VIRGIN CINNAMON APPLE

2 parts apple cider

1 part sparkling cider

Dash of cinnamon

1 cinnamon stick, for garnish

Fill a rocks glass with ice and add the ciders and cinnamon. Stir until mixed and garnish with a cinnamon stick.

RAW BEET SALAD WITH BLOOD ORANGE

Makes 4 to 6 Servings   Active Time: 30 to 40 Minutes   Total Time: 16 Hours

5 to 7 red beets, peeled and shredded, stems and greens reserved

1 jalapeño pepper, minced (remove seeds if you don't want the extra spice)

½ teaspoon kosher salt

Zest, segments, and juice of 1 blood orange

3 tablespoons extra virgin olive oil

3 tablespoons honey

1 tablespoon rice vinegar

2 pounds arugula

½ pound Brie, sliced

1. Place the beet greens and stems in a bowl of ice water to remove any dirt. Place the shredded beets and the jalapeño in a salad bowl. Remove the beet greens and stems from the ice water and dice the stems. Set the greens aside. Add the beet stems to the salad bowl. Add the salt and stir.

2. Remove the fruit from the membranes of the blood orange. Add the fruit to the salad bowl and then squeeze the juice from the remnants of the orange into the bowl.

3. In a separate small bowl, whisk the oil, honey, and vinegar together and pour over the beet mixture. Cover the salad bowl and refrigerate overnight.

4. When ready to serve, mix the beet greens with arugula and place them in the salad bowl. Top with the Brie and serve.

CHEESE GOUGERES

Makes 4 to 6 Servings   Active Time: 15 Minutes
Total Time: 45 Minutes

¾ cup milk

¾ cup water, plus 2 tablespoons

⅛ teaspoon salt

7 tablespoons butter

1¼ cups all-purpose flour

5 eggs, plus 1 egg for egg wash

1¼ cups Gruyère cheese, grated

1. Preheat oven to 400°F. In a medium saucepan, add the milk, ¾ cup of the water, salt, and butter and bring to a boil. Add the flour and stir constantly until a ball of dough forms. Remove dough from pan and place in a standing mixer. Mix slowly until dough stops steaming.

2. Add the 5 eggs one at a time. Add the cheese and mix until combined.

3. Place spoonfuls of the dough onto a parchment-lined baking sheet. In a small bowl, add the remaining egg and water and whisk until combined. Brush this wash on top of dough and place in oven. Bake for 20 minutes, or until golden brown, then remove and let cool on a wire rack.

POTATOES, PEPPERS, AND EGGS

Makes 4 to 6 Servings   Active Time: 20 Minutes   Total Time: 40 Minutes

1 tablespoon olive oil

1 red bell pepper, seeded and chopped

¼ onion, diced

Red pepper flakes, to taste (optional)

4 large russet potatoes, shredded and squeezed dry

Salt and black pepper, to taste

4 tablespoons butter

6 eggs

1. Heat the oil in a cast-iron skillet over medium-high heat. Add the pepper and onion and cook, while stirring, for about 4 minutes, or until the vegetables are just soft. If desired, stir in the red pepper flakes. Transfer the mixture to a large bowl containing the shredded potatoes, season with salt and pepper, and stir to combine.

2. Add the butter to the skillet and cook until bubbling. Add the potato-and-onion mixture, press it into the skillet, and cook for 5 minutes.

3. Create six indentations in the potatoes and break the eggs into them. Reduce the heat slightly, cover, and cook for about 5 minutes, until the eggs are cooked through and the yolks are set.

LAVENDER ICE CREAM

Makes 1 Quart   Active Time: 20 Minutes   Total Time: 8 Hours

2 cups heavy cream

1 cup half-and-half

⅔ cup honey

2 tablespoons dried lavender

Yolks from 2 large eggs

⅛ teaspoon sea salt

1. Place the cream, half-and-half, honey, and lavender in a medium saucepan and cook until it is about to boil. Remove from heat and let stand for at least 30 minutes. When cool, pour the mixture through a fine mesh sieve to remove the lavender.

2. Place the mixture in a clean saucepan and cook over medium-low heat. Beat the egg yolks in a bowl, add the salt, and then add 1 cup of the saucepan's contents to the yolks while whisking constantly. Place the tempered eggs in the saucepan and cook over medium-low heat while stirring constantly to ensure that the mixture does not come to a boil.

3. When the mixture is thick enough to coat the back of a wooden spoon, remove the pan from the heat and pour through a fine mesh sieve. Let cool while stirring a few times. Cover with plastic and place in the refrigerator for at least 4 hours.

4. Pour mixture into an ice-cream maker or food processor and churn until it reaches the consistency of soft-serve ice cream. Transfer to an airtight container and freeze for 2 to 3 hours before serving.

Week 5

Don't get put off by the name; starting off with a Hairy Navel ensures that your day will be bright and sweet no matter what it's doing outside. The Bacon Deviled Eggs and the French Onion Soup are two rich classics that are enjoying a much-deserved renaissance. Once you encounter their ease of preparation and considerable flavor, you'll understand why.

Hairy Navel

Bacon Deviled Eggs

French Onion Soup

Five-Bean Salad
with Gooseberry Vinaigrette

Almond and
Pine Nut Macaroons

HAIRY NAVEL

1½ oz. vodka

1½ oz. peach schnapps

4 oz. orange juice

Splash of pineapple juice

1 orange slice, for garnish

1. Fill a mason jar with the desired amount of ice, add the vodka and schnapps, and stir to combine.

2. Top with the orange juice and the pineapple juice and garnish with the orange slice.

BACON DEVILED EGGS

Makes 6 Servings   Active Time: 15 Minutes
Total Time: 30 Minutes

Yolks from 2 eggs, at room temperature

Juice from ¼ lemon

1 cup olive oil

10 large hard-boiled eggs, halved

6 strips of thick-cut bacon

2 tablespoons Dijon mustard

2 tablespoons parsley, finely chopped

Sea salt and freshly ground black pepper,
to taste

1 teaspoon paprika, for dusting (optional)

1. In a food processor, add the 2 egg yolks and the
    lemon juice, and puree for 30 seconds. Add the
    olive oil slowly until the mixture has a thick,
    mayonnaise-like consistency.

2. Remove the yolks from the hard-boiled eggs and
    place them in a small bowl. Whisk in the lemon
    juice mixture, Dijon mustard, and parsley, season
    with salt and pepper, and set aside.

3. Place a medium skillet over medium-high heat,
    add the bacon, and cook until crispy, about 6 to 8
    minutes. Remove and set to drain on paper towels.

4. Transfer the bacon to a cutting board and chop.
    Whisk into the lemon juice-and-yolk mixture and
    then spoon the mixture into the cavities of the
    hard-boiled eggs. If desired, dust with paprika.
    Chill in refrigerator until ready to serve.

FRENCH ONION SOUP

Makes 4 Servings   Active Time: 30 Minutes   Total Time: 1 Hour and 15 Minutes

---

2 tablespoons vegetable oil

4 onions, sliced very thin

½ cup sherry

1 tablespoon Worcestershire sauce

2 teaspoons thyme, chopped

8 cups Chicken Stock
(see page 24)

Salt and black pepper, to taste

4 slices of sourdough bread

1½ cups Gruyère cheese, grated

1. Place the oil in a medium saucepan. Add the onions and cook on the lowest heat setting for 30 minutes, or until golden brown. Stir the onions every few minutes, and add small amounts of water if they begin to stick.

2. Deglaze the pan with the sherry and Worcestershire sauce. Cook until liquid has been reduced by half. Add the thyme and stock and cook until reduced by half.

3. Meanwhile, preheat your oven to its broiler setting. Season the soup with salt and pepper and pour into ceramic bowls. Divide the bread and the cheese between the bowls. Place bowls under the broiler and cook until the cheese has melted.

FIVE-BEAN SALAD WITH GOOSEBERRY VINAIGRETTE

Makes 6 Servings   Active Time: 30 Minutes   Total Time: 2 Days

For the Salad

¼ pound kidney beans, soaked overnight

¼ pound cannellini beans, soaked overnight

¼ pound pink beans, soaked overnight

¼ pound pinto beans, soaked overnight

¼ pound whole dried green peas, soaked overnight

4 to 6 cups Chicken Stock (see page 24)

2 tablespoons granulated garlic

2 bay leaves

Pinch of red pepper flakes

3 tablespoons kosher salt

2 cups celery, minced

¼ cup red radishes, grated (about 2 large radishes)

1½ cups parsnip, peeled and minced (about 1 medium parsnip)

½ cup parsley, chopped

1 cup scallion greens, chopped

Juice of ½ lemon

For the Gooseberry Vinaigrette

3½ oz. gooseberries, washed

¼ cup red wine vinegar

¼ cup honey

½ cup extra virgin olive oil

1 tablespoon kosher salt

1. Drain and rinse the beans and peas, and transfer them to a slow cooker. Add the chicken stock, granulated garlic, bay leaves, red pepper flakes, and kosher salt and cook on low for 8 hours, or until the beans are tender. Turn off the slow cooker and let the beans rest until they come to room temperature. Place the beans in the refrigerator overnight.

2. Prepare the Gooseberry Vinaigrette. Place all of the vinaigrette ingredients into a blender and puree until the consistency is silky. The dressing should be thick enough to coat a spoon. Set the dressing aside.

3. Place all of the remaining salad ingredients in a large salad bowl. Stir until combined.

4. Drain the beans. Place the beans in the salad bowl, add half of the vinaigrette, and toss. Serve with the remaining vinaigrette on the side.

ALMOND AND PINE NUT MACAROONS

Makes 36 Cookies   Active Time: 15 Minutes
Total Time: 40 Minutes

1 (8 oz.) can of almond paste

1¼ cups sugar

Whites from 2 large eggs, at room temperature

¾ cup pine nuts

1. Preheat the oven to 325°F. Line two baking sheets with parchment paper.

2. Break almond paste into small pieces and place it in a mixing bowl along with the sugar. Beat at medium speed with an electric mixer until combined. Increase the speed to high, add the egg whites, and beat until mixture is light and fluffy.

3. Drop heaping tablespoons of dough onto the prepared baking sheets. Pat pine nuts into the top of each cookie. Bake for 18 to 20 minutes, or until lightly browned. Place baking sheets on wire racks and let cool completely.

Tip: *When buying almond paste, make sure it's almond paste and not marzipan, which is already sweetened.*

Chinese New Year

A glass of the Plumdemonium sangria, a few Pot Stickers, and the Peanut Satay Dip are sure to get the party started on this increasingly popular holiday. If inclined, chop up a few hard-boiled eggs and toss them into the Rice Noodle Salad, which is a perfect stage setter for the elegant Salmon with Chinese Eggplants. Some might be at capacity following such a bountiful meal, but we're betting that no one will be able to resist the spicy sweetness of the Pear-Ginger Crumble.

Plumdemonium

Cucumber-Ginger-Lemongrass Water

Pot Stickers

Peanut Satay Dip

Rice Noodle Salad with Peanut Sauce

Salmon with Chinese Eggplants

Pear-Ginger Crumble

PLUMDEMONIUM

Makes 4 to 6 Servings

1 (750 ml) bottle of dry red wine

2 plums, pitted, cut into thin wedges, and frozen

1 apricot, cut into bite-sized pieces

1 cup cranberry juice

¼ cup brandy

1 cup seltzer

1. Combine all ingredients except the seltzer in a large pitcher. Cover and refrigerate for at least 4 hours.

2. After removing from refrigerator, add ice and the seltzer. Stir and serve.

CUCUMBER-GINGER-LEMONGRASS WATER

Makes 8 Servings

2 lemongrass stalks

½ cucumber, seeded and thinly sliced

1-inch piece of ginger, peeled and smashed

8 cups cold, filtered water

1. Cut the lemongrass into 3- to 4-inch pieces. Bend them without breaking to help release their oils and juices. Place in a jar or pitcher with the cucumber and ginger.

2. Cover with water. Let sit for 1 to 2 hours at room temperature for a quick infusion, or refrigerate for anywhere from 4 hours to overnight.

3. Serve chilled.

POT STICKERS

Makes 4 Servings   Active Time: 30 Minutes   Total Time: 1 Hour

6 oz. ground pork or shrimp

½ cup cabbage, minced

1 tablespoon ginger, minced

4 scallions, sliced, whites and greens separated

1 tablespoon soy sauce, plus more for serving

4 tablespoons water

24 wonton wrappers

1 egg, beaten

2 tablespoons oil

Chili-garlic sauce, for serving

1. In a bowl, add the pork or shrimp, cabbage, ginger, scallion whites, soy sauce, and 2 tablespoons of the water and stir until combined.

2. Lay 6 wrappers on a clean, dry work surface. Dip a finger into the egg and rub it over the edge of each wonton wrapper. Place a teaspoon of the filling in the middle of each wrapper. Fold the wrapper over and seal by pinching the edges together. Repeat with the remaining wrappers.

3. Warm a large skillet over medium-high heat. Add the oil and warm for 1 minute. Add the pot stickers and cook for 2 minutes, or until nicely browned.

4. Add the remaining water to the pan, cover, and cook for 3 minutes. Remove and place in serving bowls or refrigerate if using later. Serve with additional soy sauce, chili-garlic sauce, and the scallion greens.

Peanut Satay Dip

Makes 1 Cup   Active Time: 10 Minutes   Total Time: 1 Hour and 10 Minutes

1 cup creamy peanut butter

2 tablespoons rice wine vinegar

¼ cup soy sauce

1 tablespoon honey

¼ cup boiling water

Juice of 2 limes

1 teaspoon red chili sauce

1 teaspoon freshly ground black pepper

Place all ingredients in a bowl and stir until well combined. Refrigerate for 1 hour before serving.

RICE NOODLE SALAD WITH PEANUT SAUCE

Makes 6 Servings   Active Time: 10 Minutes   Total Time: 40 Minutes

For the Peanut Sauce

Juice of 2 limes

2 tablespoons fresh ginger, peeled and minced

1 garlic clove

¼ cup brown sugar

2 to 3 tablespoons fish sauce

2 tablespoons dark soy sauce

½ cup peanut butter

For the Salad

1 pound rice stick noodles

½ pound carrots, peeled and julienned

1 red bell pepper, seeded and julienned

1 red Fresno pepper, seeded and julienned

1 to 2 jalapeño peppers, seeded and julienned

4 scallions, sliced thin on a bias

1 cup basil, chopped

¼ cup cilantro, chopped

1 to 2 tablespoons fresh mint, chopped

Peanuts, crushed, for garnish

1. Prepare the sauce. Place the ingredients in a food processor and puree. Transfer to a refrigerator and chill for 30 minutes.

2. In a large stockpot, bring water to a boil and add the noodles. Cook, while stirring, for 3 minutes, or until the noodles are tender. Drain the noodles and rinse with cold water.

3. Place the noodles and the remaining ingredients in a salad bowl. Stir to combine, add the peanut sauce, and toss to coat. Garnish with the crushed peanuts and serve.

SALMON WITH CHINESE EGGPLANTS

Makes 4 Servings   Active Time: 20 Minutes   Total Time: 20 Minutes

For the Sauce

1 tablespoon fresh ginger, peeled and minced

2 to 3 garlic cloves, minced

1 tablespoon rice vinegar

2 tablespoons light brown sugar

¼ cup light soy sauce

1 tablespoon tapioca starch or cornstarch

½ cup water

For the Salmon & Eggplants

3 tablespoons canola oil

4 Chinese eggplants, cut into ½-inch-thick slices on a bias

1 red bell pepper, seeded and julienned

2 tablespoons scallions, chopped, greens reserved for garnish

1 cup bean sprouts

1½ pounds Atlantic salmon, skin removed

Salt and black pepper, to taste

1. Prepare the sauce. Place all of the ingredients in a blender and puree until smooth. Transfer to a small saucepan and cook while stirring until the sauce starts to thicken. Remove from heat and set aside.

2. Preheat your oven to 375°F. Place the oil in a cast-iron skillet and warm over medium-high heat. Add the eggplants, bell pepper, and scallion whites to the pan and cook for 5 minutes while stirring occasionally. Add bean sprouts and stir until all the vegetables are evenly coated by the oil.

3. Place the salmon on the vegetables, flesh side up, season with salt, pepper, and some of the sauce, and transfer the pan to the oven. Cook for 8 to 10 minutes, remove pan from the oven, top with more sauce, and garnish with the scallion greens.

PEAR-GINGER CRUMBLE

Makes 4 to 6 Servings   Active Time: 30 Minutes
Total Time: 1½ Hours

---

9 tablespoons unsalted butter, chilled

4 pears

1 teaspoon ground ginger

1 cup all-purpose flour

½ cup dark brown sugar

½ cup rolled oats

Vanilla ice cream or whipped cream,
for serving

1. Preheat oven to 350°F. Melt 1 tablespoon of the butter in a cast-iron skillet over medium heat.

2. Trim the tops and bottoms from the pears, cut into quarters, remove the cores, and slice thin. Lay the slices in the melted butter. Sprinkle the pear slices with the ginger and remove the skillet from heat.

3. In a bowl, combine the flour and brown sugar. Cut the remaining butter into slices. Using your fingers, work the butter into the mixture until a coarse meal forms. Add the rolled oats, combine, and then spread the mixture over the pears. Put the skillet in the oven and bake for 15 minutes, until the contents of the saucepan are melted and bubbly. Remove the skillet from the oven and let cool for a few minutes before serving with ice cream or whipped cream.

Variation:

To add a touch of presentation, divide
the crumble between individual ramekins
or crocks when serving.

Week 6

These dishes work so well together that it will be tough to single one out as a favorite. The slightly minty flavor of gin puts a refreshing twist on the simple, well-treaded cup of hot chocolate. While Classic Stout Bread can certainly stand on its own, it's great with some of the Whipped Herb Butter (see page 33) or Curried Chicken Salad. If you're worried about having room for the delicious Honey-Roasted Figs, don't hesitate to toss the Curried Chicken Salad over greens.

Christmas Cocoa

Virgin Mule

Classic Stout Bread

Curried Chicken Salad

Baked Egg Casserole

Honey-Roasted Figs

CHRISTMAS COCOA

1 part gin

3 parts hot chocolate

1 part cream liqueur

Dollop of whipped cream (optional)

Add the gin and hot chocolate to an Irish coffee glass, stir in the cream liqueur, and top, if desired, with the dollop of whipped cream.

VIRGIN MULE

Juice of ½ lime

1 cup ginger beer

1 lime wheel, for garnish

1. Place the lime juice and ice in a highball glass.

2. Fill with the ginger beer and then garnish with the lime wheel.

CLASSIC STOUT BREAD

Makes 2 Loaves Active Time: 10 Minutes
Total Time: 1 Hour and 10 Minutes

2¼ cups whole wheat flour

1 cup rolled oats, plus more for topping

½ cup brown sugar

2¼ teaspoons baking soda

1 teaspoon baking powder

½ teaspoon salt

⅓ cup butter, melted

1 cup buttermilk

1 bottle of Guinness or other stout

1. Preheat oven to 400°F and grease 2 standard loaf pans. Combine the dry ingredients in a bowl and set aside. In a separate bowl, combine the butter, buttermilk, and beer.

2. Place the wet and dry mixtures together and stir until well combined. Divide the mixture between the prepared loaf pans and sprinkle with additional oats.

3. Bake for 1 hour, or until a knife inserted into the middle of the loaves comes out clean. Let cool on a wire rack before serving.

CURRIED CHICKEN SALAD

Makes 6 Servings   Active Time: 15 to 20 Minutes   Total Time: 45 Minutes

1½ pounds boneless, skinless chicken breasts, cut into ½-inch-thick cutlets

Salt and pepper, to taste

Dash of olive oil

1 cup mayonnaise

3 tablespoons fresh lime juice

¼ cup Madras curry powder

1 tablespoon cumin

1 tablespoon granulated garlic

½ teaspoon cinnamon

½ teaspoon turmeric

2 cups celery, minced

2 Granny Smith apples, minced

½ red bell pepper, seeded and minced

½ cup pecans, plus ¼ cup for garnish, chopped

1. Preheat oven to 350°F. Place the chicken on a baking sheet. Season with salt and pepper and drizzle with enough olive oil to coat. Place the chicken in the oven and bake for 30 minutes, or until the center of the cutlets reaches 160°F. Remove from the oven and let rest for 10 minutes.

2. In a large salad bowl, combine the mayonnaise, lime juice, and all of the spices. Add the celery, apples, red pepper, and the pecans and stir until well combined.

3. Once the chicken is cool, dice into small cubes and add to the bowl. Toss to combine and garnish with additional pecans.

BAKED EGG CASSEROLE

Makes 6 Servings   Active Time: 15 Minutes   Total Time: 1 Hour and 10 Minutes

12 large eggs

¼ cup water

½ cup half-and-half

3 plum tomatoes, quartered and sliced into wedges

1 cup spinach, roughly chopped

½ cup scallions, chopped

1 cup Parmesan cheese, grated, plus more for topping

1 tablespoon fresh thyme, chopped

Salt and pepper, to taste

1. Preheat oven to 350°F. In a mixing bowl, whisk the eggs, water, and half-and-half together.

2. Place all of the other ingredients, except for the salt and pepper, in the mixing bowl and stir to combine. Pour the mixture into a greased 8 x 8–inch baking pan.

3. Season with salt and pepper. Put in the oven for 1 hour, or until the eggs are set in the middle. Remove the pan from the oven and let the casserole stand for 5 minutes before serving. Grate additional Parmesan onto the top and serve.

HONEY-ROASTED FIGS

Makes 4 Servings   Active Time: 5 Minutes   Total Time: 10 Minutes

2 tablespoons honey

4 Black Mission figs, halved

⅛ teaspoon cinnamon

Goat cheese, crumbled, to taste

1. In a medium nonstick sauté pan, add the honey and warm over medium heat.

2. Place the cut figs face down and cook for 5 minutes, or until golden brown.

3. Sprinkle the cinnamon over the figs and gently stir to coat. Remove figs from the pan, top with the goat cheese, and serve.

Week 7

Advocaat is essentially the European version of eggnog, making it the perfect base for a winter warmer. For those put off by the unorthodox combination of peanut butter and bacon, the earthy Mushroom and Swiss Cheese Quiche provides a safe space to hide. Unfortunately, there's no place they can get away from the regret that will come when they hear everyone else's enthusiastic responses to the Peanut Butter and Bacon Oats.

Snowball

Mushroom and
Swiss Cheese Quiche

Peanut Butter and Bacon Oats

Cinnamon Twists with
Caramel Dipping Sauce

SNOWBALL

1 part advocaat

Dash of lime juice

Dash of maple syrup

1 part lemonade

Dollop of whipped cream, for garnish

1 maraschino cherry, for garnish

1. Place the advocaat and lime juice in a cocktail shaker filled with ice and shake thoroughly.

2. Strain the resulting mixture into a mason jar and then add the maple syrup.

3. Top off the glass with lemonade and garnish with the whipped cream and maraschino cherry.

MUSHROOM AND SWISS CHEESE QUICHE

Makes 6 to 8 Servings   Active Time: 30 Minutes   Total Time: 1½ Hours

---

1 Flaky Pastry Crust (see page 28)

4 tablespoons butter

½ pound mushrooms, sliced thin
(a mixture of portobello, shiitake,
and white mushrooms is ideal)

1 small leek, white part only,
thinly sliced

4 eggs

2 cups whole milk

1 teaspoon salt

½ teaspoon pepper

⅛ teaspoon nutmeg

1 cup Swiss cheese, shredded

1. Preheat the oven to 350°F and place the crust in a greased 9" pie plate. In a cast-iron skillet over medium heat, melt the butter and add the mushrooms and leek. Cook, while stirring, until vegetables are soft, about 5 minutes. Remove from heat and set aside.

2. In a large bowl, whisk the eggs until thoroughly combined. Add the milk, salt, pepper, and nutmeg and whisk to combine.

3. Sprinkle half of the Swiss cheese onto the crust. Distribute the mushroom-and-leek mixture over the cheese. Pour the egg mixture over everything and shake gently to evenly distribute the liquid. Sprinkle the remaining Swiss cheese on top.

4. Place the quiche in the oven and bake for 30 to 40 minutes, or until the quiche is puffy and golden brown and the eggs are set. Remove from the oven and allow to sit for 20 minutes before slicing and serving.

PEANUT BUTTER AND BACON OATS

Makes 4 to 6 Servings   Active Time: 5 Minutes   Total Time: 10 to 20 Minutes

6 slices of thick-cut bacon

4 to 6 eggs

2 cups oats

6 cups water

1 tablespoon kosher salt

¼ cup peanut butter

1. Cook the bacon in a cast-iron skillet over medium heat. Remove the bacon from the skillet and use the bacon grease to fry the eggs.

2. Once the eggs are fried, remove them from the skillet and set aside. Add oats, water, and salt to a Dutch oven and cook for 7 to 10 minutes over medium heat until the oats are the desired consistency.

3. While the oats are cooking, chop the bacon. Add the bacon and peanut butter to the oatmeal. Stir to combine. Top each portion with a fried egg and serve.

CINNAMON TWISTS
WITH CARAMEL DIPPING SAUCE

Makes about 24 Twists   Active Time: 15 to 20 Minutes   Total Time: 30 Minutes

2 sheets of frozen puff
pastry, thawed

1 cup sugar

3½ tablespoons cinnamon

1 teaspoon nutmeg, grated

1 egg

1. Preheat oven to 375°F. Roll out the puff pastry sheets until each is 10 x 12 inches.

2. Combine the sugar, cinnamon, and nutmeg in a bowl. Beat the egg in a separate bowl.

3. Lightly brush the top of each pastry sheet with the egg. Then, sprinkle the sugar-and-spice mixture evenly across the tops of both sheets.

4. Cut the pastries into long strips and twist. Place strips on a baking sheet and bake for 12 to 15 minutes, or until golden brown. Flip each pastry over and allow to cook for an additional 2 to 3 minutes.

5. Remove twists from oven and allow to cool until just slightly warm. Serve with the Caramel Dipping Sauce.

Caramel Dipping Sauce

Makes 1 Cup   Active Time: 5 Minutes   Total Time: 10 Minutes

1 cup sugar

¼ cup water

3 tablespoons butter

½ teaspoon sea salt

1. Add the sugar, water, butter, and salt to a small saucepan and cook over medium-high heat until it is light brown. Be sure not to stir the mixture; instead, swirl the pan a few times.

2. Reduce heat to medium and cook for about 3 to 5 minutes, or until the mixture caramelizes. Stir the mixture once or twice to make sure it does not burn.

Week 8

To help you navigate the homestretch of the winter slog, we turn to the Mimosa: the quintessential brunch cocktail. It's airy, slightly sweet quality is more than enough to lift you out of the doldrums. The Roasted Brussels Sprouts with Cranberry and Walnut Honey and the Szechuan Ramen keep you on the right path, adding a bit of brightness to the gray you've been facing every day. As ramen is an incredibly accepting dish, feel free to add Pot Stickers (see page 78), poached, fried, or hard-boiled eggs, or slices of steak to the bowls.

Mimosa

Apple-Fennel Water

Roasted Brussels Sprouts
with Cranberry and Walnut Honey

Szechuan Ramen

White Chocolate Almond Squares

MIMOSA

1 part orange juice

1 part Champagne

1 orange slice, for garnish

1. Fill your champagne flute halfway with orange juice.

2. Top with Champagne. Stir if you want, or let them combine on their own. Garnish with the slice of orange.

APPLE-FENNEL WATER

Makes 8 Servings

½ small fennel bulb, thinly sliced

1 medium apple, cored and thinly sliced

8 cups cold, filtered water

1. Place the fennel and apple in a pitcher or jar and cover with water.

2. Let sit for 1 to 2 hours at room temperature for a quick infusion, or refrigerate for anywhere from 4 hours to overnight.

3. Serve chilled.

ROASTED BRUSSELS SPROUTS
WITH CRANBERRY AND WALNUT HONEY

Makes 6 to 8 Servings   Active Time: 15 Minutes   Total Time: 45 Minutes to 1 Hour

3 pounds Brussels sprouts

2 tablespoons olive oil

Pinch of salt

6 oz. honey

3 tablespoons cranberry sauce or dried cranberries

4 oz. walnuts, chopped

1 teaspoon pepper

1. Preheat oven to 425°F. Wash and cut the Brussels sprouts in half lengthwise.

2. Toss the cut sprouts in a bowl with the olive oil and salt. Place the sprouts on a baking sheet and cook in the oven for 25 to 35 minutes, or until brown.

3. While the sprouts are baking, place the honey and the cranberry component in a bowl, and stir until combined.

4. Toss the finished sprouts in a bowl along with the honey mixture and half of the walnuts. Season with the pepper and top with the remaining walnuts.

SZECHUAN RAMEN

Makes 4 Servings   Active Time: 30 Minutes
Total Time: 1 Hour and 15 Minutes

2 tablespoons sesame oil

4 garlic cloves, minced

3-inch piece of ginger, minced

2 tablespoons chili bean sauce

3 cups Chicken Stock (see page 24)

3 cups Dashi Stock (see recipe)

¼ cup soy sauce

1 tablespoon sake

2 teaspoons sugar

Salt and pepper, to taste

Noodles from 2 packets of Ramen

Scallion greens, for garnish

Szechuan Peppercorn and Chili Oil
(see recipe), for garnish

1. In a medium saucepan, add the sesame oil and
    warm over medium heat. Add the garlic and
    ginger and cook for 3 minutes, or until fragrant.
    Add the chili bean sauce and cook for 1 minute.

2. Add the Chicken Stock, Dashi Stock, soy sauce,
    and sake. Bring to a boil and then reduce heat so
    that the soup simmers. Cook for 5 minutes, adjust
    the seasoning with sugar, salt, and pepper, and
    then turn off the heat.

3. Meanwhile, cook the Ramen noodles according
    to the manufacturer's instructions. When cooked,
    place in warm bowls.

4. Bring the broth to a boil and then pour over
    the Ramen noodles. Garnish with Szechuan
    Peppercorn and Chili Oil.

Szechuan Peppercorn and Chili Oil

1½ cups vegetable oil	3 tablespoons Szechuan peppercorns
5 star anise	
1 cinnamon stick	⅓ cup red pepper flakes
2 bay leaves	1 teaspoon salt

1. In a small saucepan, add the vegetable oil, star
    anise, cinnamon stick, bay leaves, and Szechuan
    peppercorns. Cook over the lowest-possible heat
    for 20 minutes, being careful not to burn.

2. Place the red pepper flakes in a small bowl. Strain
    the warm oil over the flakes. Let cool, season with
    salt, and reserve until ready to use.

Dashi Stock

Makes 6 Cups   Active Time: 10 Minutes
Total Time: 40 Minutes

8 cups cold water

2 oz. kombu

1 cup bonito flakes

1. In a medium saucepan, add the water and the
    kombu. Soak for 20 minutes, remove the kombu,
    and score gently with a knife.

2. Return the kombu to the saucepan and bring to a
    boil. Remove the kombu as soon as the water boils,
    so that the stock doesn't become bitter.

3. Add the bonito flakes and return to a boil.
    Turn off heat and let stand.

4. Strain through a fine sieve and chill in refrigerator.

WHITE CHOCOLATE ALMOND SQUARES

Makes 12 to 16 Squares   Active Time: 10 Minutes
Total Time: 45 Minutes

---

1 cup almonds, blanched and chopped

1 cup butter

1 cup dark brown sugar, firmly packed

Yolk of 1 large egg, at room temperature

1 teaspoon vanilla extract

2 cups all-purpose flour

¼ teaspoon salt

½ pound quality white chocolate, chopped

1. Preheat the oven to 350°F. Line a 9 x 13–inch baking pan with parchment paper. Place almonds on a baking sheet and toast for 5 to 7 minutes, until lightly browned.

2. Combine the butter and sugar in a mixing bowl and beat at low speed with an electric mixer to blend. Increase the speed to high and beat for 3 to 4 minutes, until light and fluffy. Add the egg yolk and vanilla, and beat for 1 minute. Slowly add the flour and salt, and beat until a stiff dough forms. Pat the dough evenly into the baking pan and prick it with the tines of a fork. Place the pan on the middle rack in the oven and cook for 20 minutes, or until light brown.

3. Remove the pan from the oven and scatter the white chocolate evenly over the crust. Return the pan to the oven for 1 minute, remove, and spread the chocolate into an even layer. Sprinkle the almonds on top, allow to cool in the pan, and then cut into bars.

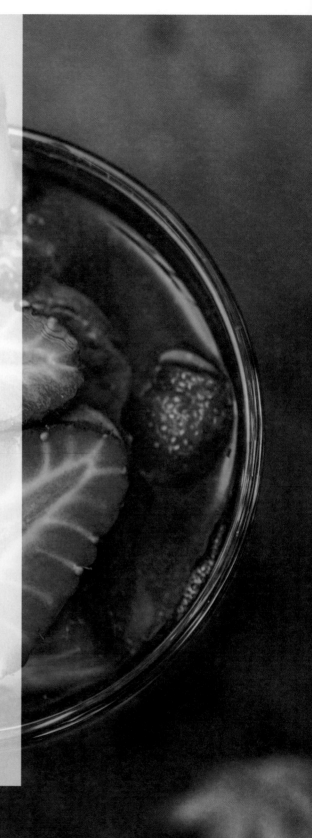

Week 9

You may think that stuffing looks strange without a turkey to stand beside, but this decadent Challah, Sautéed Onion, and Goat Cheese Stuffing is good enough to strike out on its own. It'll be tempting to go for a second serving of that, but the Quiche Lorraine and Chicken and Corn Succotash Soup are too intriguing to ignore. After that scintillating sojourn, the Rajndling will feel like a return to the comfort of home. Also, don't make plans for next weekend: there's a good chance whomever you invite will want you to cook for them again.

Sage Advice

Challah, Sautéed Onion,
and Goat Cheese Stuffing

Quiche Lorraine

Chicken and
Corn Succotash Soup

Rajndling

SAGE ADVICE

1 part orange vodka

1 part strawberry/sage kombucha

1 part strawberry seltzer

Splash of grenadine

1 handful of sliced strawberries, for garnish

1. Add the vodka, kombucha, and seltzer to a highball glass filled with ice.

2. Stir thoroughly, top with the splash of grenadine, and garnish with the handful of strawberries.

CHALLAH, SAUTÉED ONION, AND GOAT CHEESE STUFFING

Makes 6 to 8 Servings   Active Time: 15 Minutes   Total Time: 1 Hour

---

13 cups challah bread, cubed and dried

3 tablespoons unsalted butter

2 medium onions, sliced

4 celery stalks, chopped

1 cup Chicken Stock (see page 24)

1 tablespoon salt

1 teaspoon pepper

1 tablespoon dried sage

2 tablespoons fresh thyme

8 oz. goat cheese

1. Preheat oven to 350°F. Grease a 3-quart baking dish and place the bread in the dish.

2. In a large pan over medium heat, melt the butter. Add the onions and celery and cook until they start to brown, about 10 minutes. Add the stock to the pan along with the salt, pepper, sage, and thyme. Bring to a boil, and then reduce heat to a simmer for 10 minutes.

3. Pour the mixture over the bread in the baking dish. Crumble the goat cheese and mix it into the stuffing. Cover the dish and bake for 30 minutes.

4. Uncover the dish and bake for an additional 25 to 30 minutes, until the top of the mixture begins to brown.

QUICHE LORRAINE

Makes 6 to 8 Servings   Active Time: 30 Minutes   Total Time: 1 Hour

---

1 Flaky Pastry Crust (see page 28)

3 large eggs

2 cups heavy cream

¾ teaspoon coarse salt

¼ teaspoon freshly ground pepper

½ pound thick-cut bacon, cooked and chopped

1. Preheat the oven to 400°F. Place the crust in a 9" pie plate and press it gently into place. Crimp the edges at the top for a decorative touch.

2. In a large bowl, whisk the eggs and cream until thoroughly combined. Add the salt and pepper and stir.

3. Pour the egg mixture into the crust and sprinkle with the bacon pieces. Put the quiche in the oven and bake for about 30 minutes, or until the quiche is puffy and golden brown, and the eggs are set. Remove from oven and allow to sit for 20 minutes before slicing and serving.

CHICKEN AND CORN SUCCOTASH SOUP

Makes 4 Servings   Active Time: 20 Minutes
Total Time: 1 Hour

¼ cup butter

4 slices of thick-cut bacon, cut into
¼-inch pieces

2 onions, chopped

2 garlic cloves, minced

2 chicken breasts, skin removed and chopped
into ½-inch pieces

¼ cup all-purpose flour

4 cups Chicken Stock (see page 24)

4 ears of corn, kernels removed

1 (14 oz.) can of kidney beans, rinsed
and drained

1 cup heavy cream

3 tablespoons parsley, chopped

Salt and black pepper, to taste

1. In a medium saucepan, add the butter and cook
   over medium heat until melted. Add the bacon,
   onions, and garlic and cook for 5 minutes. Add
   the chicken breasts and cook for 5 minutes.

2. Add the flour and cook, while stirring
   constantly, for 5 minutes. Add the Chicken Stock
   slowly, whisking constantly to prevent lumps
   from forming. Bring to a boil. Reduce heat so
   that the soup simmers. Add the corn kernels and
   kidney beans and simmer for 5 minutes.

3. Add the cream and return to a simmer. Add the
   parsley, season with salt and pepper, and serve in
   warm bowls.

RAJNDLING

Makes 6 Servings   Active Time: 20 Minutes   Total Time: 2 Hours

2¼ cups all-purpose flour

1 cup milk

5 teaspoons yeast

2 eggs

½ cup sugar

Pinch of salt

8 tablespoons (1 stick) butter, chopped into small pieces

¾ cup light brown sugar, firmly packed

1 teaspoon cinnamon

½ cup walnuts, chopped

½ cup cranberries, chopped

Powdered sugar, for topping

1. Preheat the oven to 375°F. Combine the flour, 1 tablespoon of the milk, yeast, eggs, and 1 teaspoon of the sugar in a large mixing bowl and stir gently. Cover with a cloth and let stand in a naturally warm area for 30 minutes.

2. Add the remaining milk and sugar, salt, and the butter to the mixture and work it into a smooth dough. Let stand for 10 minutes, and then roll out the dough until it is roughly as thick as your thumb.

3. Sprinkle the brown sugar and cinnamon over the dough and then add the walnuts and cranberries. Roll the dough up from a long side. Cut into 1-inch-thick slices.

4. Thoroughly coat a Bundt pan with cooking spray to prevent sticking, or line the bottom with parchment paper. Layer the slices along the bottom of the Bundt pan with the swirled side facing up. If not all of the slices will rest flat, slightly overlap the slices on one side.

5. Bake for about 35 minutes, until the rolls are cooked through. Remove from the oven and allow to cool before topping with the powdered sugar.

Week 10

The days are getting longer, the air is getting warmer—sounds like the perfect time to break out the cast-iron skillet and whip up some Southern classics. This classic cookware is essential to getting the outsides of the Biscuits crispy and the insides soft and warm. Following the richness of the Country Fried Steaks and Gravy, the light landing provided by the Lemon Curd will be welcomed by all.

Spice Cake

Orange Chai

Biscuits

Country Fried Steaks and Gravy

Lemon Curd

SPICE CAKE

1 part spiced rum

2 parts apple juice

Dash of Simple Syrup (see page 32)

Dusting of cinnamon

1 cinnamon stick, for garnish

1. Combine the rum, apple juice, syrup, and cinnamon in a cocktail shaker filled with ice and shake vigorously.

2. Strain the resulting mixture into a cocktail glass and garnish with a cinnamon stick.

ORANGE CHAI

Makes 8 Servings

1 orange, sliced

2 cardamom pods, cracked

1 cinnamon stick

2 whole cloves

1 bay leaf

3 to 4 whole black peppercorns

1-inch piece of ginger, peeled and smashed

8 cups cold, filtered water

1. Place the orange, cardamom pods, cinnamon stick, cloves, bay leaf, peppercorns, and ginger in a pitcher or jar and cover with the water.

2. Infuse for at least 4 hours. Strain and serve chilled.

BISCUITS

Makes 4 to 6 Servings   Active Time: 20 Minutes
Total Time: 40 Minutes

---

2 cups all-purpose flour, plus more for dusting

1 teaspoon sugar

1 teaspoon salt

1 tablespoon baking powder

8 tablespoons (1 stick) butter, cut into pieces

½ cup buttermilk, plus more as needed

1. Preheat oven to 450°F. In a large bowl, combine the flour, sugar, salt, and baking powder. Using a fork or pastry knife, blend in 6 tablespoons of the butter to form a crumbly dough. Form a well in the middle and add the buttermilk. Stir until a stiff dough forms. If the mixture seems too dry, add 1 tablespoon more of the buttermilk, going to 2 tablespoons if necessary.

2. Put the remaining butter in a cast-iron skillet and then place the skillet in the oven.

3. Put the dough on a lightly floured surface and press out to a thickness of about 1 inch. Cut out biscuits using an inverted water glass. Place the biscuits in the skillet and bake for about 10 minutes, until golden on the bottom.

COUNTRY FRIED STEAKS AND GRAVY

Makes 4 Servings   Active Time: 40 Minutes   Total Time: 40 Minutes

For the Steaks

4 (4 oz.) cube steaks

Kosher salt, to taste

2 cups flour

1 teaspoon freshly ground
black pepper

1 cup peanut, vegetable, or
canola oil

4 tablespoons unsalted butter,
cut into pieces

For the Gravy

4 tablespoons pan drippings

4 tablespoons flour

1 cup milk, plus more as needed

Kosher salt and freshly ground
black pepper, to taste

1. Prepare the steaks. Preheat the oven to 200°F. Pat the steaks dry and then season both sides with the kosher salt. Combine the flour and pepper in a bowl and then dredge the steaks in the mixture. Heat a cast-iron skillet over medium-high heat and add the oil and the butter. Place the steaks in the pan and cook for about 5 minutes a side. Transfer steaks to a platter in the oven to keep them warm as you make the gravy.

2. Prepare the gravy. Reduce the heat and pour out all but 4 tablespoons of the leftover pan drippings. Mix in the flour to create a roux. Continue to stir while raising the heat to medium. Once the roux is smooth, slowly add the milk, stirring constantly until incorporated. If the gravy is too thick, add more milk. If too thin, continue to cook it until it reduces. Season with salt and plenty of black pepper.

3. Place the steaks on a plate and pour the gravy over them.

LEMON CURD

Makes 1 Cup   Active Time: 10 to 15 Minutes
Total Time: 20 to 30 Minutes

½ cup fresh lemon juice

2 teaspoons lemon zest

3 large eggs

⅔ cup sugar

8 tablespoons (1 stick) butter

Graham crackers, for serving (optional)

Nilla wafers, for serving (optional)

1. Combine all ingredients in a standing mixer and mix until well combined. Pour mixture into saucepan and cook over low heat for about 10 minutes, until the mixture has thickened.

2. Pour into serving dish and place in the refrigerator. Chill until it thickens further. Serve with graham crackers or Nilla wafers, if desired.

Week 11

St. Patrick's is one of those days where it seems like everyone's ready to celebrate. This year, retreat from the crowds of revelers and put on your own party. To accommodate the festive feelings that attend this day, we've included two cocktails that have the Emerald Isle in mind: Irish Coffee and the Stout 'N' Cider. To keep everything running smoothly, the hearty spread of Corned Beef Hash, Shepherd's Pie, and Dark Chocolate Stout Brownies ensures that everyone has a solid foundation from which to proceed.

Irish Coffee

Stout 'N' Cider

Corned Beef Hash

Shepherd's Pie

Dark Chocolate Stout Brownies

IRISH COFFEE

3 parts coffee

Dash of sugar

1 part Irish whiskey

1 part Baileys Irish Cream

Dollop of whipped cream, for garnish

Dash of cinnamon, for garnish (optional)

1. Pour the coffee into a mug and add the sugar. Stir until the sugar has dissolved.

2. Add the whiskey and stir again. Top with Baileys Irish Cream. If you can, layer the cream on top rather than stirring it in. Garnish with the dollop of whipped cream and, if desired, a dash of cinnamon.

STOUT 'N' CIDER

1 part hard cider

1 part stout

1. Pour the cider into a pint glass.

2. Add the stout by pouring it over the back of an upside-down spoon. This will prevent the drink from becoming extremely fizzy.

CORNED BEEF HASH

Makes 4 to 6 Servings   Active Time: 40 Minutes   Total Time: 1 Hour and 15 Minutes

2 large russet potatoes, peeled and cubed

1 teaspoon salt, plus more to taste

3 tablespoons butter

½ Vidalia onion, diced

3 garlic cloves, minced

1 red bell pepper, seeded and diced

1 pound corned beef, cut into bite-sized pieces

½ teaspoon dried thyme

Freshly ground black pepper, to taste

1. Place the potatoes in a saucepan and cover with cold water. Add the salt, bring the water to a boil, and then lower the heat and cook for about 10 minutes. Drain them in a colander, rinse with cold water, and set aside.

2. Heat the butter in a skillet over medium-high heat. Add the onion, garlic, and red pepper and cook, while stirring, until the vegetables soften, about 3 minutes. Add the potatoes and press them down into the skillet around the vegetables. Allow them to cook for about 5 minutes, then start turning sections over with a spatula while stirring in the corned beef. Sprinkle with the thyme and season with salt and pepper. Continue to cook for about 5 minutes so that the potatoes are browned and the corned beef is warmed through.

Variation:
If you like eggs with your corned beef hash, once the potatoes are browned, make 4 to 6 indentations in the top of the hash and break the eggs into them. Lower the heat and cover the skillet. Continue cooking until the eggs are set, about 3 minutes.

SHEPHERD'S PIE

Makes 4 to 6 Servings   Active Time: 45 Minutes   Total Time: 1½ Hours

---

6 russet potatoes, peeled
and cubed

½ teaspoon salt, plus more to taste

8 tablespoons (1 stick) butter, cut
into individual tablespoons

½ cup milk

¼ cup yogurt

Black pepper, to taste

1 tablespoon olive oil

½ yellow onion, minced

1 pound ground beef

1 (15 oz.) can of peas, drained; or
2 cups high-quality frozen peas

½ (15 oz.) can of corn, drained
(optional)

1. Preheat the oven to 350°F. Put the potato pieces in a large pot and cover with cold water. Add the salt, bring the water to a boil, and reduce to a simmer. Cook the potatoes for about 20 minutes, until they can be easily pierced with a sharp knife.

2. Drain the potato pieces and put them in a large bowl. Add 6 table-spoons of the butter and the milk, and use a potato masher to make mashed potatoes. Add the yogurt, season with salt and pepper, and stir to combine.

3. Warm a skillet over medium heat, add the tablespoon of olive oil, and cook the onion, stirring to just soften, about 2 minutes. Add the ground beef and stir to break apart while it browns. When there is just a little pink left in the meat, drain the fat from the skillet. Stir in the peas and, if desired, the corn kernels. Season with salt and pepper and remove the skillet from the heat.

4. Place the ground beef mixture in an even layer in a 9 x 13–inch baking dish. Spread the mashed potatoes on top, cut the remaining 2 tablespoons of butter into slivers, and dot the potatoes with them.

5. Cover with foil and bake for 30 minutes. Remove the foil and cook for another 10 minutes until the potatoes are just browned. Remove from the oven and let cool for 5 minutes before serving.

DARK CHOCOLATE STOUT BROWNIES

Makes 16 Brownies   Active Time: 15 Minutes   Total Time: 1 Hour and 15 Minutes

12 oz. Guinness or other stout

12 oz. dark chocolate chips

2 sticks of butter

1½ cups sugar

3 large eggs

1 teaspoon vanilla extract

¾ cup all-purpose flour

1¼ teaspoons kosher salt

Cocoa powder, for dusting

1. Preheat your oven to 350°F and grease a 9 x 9–inch baking pan. Place the stout in a medium saucepan and bring to a boil. Cook until it has reduced by half. Remove pan from the heat and let cool.

2. Place the chocolate chips and the butter in a microwave-safe bowl and microwave until melted, removing to stir every 20 seconds.

3. Place the sugar, eggs, and vanilla in a large bowl and stir until combined. Slowly whisk in the chocolate-and-butter mixture, and then whisk in the stout.

4. Fold in the flour and salt. Pour batter into greased pan, place in oven, and cook for 35 to 40 minutes, until the surface begins to crack and a toothpick inserted in the center comes out with a few moist crumbs attached. Remove the pan from the oven, place on a wire rack, and let cool for at least 20 minutes. When cool, sprinkle the cocoa powder over the top and cut the brownies into squares.

Spring

Making it through another winter in one piece is enough cause for celebration. But too often, our relief at what has passed eclipses the brilliance that is unfurling right under our noses. As the world moves into its period of regeneration, we recommend taking some time to sit back and appreciate the miracle that arrives at the end of each and every winter: spring.

What better way to ensure that you take this time than a brunch hosted at your home? Sitting around with your loved ones and enjoying delicious food as you gaze out at the world coming back to life, you can't help but become a little more optimistic about the state of things.

Featuring menus freighted with freshness and warmth—including a revolutionary Easter menu and a Mother's Day spread sure to melt hearts the world over—we put you and your loved ones in position to renew yourself every Sunday.

Week 12

You made it. To celebrate the end of your incredible ordeal, we wanted to provide you with a number of easy-to-prepare recipes that will fill your table with fresh flavors and beautiful colors. The Lemon Cooler and the Strawberry-Chamomile Water will erase all memory of the brutal winter and set your sights squarely on the warmth to come. The Blini is traditionally served with sour cream and smoked salmon, but it is versatile enough for you to accommodate anyone who may show up at your table.

Lemon Cooler

Strawberry-Chamomile Water

Blini

Ham, Herb, and Tomato Frittata

Rice Pudding

LEMON COOLER

6 oz. beer
(lager, pilsner, or wheat beer)

2 oz. lemonade

1 oz. whiskey

Spoonful of honey

Dash of lemon juice

1 lemon slice, for garnish

1. Place ice in a pint glass and add the beer. Top with the lemonade.

2. Add the whiskey, honey, and lemon juice and stir until well combined. Garnish with the slice of lemon.

STRAWBERRY-CHAMOMILE WATER

Makes 8 Servings

¼ cup dried chamomile flowers

1 pint fresh strawberries, hulled and sliced

8 cups cold, filtered water

1. Place the chamomile flowers and strawberries in a pitcher or jar and cover with the water.

2. Let sit for 1 to 2 hours at room temperature for a quick infusion, or refrigerate for anywhere from 4 hours to overnight. Serve at room temperature.

BLINI

Makes 6 to 8 Servings   Active Time: 1 Hour   Total Time: 1 Hour

½ cup whole wheat flour

1 tablespoon sugar

¼ teaspoon salt

½ teaspoon baking powder

2 eggs, beaten

2½ cups milk

2 tablespoons vegetable oil

1. Preheat the oven to 200°F. In a large bowl, whisk together the flour, sugar, salt, and baking powder.

2. In a smaller bowl, combine the eggs and milk. Add the liquid mixture to the dry mixture and stir until well combined.

3. Heat a skillet over medium-high heat and brush with some of the vegetable oil. Spoon just about a tablespoon of batter to form each blini. You should be able to fit about 4 at a time in the skillet. Cook for about 2 minutes a side and flip them over when the edges start to crisp. If the skillet looks dry, brush it with more of the vegetable oil. Keep the cooked blinis warm in the oven until ready to serve.

Tip: If you like caviar of any kind, you have to try these with a dollop of sour cream or crème fraîche topped with caviar. Other great toppings include jams, sour cream with a sprig of dill, scrambled eggs and hot sauce, bacon bits and sour cream, and butter and honey.

HAM, HERB, AND TOMATO FRITTATA

Makes 4 Servings   Active Time: 20 Minutes   Total Time: 40 Minutes

2 tablespoons butter

½ pound thick-sliced deli ham, cut into pieces

¼ cup milk or heavy cream

6 eggs, beaten

1 teaspoon salt, plus more to taste

Freshly ground black pepper, to taste

6 cherry tomatoes, halved

½ cup parsley, coarsely chopped

1 teaspoon fresh thyme, minced

1. Preheat the broiler to low. Heat a cast-iron skillet over medium-high heat and melt the butter, being careful not to let it burn. Add the ham to the pan and stir, cooking until just browned, about 3 minutes.

2. Add the milk or cream to the beaten eggs, stir to combine, and season with salt and pepper.

3. Pour the egg mixture into the skillet. After a couple of minutes, as the eggs begin to set, add the cherry tomato halves and sprinkle the herbs over everything. Lower the heat to medium or low, cover, and cook until eggs are set, another 10 minutes.

4. Place the skillet under the broiler for just a couple of minutes to toast the top. Remove from the oven and allow to sit for a few minutes before serving.

RICE PUDDING

Makes 6 to 8 Servings   Active Time: 30 Minutes   Total Time: 30 to 35 Minutes

---

4½ cups whole milk

½ cup heavy cream

1 cup Arborio rice

½ cup sugar

1 teaspoon ground cinnamon

½ teaspoon nutmeg, grated

3 strips of orange zest

1 vanilla bean, halved lengthwise;
or 1 teaspoon pure vanilla extract

½ teaspoon sea salt

Yolk of 1 egg

1. Combine milk, cream, rice, sugar, cinnamon, nutmeg, orange zest, vanilla component, and salt in a medium saucepan and bring to a gentle boil. Reduce heat to low and cook for approximately 25 minutes, until rice is tender and mixture is thick. Stir while cooking to make sure rice doesn't stick to the bottom of the pan.

2. Remove the pan from heat and remove the orange zest and vanilla bean. Let stand for 3 to 5 minutes. Whisk in the egg yolk until very well combined. Serve warm or place in refrigerator for 5 minutes.

Week 13

The end of March is always tricky—you want to be outside, but often it's nowhere near as warm as it looks, and you end up shivering the second you stop moving. To counter this, we've decided to bring the outdoors inside and curate a series of selections that would be perfect for a picnic: the Salty Mutt, Herb-Roasted Almonds, and Bruschetta. The Miso Broth with Fried Tofu and Crispy Wonton Skins is a nod to reality, as it will cut through the chill you picked up while grilling the tomatoes for the Bruschetta.

Salty Mutt

Herb-Roasted Almonds

Bruschetta

Miso Broth with Fried Tofu
and Crispy Wonton Skins

Rose Water Pound Cake
with Vanilla Peach Compote

SALTY MUTT

Salt, for the rim

1 part gin

1 part grapefruit juice

1 part cranberry juice

1 grapefruit wedge, for garnish

1. Wet the rim of a rocks glass and then dip the rim into the salt.

2. Add the gin, grapefruit juice, and cranberry juice to a cocktail shaker filled with ice. Shake vigorously.

3. Strain the resulting mixture over ice into the rocks glass and garnish with the grapefruit wedge.

HERB-ROASTED ALMONDS

Makes 2 Cups   Active Time: 10 Minutes
Total Time: 30 Minutes

½ teaspoon salt

1½ teaspoons water

2 cups whole raw almonds

3 sprigs of thyme, leaves only

1 sprig of summer savory, leaves only

2 teaspoons olive oil

1. Preheat oven to 375°F. Dissolve the salt in the water.

2. Combine the salt water, almonds, and herbs in a small bowl.

3. Place the almonds in a single layer on baking sheet and roast for 15 to 20 minutes, removing to stir every 5 minutes. Once the almonds have browned, remove them from the oven immediately. Let stand until cool.

4. Transfer to a bowl. Add the olive oil and toss to coat.

BRUSCHETTA

Makes 6 Servings   Active Time: 10 Minutes   Total Time: 25 Minutes

4 tomatoes, cut into wedges

5 garlic cloves, minced

½ cup olive oil

15 slices of French bread

6 basil leaves, torn

1 teaspoon oregano, minced

1 teaspoon parsley, minced

1. In a large bowl, add the tomatoes, garlic, and half of the olive oil and toss to coat.

2. Preheat your gas or charcoal grill to 400°F. Place the tomatoes on the grill and cook for 8 to 10 minutes, turning occasionally. When the tomatoes are tender, remove from heat and let cool. When cool enough to handle, chop into bite-sized pieces, combine in a bowl, and set aside.

3. Brush both sides of the bread slices with the remaining olive oil. Grill each piece for about 1 minute per side, or until the bread is lightly toasted.

4. Spoon the grilled tomatoes onto the toasted bread. Sprinkle the basil leaves, oregano, and parsley on top and serve.

MISO BROTH WITH FRIED TOFU
AND CRISPY WONTON SKINS

Makes 4 Servings   Active Time: 30 Minutes   Total Time: 1 Hour

For the Miso Broth

4 scallions, whites thinly sliced, greens reserved for broth

4 sprigs of cilantro, leaves reserved for garnish, stalks reserved for broth

1-inch piece of ginger, sliced

1 star anise

1 cinnamon stick

4 cardamom pods, seeds removed from shell and crushed

1 bay leaf

½ teaspoon red pepper flakes

4 cups Dashi Stock (see page 99)

3 bok choy, cut lengthwise into eighths

¼ cup red miso

2 tablespoons soy sauce

Thai chili, seeded and thinly sliced, for garnish

For the Fried Tofu

2 cups vegetable oil

2 eggs, beaten

¼ cup all-purpose flour

1½ cups panko bread crumbs, finely ground

5 oz. tofu, cubed

Salt, to taste

For the Crispy Wonton Skins

4 wonton wrappers, cut into triangles

Salt, to taste

1. Prepare the broth. In a stockpot, add the scallion greens, cilantro stalks, ginger, star anise, cinnamon stick, cardamom seeds, bay leaf, red pepper flakes, and Dashi Stock. Cook over medium heat until boiling, reduce the heat, and simmer for 15 minutes.

2. Prepare the tofu. Place oil in a medium saucepan and heat to 350°F. Place the eggs, flour, and panko bread crumbs in 3 separate bowls. Dredge the tofu in the flour, remove, and shake to remove any excess flour. Place the coated tofu in the egg wash. Remove from egg wash, shake to release any excess egg, and gently coat with bread crumbs. If there is any tofu exposed, return to the egg mix and repeat with bread crumbs.

3. Once all the tofu is coated, place in oil and fry in batches until golden brown. Remove with a slotted spoon, place on a paper towel, and season with salt. Reduce the heat of the oil to 300°F and reserve for the Crispy Wonton Skins.

4. Prepare the wonton skins. Place the wonton wrappers in the reserved oil and turn frequently until they are crisp and golden brown. Use a slotted spoon to remove the fried wonton wrappers from oil and set on paper towels to drain. Season with salt and set aside.

5. Strain the broth through a fine sieve. Return to the stockpot and bring to a simmer. Add the bok choy and cook for 5 minutes. Add the scallion whites and cook for an additional 2 minutes. Place the miso in a small bowl, add a bit of the hot stock, and then place the tempered miso in the soup.

6. Add the soy sauce. Ladle into warm bowls, garnish with the cilantro and Thai chili, and serve with Fried Tofu and Crispy Wonton Skins.

ROSE WATER POUND CAKE
WITH VANILLA PEACH COMPOTE

Makes 8 to 10 Servings   Active Time: 30 Minutes   Total Time: 1 Hour and 10 Minutes

For the Rose Water Pound Cake

1 cup butter, at room temperature, plus more for pan

2 cups all-purpose flour, plus more for dusting

1 cup sugar

5 eggs, at room temperature

2 teaspoons rose water

1½ teaspoons baking powder

½ teaspoon salt

For the Vanilla Peach Compote

7 medium peaches, peeled and chopped

¼ cup sugar

½ vanilla bean, halved and scraped

2 teaspoons rose water

1. Prepare the pound cake. Preheat oven to 350°F. Liberally coat a Bundt pan with butter and lightly coat with flour. In a standing mixer with a paddle attachment, cream together the butter and sugar until the mixture is light and fluffy. Once finished, add the eggs one at a time and beat until thoroughly incorporated, scraping down the sides of the bowl after each egg. Add the rose water.

2. In a separate medium mixing bowl, combine the flour, baking powder, and salt. Add the flour mixture to the egg mixture and stir briefly. Transfer the batter to your prepared Bundt pan and spread evenly. Bake for 45 to 50 minutes, or until a toothpick comes out mostly clean. Remove, allow the cake to rest in the pan for 15 minutes, then remove from the pan and let cool on a wire rack.

3. Prepare the compote. Place the peaches, sugar, vanilla bean, and half of the rose water in a medium saucepan and simmer for 10 minutes over medium heat.

4. Remove the saucepan from heat and add the remaining rose water. Transfer the mixture to a small bowl and let cool. When cool, drizzle over the slices of pound cake.

Week 14

It's a good week to invite over your more adventurous friends, those who won't turn their nose up at the unique union of tequila and Champagne in the Unlikely Allies. Those who will nod approvingly when they see the bold pairing of Bacon, Cheddar, and Jalapeño Scones and Green Chili Chow Chow. The Smoked Salmon and Dill Quiche is more on the traditional side of things, but no one's going to complain once they taste the combination of smoke and the warm, almost-anise flavor of dill. Because this menu favors the bold, we've decided to double down on the sweet-and-tart citrus in the Double Lemon Tart.

Unlikely Allies

Virgin Fizz

Bacon, Cheddar, and Jalapeño Scones

Green Chili Chow Chow

Smoked Salmon and Dill Quiche

Double Lemon Tart

UNLIKELY ALLIES

1 part tequila

1 part grapefruit soda

2 parts Champagne

1. Add tequila to a champagne flute. Pour in the grapefruit soda and lightly swirl the glass to stir.

2. Top with Champagne and serve.

VIRGIN FIZZ

1 part ginger ale

2 parts seltzer

Raspberries, for garnish

Pour the ginger ale and seltzer into a champagne flute. Drop in the raspberries for garnish.

BACON, CHEDDAR, AND JALAPEÑO SCONES

Makes 4 to 6 Servings   Active Time: 30 Minutes   Total Time: 50 Minutes

2 cups all-purpose flour, plus more for dusting

1 teaspoon baking powder

½ teaspoon salt

1 teaspoon freshly ground black pepper

4 tablespoons butter, chilled, cut into small pieces, plus more for greasing pan

¾ cup sharp cheddar cheese, grated

½ cup jalapeño peppers, sliced or chopped

½ cup milk

4 slices of thick-cut bacon, cooked and chopped

1 egg, beaten with a little milk

1. Preheat the oven to 400°F. Position a rack in the middle of the oven. In a large bowl, whisk together the flour, baking powder, salt, and pepper. Add the butter pieces and mix with an electric mixer until just blended, or mix with a fork so that the dough is somewhat crumbly. Stir in the cheese, peppers, milk, and bacon, being careful not to overmix.

2. With flour on your hands, transfer the dough to a lightly floured work surface. Form the dough into a ½-inch-thick circle. With a long knife, cut the dough into 6 to 8 wedges. Butter a cake pan, and place the wedges into it, leaving some space between the pieces.

3. Brush with the beaten egg. Bake for 20 to 25 minutes, or until golden brown.

Variation:

Ramp up the heat by substituting pepper jack cheese for the cheddar, or substitute a serrano pepper for the jalapeño.

GREEN CHILI CHOW CHOW

Makes 2 Cups   Active Time: 5 Minutes   Total Time: 40 Minutes

1 cup distilled vinegar

¼ tablespoon mustard powder

2 tablespoons yellow mustard seeds

¼ cup sugar

½ bay leaf

¼ bunch of cilantro, stems only, chopped

1 (13.5 oz.) can of Hatch green chilies

2 tablespoons Dijon mustard

Salt, to taste

Hatch chili powder, to taste

1. Combine vinegar, mustard powder, mustard seeds, sugar, bay leaves, and cilantro in a medium saucepan. Cook until reduced by one-third. Add chilies and cook for another 5 minutes.

2. Add the Dijon mustard. Season with salt and the chili powder and remove the pan from heat. Let cool until the mixture starts to look gelatinous.

Tip: This Chow Chow, which comes courtesy of Joe Frietze at Publican Quality Meats in Chicago, will go well with the scones or even on the quiche.

SMOKED SALMON AND DILL QUICHE

Makes 6 to 8 Servings   Active Time: 30 Minutes   Total Time: 1½ Hours

1 Flaky Pastry Crust (see page 28)

1 teaspoon Dijon mustard

1 pound smoked salmon, cut into nickel-sized pieces

4 eggs

1 cup half-and-half

1 teaspoon salt

½ teaspoon ground black pepper

1 tablespoon dill, minced

1 (3 oz.) package of cream cheese, cubed

1. Preheat the oven to 350°F. Working with the crust in a greased pie plate, brush the mustard over the bottom of the dough. Place the salmon pieces in the pie. In a large bowl, whisk the eggs until thoroughly combined. Add the half-and-half, salt, and pepper, and whisk to combine. Add the dill and mix well.

2. Pour the egg mixture over the salmon pieces, shaking the pie plate gently to distribute evenly. Sprinkle the cubes of cream cheese evenly on top. Put the quiche in the oven and bake for 35 to 40 minutes or until the quiche is puffy and golden brown and the eggs are set. Remove from the oven and let stand for 10 minutes before slicing and serving.

DOUBLE LEMON TART

Makes 6 to 8 Servings   Active Time: 30 Minutes
Total Time: 1 Hour

1 (14 oz.) can of sweetened condensed milk

½ cup fresh lemon juice

4 large egg yolks

1 tablespoon vanilla extract

1 Graham Cracker Crust (see page 29)

1 lemon, seeded and very thinly sliced

1. Preheat the oven to 325°F. In a medium bowl, combine the condensed milk, lemon juice, egg yolks, and vanilla. Working with the crust in a 9" pie plate, pour the filling into the crust. Top with the very thin slices of lemon, arranged in a decorative pattern.

2. Put the tart in the oven and bake for about 15 to 20 minutes, until the filling has set into a soft custard. Remove from the oven and allow to cool completely before serving.

Week 15

It's tough to improve on a mound of Cheesy Hash Browns and a cup of spiked coffee to start the day, but the decadent Bananas Foster French Toast manages to pull off this arduous task. The hash browns are the perfect place to stash an egg or two, so make sure you're ready to accommodate those who like a little protein in their breakfast, or prefer to start the day with something savory instead of something sweet.

Ice Age

Cheesy Hash Browns

Bananas Foster French Toast

Plum Galette

ICE AGE

Splash of Simple Syrup (see page 32)
Dash of bitters
1 part bourbon
2 parts iced coffee

1. Add the Simple Syrup and bitters to a rocks glass filled with ice.

2. Add the bourbon and iced coffee and stir.

CHEESY HASH BROWNS

Makes 4 to 6 Servings
Active Time: 20 Minutes
Total Time: 1 Hour

4 tablespoons butter

4 large russet potatoes, shredded and squeezed dry

1 teaspoon salt

Black pepper, to taste

6 eggs

½ cup milk

1 cup cheese, shredded

1. Preheat the oven to 375°F. Place the butter in a cast-iron skillet and cook over medium-high heat. When the butter starts bubbling, add the potatoes and season with the salt and pepper. Press the potatoes into the bottom of the pan. Cook for about 5 minutes.

2. In a mixing bowl, whisk the eggs and milk together. Pour the mixture over the potatoes, shaking the pan to help them penetrate to the bottom. Sprinkle liberally with the cheese and then transfer the skillet to the oven. Cook until just set, about 10 minutes, and serve immediately.

Note: *Use a blend of cheddar, Swiss, mozzarella, Monterey Jack, and/or Provolone for the cheese.*

BANANAS FOSTER FRENCH TOAST

Makes 4 to 6 Servings   Active Time: 10 Minutes   Total Time: 10 Minutes

For the French Toast

3 tablespoons butter

8 eggs

2 tablespoons sugar

½ cup heavy cream

1 tablespoon cinnamon

1 tablespoon vanilla extract

Pinch of salt

1 loaf of brioche, cut into
10 to 12 slices

For the Bananas Foster

8 tablespoons (1 stick) butter

½ cup light brown sugar,
firmly packed

3 bananas, cut lengthwise
and halved

¼ cup dark rum

½ cup heavy cream

Powdered sugar, for topping

1. Prepare the French toast. Preheat the oven to 200°F. Heat a large skillet over medium-high heat and melt 1 tablespoon of butter per batch of French toast.

2. Place the eggs, sugar, heavy cream, cinnamon, vanilla, and salt in a mixing bowl and stir to combine. Dunk the slices of bread in the batter to cover both sides. Cook the bread in batches for 1 minute per side, or until a brown crust forms. Remove from the pan and keep warm in the oven.

3. Prepare the Bananas Foster. Place the skillet over medium-high heat and add the stick of butter and the brown sugar. Once the butter and sugar are melted, add the bananas to the pan and cook for 3 minutes. Shake the pan and spoon the sauce over the bananas.

4. Pull the pan away from the heat and add the rum. Using a long match or a lighter, carefully light the rum on fire. Place the pan back on the heat and shake the pan until the flames are gone. Add the cream. Stir to blend and pour over the French toast. Sprinkle with powdered sugar and serve.

PLUM GALETTE

Makes 4 to 6 Servings   Active Time: 40 Minutes
Start to Finish: 1½ Hours

1 Flaky Pastry Crust (see page 28)

3 cups fresh plums, pitted and sliced

½ cup sugar, plus 1 tablespoon

Juice of ½ lemon

3 tablespoons cornstarch

Pinch of salt

2 tablespoons blackberry jam

1 egg, beaten

1. Preheat the oven to 400°F. Roll the crust out to 10 inches and place it on a baking sheet. In a large bowl, add the plums, the ½ cup of sugar, lemon juice, cornstarch, and salt. Stir well to coat all the fruit.

2. Brush or smear the jam in the center of the crust. Place the fruit mixture in a mound in the center. Fold the edges of the crust over to cover about 1 inch of the filling. Brush the top of the crust with the beaten egg and sprinkle it with the remaining sugar.

3. Put the galette in the oven and bake until the filling is bubbly, which is necessary for it to thicken sufficiently, about 35 to 40 minutes. Remove from the oven and allow the galette to cool before serving.

Week 16
Easter

Ham. Potatoes. Peas. Most Easter meals will roll this trio out,
but we've put a twist on the flavors typically associated with
the holiday to inject a little bit of life into your gathering. The
Gin Waterfall and Kombucha Sangria are the perfect beverages
to get people thinking outside of the box, and peas on a bed of
crusty bread and creamy, salty ricotta will have them wondering
how they've never truly appreciated this legume before. Follow
up with a beautiful bowl of Ham Hock and Collard Green Soup
and no one will be able to question the break from tradition.
And, while challenging convention is fun, we can't let it stamp
out classics such as Baklava. This flaky, buttery masterpiece will
send everyone into a full-on food coma.

Gin Waterfall

Kombucha Sangria

Lemon-Rose Water

Crostini with Ricotta and Pea Pods

French Potato Tart

Ham Hock and Collard Green Soup

Lemon Brûlée Pie

Baklava

GIN WATERFALL

1 part gin

1 part Champagne

2 parts Sprite

Juice of ½ lemon

1 lemon wheel, for garnish

Fill a highball glass with ice and add all of the liquid ingredients. Stir until thoroughly mixed and garnish with the lemon wheel.

KOMBUCHA SANGRIA

3 parts pomegranate kombucha

3 parts red wine

1 part grapefruit seltzer

1 part cranberry juice

1 handful of pomegranate seeds, for garnish

1. Add ice to a mason jar. Pour in the kombucha and red wine.

2. Add the seltzer and cranberry juice. Avoid shaking the drink around too much as the kombucha is extremely fizzy. Float some pomegranate seeds on top for garnish.

LEMON-ROSE WATER

Makes 8 Servings

1 lemon, thinly sliced

½ cup rose petals

8 cups cold, filtered water

1. Place the lemon slices and rose petals in a pitcher or jar and cover with the water.

2. Let sit for 1 to 2 hours at room temperature for a quick infusion, or refrigerate for anywhere from 4 hours to overnight. Serve chilled or at room temperature.

CROSTINI WITH RICOTTA AND PEA PODS

Makes 4 to 6 Servings   Active Time: 15 Minutes
Total Time: 35 Minutes

1 baguette, cut into ½-inch-thick slices

7 tablespoons extra virgin olive oil,
plus more for topping

3 cups whole milk ricotta

½ teaspoon sea salt, plus more
for topping

½ teaspoon freshly ground black pepper,
plus more for topping

¼ cup garlic, minced

3 tablespoons mint, minced

3 teaspoons lemon zest

Pea pods, for garnish

1. Preheat oven to 400°F. Lightly brush the baguette slices
    with 1 tablespoon of the olive oil and arrange on a baking
    sheet. Bake in oven for about 12 to 15 minutes, turning
    the slices over halfway through. When the slices are
    golden brown on both sides, remove from the oven.

2. Combine ricotta, the remaining olive oil, salt, and pepper
    in a bowl and stir until the mixture is light and fluffy. Stir
    in the garlic, mint, and lemon zest. Spread the mixture on
    the baguette slices.

3. Drizzle olive oil over the crostini. Sprinkle with a few
    grains of sea salt and black pepper. Top with the pea pods
    and serve.

FRENCH POTATO TART

Makes 4 to 6 Servings   Active Time: 45 Minutes   Total Time: 2 Hours

2 pounds Yukon Gold
potatoes, peeled

1¼ cups crème fraîche

1 tablespoon kosher salt

½ teaspoon black pepper

Pinch of nutmeg, grated

2 garlic cloves, crushed

2 teaspoons fresh thyme, chopped

2 Flaky Pastry Crusts
(see page 28)

All-purpose flour, for dusting

Yolk of 1 egg

1 tablespoon half-and-half

1. Preheat the oven to 400°F. Using a very sharp knife, a mandoline, or a spiralizer, slice the potatoes as thin as possible.

2. In a bowl, add the crème fraîche, salt, pepper, nutmeg, garlic, and thyme. Stir to combine. Add the potato slices and fold gently to cover with the creamy mixture.

3. On a lightly floured surface, roll out the one crust so that it is just larger than the bottom of a pie plate. Layer the potato slices in the crust, creating even, tight layers. Once all the potatoes are used up, use a rubber spatula to scrape the remaining cream into the pie. Tap the edges of the pie plate to distribute the mixture evenly.

4. On a lightly floured surface, roll out the top crust, place it on top of the tart, and crimp the edges of the bottom crust to seal. Blend the egg yolk with the half-and-half and brush the mixture over the top crust. Cut 4 to 5 slits in the middle. Put the tart in the oven and bake for 15 minutes. Reduce temperature to 350°F and continue to bake for 1 hour, or until potatoes are tender. Serve hot or at room temperature.

HAM HOCK AND COLLARD GREEN SOUP

Makes 4 Servings   Active Time: 30 Minutes   Total Time: 1 Hour and 35 Minutes

4 quarts water

1 teaspoon salt

1 pound collard greens, chopped

1 tablespoon vegetable oil

2 oz. salt pork

½ cup onions, minced

¼ cup celery, minced

½ cup all-purpose flour

8 cups Chicken Stock
(see page 24)

2 smoked ham hocks

Sachet d'Epices (see page 32)

½ cup heavy cream

1. In a medium saucepan, add the water and salt and bring to a boil. Add the collard greens and cook for 4 minutes, or until soft. Remove with a slotted spoon and submerge in ice water. Set aside to dry.

2. In a large saucepan, add the oil and then the salt pork. Cook over medium heat until the salt pork is melted. Add the onions and celery and cook for 5 minutes, or until soft.

3. Add the flour slowly, while stirring constantly, and cook for 4 minutes. Gradually add the stock while whisking constantly to prevent any lumps from forming. Bring to a boil, reduce heat so that the soup simmers, and add the ham hocks and sachet d'epices. Cook for 1 hour.

4. Remove ham hocks and sachet d'epices and add the collard greens to the saucepan. Remove meat from the ham hocks, finely dice, and return to soup. Add the heavy cream, season to taste, and serve in warm bowls.

LEMON BRÛLÉE PIE

Makes 6 to 8 Servings   Active Time: 30 Minutes   Total Time: 2 Hours

1 Baked Crust (see page 27)

1¼ cups sugar

Zest from 2 lemons

¾ cup fresh lemon juice

2 teaspoons lemon liqueur
(optional)

6 eggs, beaten

⅔ cup heavy cream

1. Preheat the oven to 300°F and place the crust in a 9" pie plate. Add the sugar, zest, lemon juice, and lemon liqueur, if using, to the beaten eggs and whisk until the mixture is well combined and sugar is dissolved. Stir in the heavy cream.

2. Fill the crust with the mixture and tap the plate to distribute filling evenly. Bake for 50 to 60 minutes, testing after 50 minutes to see if center is set. If it is, remove from oven. If it's still runny, return to the oven and bake in 5-minute increments until set in center. Allow to cool before serving.

BAKLAVA

Makes 48 Pieces   Active Time: 30 Minutes   Total Time: 1 Hour

---

3½ cups walnuts

2½ cups granulated sugar

1 teaspoon ground cinnamon

¼ teaspoon ground cloves

1 (1 pound) package of phyllo sheets, thawed

1½ cups butter, melted

1½ cups water

½ cup honey

½ lemon, thinly sliced

1 (3-inch) cinnamon stick

Pistachios, chopped, for garnish (optional)

1. Preheat the oven to 350°F. Place the walnuts on a baking sheet, place the sheet in the oven, and toast for 5 to 7 minutes, until lightly browned. Remove the pan from the oven and place the walnuts, ½ cup of the sugar, cinnamon, and cloves in a food processor. Pulse until chopped very finely.

2. Increase the oven's temperature to 375°F and grease a 12 x 16–inch rimmed baking sheet. Place the phyllo sheets on a plate and cover with plastic wrap or a damp paper towel to keep them from drying out. Place 1 sheet of phyllo on the baking sheet and brush with the melted butter. Repeat with 7 more sheets, and spread one-third of the walnut mixture on top. Place 4 more sheets of phyllo dough on top, brushing each with butter. Spread one-third of the walnut mixture on top, and then repeat with the phyllo, butter, and walnut mixture. Top the last layer of walnut mixture with the remaining sheets of phyllo dough, brushing each one with butter. Trim the edges to make a neat rectangle. Cut pastry into 2-inch squares or triangles, taking care not to cut through the bottom crust. Place in the oven and bake for 25 to 30 minutes, until the top layer of phyllo is brown.

3. While the pastry is cooking, combine the remaining sugar, water, honey, lemon, and cinnamon stick in a saucepan. Bring to a boil over medium heat, while stirring occasionally, reduce heat to low, and simmer for 5 minutes. Strain syrup and keep hot while pastry finishes baking.

4. Remove the baking sheet from the oven and pour the hot syrup over the pastry. Place the pan on a wire rack, allow to cool to room temperature, and then cut through the bottom crust. If desired, garnish with pistachios.

Week 17

There always seems to be a summery stretch toward the end of April. Celebrate this burst of warmth with the bright bite of an Elderflower Margarita. That will provide good company for when you fire up the grill for the Grilled Beets and Toasted Sunflower Seeds Salad and the Black Bean Burgers (which are the perfect bed for a couple over-easy eggs). After these temperate treats and a slice of the Peachy Keen Cake, we're betting you go and hose down the patio furniture.

Elderflower Margarita

Vanilla-Lemon-Violet Water

Grilled Beets and
Toasted Sunflower Seeds Salad

Black Bean Burgers

Peachy Keen Cake

ELDERFLOWER MARGARITA

2 oz. tequila

2 oz. St-Germain

1⅓ oz. fresh lime juice

Sea salt, for the rim

Splash of seltzer (optional)

1 lime wedge, for garnish

1. Place the tequila, St-Germain, and lime juice in a cocktail shaker filled with ice and shake until well combined.

2. Rub the lime wedge around the rim of a cocktail glass and then dip the rim in sea salt. Fill the glass to the top with ice and strain the margarita into the glass. Top with a splash of seltzer, if desired. Garnish with the lime wedge and serve.

VANILLA-LEMON-VIOLET WATER

Makes 8 Servings

½ cup violet petals

1 lemon, thinly sliced

1 vanilla bean, sliced down the center; or 1 teaspoon pure vanilla extract

8 cups cold, filtered water

1. Place the violet petals, lemon slices, and vanilla component in a pitcher or jar and cover with the water.

2. Let sit for 1 to 2 hours at room temperature for a quick infusion, or refrigerate for anywhere from 4 hours to overnight. Serve chilled or at room temperature.

Tip: If you've never used a whole vanilla bean before, don't worry, it's easy: Using a sharp knife, slice down the center of the bean lengthwise (it's okay if you accidentally cut it in half). Scrape all those tiny black seeds into your water, since that's where the flavor is. Then add the whole bean to your pitcher.

GRILLED BEETS AND
TOASTED SUNFLOWER SEEDS SALAD

Makes 6 Servings   Active Time: 15 Minutes   Total Time: 20 Minutes

⅓ pound arugula

6 red beets, peeled

¼ cup olive oil, plus 2 tablespoons

¼ cup sunflower seeds

2 tablespoons balsamic vinegar

Sea salt and freshly ground black pepper, to taste

1. Rinse the arugula and then dry thoroughly. Place in the refrigerator to chill. Cut the beets into quarters and combine with the ¼ cup of olive oil in a small bowl. Let stand for 30 minutes.

2. Place a medium cast-iron skillet on your gas or charcoal grill and pre-heat the grill to 450°F. Leave the grill covered while heating, as this will add a faint, smoky flavor to the skillet.

3. Once the grill is ready, transfer the beets onto the grill. Grill the beets until tender, about 10 minutes. Transfer the beets to a large bowl and cover it with aluminum foil.

4. Add the sunflower seeds to the cast-iron skillet and cook until browned, about 2 minutes. Remove, mix with the beets, and set aside. In a small bowl, add the remaining olive oil and the balsamic vinegar and mix thoroughly. Drizzle on top of beets and sunflower seeds and place over chilled arugula. Season with salt and pepper before serving.

BLACK BEAN BURGERS

Makes 8 Servings
Active Time: 20 Minutes
Total Time: 35 Minutes

2 (14 oz.) cans of black beans, rinsed, drained, and dried

1 red bell pepper, seeded and minced

1 small red onion, minced

4 garlic cloves, minced

4 eggs

2 teaspoons cumin

2 tablespoons chili powder

2 cups bread crumbs

1. Place the black beans in a medium bowl and mash them until they become thick and pasty. Add the bell pepper, red onion, and garlic and stir until well combined.

2. Preheat your gas or charcoal grill to 500°F. In a small bowl, combine the eggs, cumin, and chili powder. Add this to the bean-and-vegetable mixture. Add the bread crumbs and stir until the mixture sticks together.

3. Separate the mixture into 8 patties. Grill for about 8 minutes on each side, remove from heat, and serve on buns with your preferred condiments.

PEACHY KEEN CAKE

Makes 8 Servings   Active Time: 20 Minutes   Total Time: 1 Hour

---

8 tablespoons (1 stick) butter

½ pound fresh peaches, sliced; or
1 can sliced peaches with no sugar
added, drained

1 (15.25 oz.) box of yellow
cake mix

1 cup water

½ cup vegetable oil

6 oz. unsweetened applesauce

4 eggs

¼ teaspoon almond extract

1. Preheat the oven to 350°F. In a cast-iron skillet, add the
    butter and cook over medium heat. When it's melted,
    add the peaches, reduce the heat to low, and simmer
    until the butter is bubbling but not browning. In a large
    bowl, add the cake mix, water, oil, applesauce, eggs, and
    almond extract and stir to combine. When the butter
    in the skillet is bubbling, turn off the heat and pour the
    batter over the fruit.

2. Place the skillet in the oven and bake for 35 to 40
    minutes until the cake is browned on the top and a
    toothpick inserted in the middle comes out clean.
    Remove the skillet from the oven and allow to cool. Put
    a large serving plate on the counter and, working quickly
    and purposefully, flip the skillet so the cake is inverted
    onto the plate.

Week 18

It's unclear how many of the revelers who gather on Cinco de Mayo know that it's a celebration of the Mexican Army's unlikely victory over the French Empire at the Battle of Puebla in 1862. But only a fool can overlook the gifts this culture has given to us. To celebrate this incredible bounty, we've gathered a small collection of Mexican-inspired offerings. The entire menu is bursting with intriguing flavors, but there are two real standouts on it: the Classic Michelada, which just may supplant the Bloody Mary as your favorite tomato-y morning cocktail; and the Pozole Rojo, which is so good that your friends will be clamoring for it to become an annual tradition.

Classic Michelada

Cilantro-Jalapeño-Lime Water

Grilled Mexican Street Corn

Pozole Rojo

Chocolate-Cinnamon Bread

CLASSIC MICHELADA

1 part beer (Mexican-style lager or pilsner)

1 part tomato juice

Dash of Worcestershire sauce

Dash of lime juice

Salt, for the rim

1 lime wedge, for garnish

1. Add the beer, tomato juice, Worcestershire sauce, and lime juice to a pint glass filled with ice and stir until thoroughly mixed.

2. Salt the rim of a separate pint glass and add ice as desired. Strain the beer-and-tomato juice mixture into the salt-rimmed pint glass and garnish with the lime wedge.

CILANTRO-JALAPEÑO-LIME WATER

Makes 8 Servings

1 to 2 jalapeño peppers

3 sprigs of cilantro

1 lime, thinly sliced

8 cups of cold, filtered water

1. Remove the stems from the peppers and cut in half lengthwise. Remove the seeds and then muddle lightly to break up the skin and extract some of the juice.

2. Place the peppers, cilantro, and lime slices in a pitcher or jar and cover with the water.

3. Let sit for 1 to 2 hours at room temperature for a quick infusion, or refrigerate for anywhere from 4 hours to overnight. Serve chilled.

GRILLED MEXICAN STREET CORN

Makes 4 to 6 Servings   Active Time: 30 Minutes   Total Time: 30 Minutes

½ cup mayonnaise

½ cup sour cream

1 cup Cotija or feta cheese, plus more to taste

1 teaspoon ancho chili powder, plus more to taste

2 garlic cloves, minced

½ cup cilantro, minced, plus more to taste

8 ears of corn, shucked

2 limes, cut into wedges

1. Preheat your gas or charcoal grill to 450°F. Place the mayonnaise, sour cream, cheese, ancho chili powder, garlic, and cilantro in a large bowl, stir until well combined, and set aside.

2. When the grill is 450°F, place the ears of corn on the grill and cook, while rotating them occasionally, until they are cooked through and charred. This should take about 8 minutes.

3. Drizzle the mayonnaise-and-cheese mixture over the ears of corn. Sprinkle with additional cheese, chili powder, and cilantro and serve alongside the lime wedges.

POZOLE ROJO

Makes 6 Servings   Active Time: 30 Minutes   Total Time: 6½ to 8½ Hours

---

2 cups water

3 Pasilla peppers, seeded

8 árbol chilies, seeded

2 tablespoons vegetable oil

2 pounds pork shoulder, cut into 1-inch cubes

1 large yellow onion, diced

3 tablespoons cumin

6 garlic cloves, minced

3 tablespoons dried oregano

5 dashes of Tabasco

3 tablespoons kosher salt

5 cups Chicken Stock (see page 24)

1 green bell pepper, seeded and diced

1. In a cast-iron skillet, bring the water to a boil. Place the Pasilla peppers and árbol chilies in a bowl, pour the boiling water over them, and cover with plastic wrap. Set aside for 30 minutes, until the chilies are soft.

2. Place the vegetable oil in the skillet and warm it over medium-high heat. Add the pork, being careful not to overcrowd the pan, and sear for 3 minutes per side. Transfer the seared pork to a slow cooker. Add the onion, cumin, garlic, oregano, Tabasco, salt, and chicken stock.

3. Place the green pepper, Pasilla peppers, árbol chilies, and the water in a blender and puree until smooth. Add the sauce to the slow cooker and cook on high for 6 to 8 hours, until the pork is extremely tender.

Tip: Step 2 is optional but highly recommended. Searing the meat first will help cook off some of the fat before adding it to the pot, which will keep the soup from being too greasy. If you are going to skip this step, try to remove as much of the fat as possible from the pork before adding it to the slow cooker and add 2 hours to the cooking time.

CHOCOLATE-CINNAMON BREAD

Makes 1 Small Round   Active Time: 25 Minutes   Total Time: 3 Hours

¼ teaspoon active dry yeast

¼ teaspoon sugar

1½ cups lukewarm water
(90 to 100°F)

2 tablespoons unsalted butter,
cut into small pieces

1 cup semi-sweet chocolate
morsels

1 teaspoon cinnamon

3 cups all-purpose flour, plus
more for kneading and dusting

1 teaspoon salt

1. Put the yeast and sugar in a measuring cup, and add about ½ cup of the water in a drizzle. Cover the measuring cup with plastic wrap and set it aside for about 15 minutes. If the yeast doesn't foam, it is not alive and you'll need to start over.

2. Place the butter and the chocolate morsels in a medium-sized, microwave-safe bowl. Melt the chocolate and butter in the microwave, working in 20-second increments. After each 20 seconds, stir the mixture. Microwave just until melted, about 40 to 60 seconds. Stir in the cinnamon and set aside to cool. It must be cool when added to the dough.

3. When the yeast is proofed, pour the mixture into a large bowl and add the remaining water. Stir gently to combine. Combine the flour and salt in a separate bowl, and then add to the yeast mixture. Stir with a wooden spoon until combined. The dough should be wet and sticky.

4. Put a dusting of flour on a flat surface and lift out the dough. With flour on your hands and more at the ready, begin kneading the dough so that it loses its stickiness. Don't overdo it, and don't use too much flour—just enough that it becomes more cohesive. While kneading, add the chocolate mixture in small increments. Place the dough in a large bowl, cover the bowl with plastic wrap, and allow to rise for at least 1 hour. Gently punch it down, re-cover with the plastic, and allow to rise for another 30 minutes or so.

5. While the dough is on its final rise, preheat the oven to 450°F. Put a piece of parchment paper on the bottom of a Dutch oven, cover it, and place it in the oven. When the oven is ready, use potholders to remove the lid of the Dutch oven, scoop the dough into the pot, put the lid back on, and bake with the lid on for 15 minutes. Remove the lid and bake for another 15 to 20 minutes, until the top is golden and the bread sounds hollow when tapped. Remove the pot from the oven and use tea towels to carefully remove the bread. Allow to cool before slicing.

Week 19
Mother's Day

Our mothers deserve the world, right? A meal full of seasonal favorites will show them that you believe that to be the case. A beautiful trio of drinks (Roses for Alex, Orange You Pretty, and Strawberry-Hibiscus Water) and the balance of light (Greek Couscous and Shrimp Salad and Grilled Asparagus Spears) and savory (Mainly Mushroom Frittata) prove that she raised you right. The Italian Wedding Soup is a bit of a nudge to those matriarchs who always seem to have the marriages of their offspring on their mind. By the time you break out the Chocolate-Covered Strawberries, we're betting that Mom is touched enough to have a tear or two in her eye.

Roses for Alex

Orange You Pretty

Strawberry-Hibiscus Water

Greek Couscous and Shrimp Salad

Grilled Asparagus Spears

Mainly Mushroom Frittata

Italian Wedding Soup

Chocolate-Covered Strawberries

ROSES FOR ALEX

1 part white rum

1 part triple sec

2 parts club soda

Splash of grenadine

1 maraschino cherry, for garnish

1. Fill a rocks glass with ice, add the white rum and triple sec, and top with club soda.

2. Add the splash of grenadine and garnish with the maraschino cherry.

ORANGE YOU PRETTY

Makes 4 to 6 Servings

½ navel orange, cut into thin half-moons

2 tablespoons fresh lemon juice

¼ cup Grand Marnier

4 to 6 fresh raspberries

1 (750 ml) bottle of sparkling wine, very cold

1. In a bowl, combine all but six of the orange slices with the lemon juice and Grand Marnier. Cover and refrigerate for about 1 hour.

2. Place 1 raspberry in each glass. Divide the orange slices and lemon juice–liqueur mixture equally among the glasses and top with the sparkling wine.

STRAWBERRY-HIBISCUS WATER

Makes 8 Servings

3 to 4 fresh or dried hibiscus flowers

1 pint fresh strawberries, hulled and sliced

8 cups of cold, filtered water

1. Place the hibiscus flowers and strawberries in a pitcher or jar and cover with the water.

2. Let sit for 1 to 2 hours at room temperature for a quick infusion, or refrigerate for anywhere from 4 hours to overnight. Serve chilled.

GREEK COUSCOUS AND SHRIMP SALAD

Makes 6 Servings   Active Time: 40 Minutes   Total Time: 50 Minutes

¾ pound shrimp
(16/20, shell on preferred)

6 bunches of mint,
plus 2 tablespoons

10 garlic cloves, peeled

3½ cups Chicken Stock
(see page 24)

3 cups toasted Israeli couscous

3 Roma tomatoes, diced

1 tablespoon oregano, chopped

½ English cucumber, diced

Zest and juice of 1 large lemon

½ cup red onion, diced

½ cup sun-dried tomatoes,
thinly sliced

¼ cup pitted Kalamata olives,
chopped

⅓ cup extra virgin olive oil

Salt and black pepper, to taste

½ cup feta cheese, crumbled

1. Place the shrimp, 6 bunches of mint, and garlic in a stockpot and cover with water. Cook over medium heat until shrimp are cooked through. The shrimp should be firm and pink when done. Remove the shrimp from the pot, chill in the refrigerator, peel, and cut in half lengthwise. Set aside.

2. In a large stockpot, bring the chicken stock to a boil and add the couscous. Reduce the heat to a simmer, cover, and cook for 7 to 10 minutes. Strain and chill the couscous immediately to avoid overcooking.

3. Add all the remaining ingredients, besides the feta, to a salad bowl. Add the couscous and stir to combine. Top with the shrimp and the feta and serve.

GRILLED ASPARAGUS SPEARS

Makes 4 Servings   Active Time: 5 Minutes   Total Time: 15 Minutes

1 bunch of asparagus

1 tablespoon olive oil, plus more for grill

Pinch of salt

Pinch of black pepper

1. Preheat your gas or charcoal grill to 400°F. Coat the asparagus with olive oil and season with the salt and pepper.

2. When the grill is ready, place the spears on a lightly oiled grate and cook for 2 to 3 minutes, or to desired tenderness.

MAINLY MUSHROOM FRITTATA

Makes 4 Servings   Active Time: 20 Minutes
Total Time: 40 Minutes

3 tablespoons butter

½ onion, sliced

1 pound mushrooms, chopped

1 teaspoon salt

½ teaspoon pepper

1 tablespoon dry vermouth (optional)

8 eggs

½ cup milk

1 cup Swiss cheese, shredded

⅓ cup parsley, chopped

1. Place the butter in a cast-iron skillet and warm
    over medium-high heat. Add the onion and
    cook, while stirring, for about 3 minutes. Add the
    mushrooms, lower the heat slightly, and cook until
    soft, about 5 to 10 minutes. Drain the liquid from
    the pan. Season the mushrooms with the salt and
    pepper, and, if desired, add the vermouth.

2. Preheat the broiler to low. In a bowl, whisk the
    eggs and the milk together. Pour the egg mixture
    over the mushrooms and onion. Sprinkle the
    cheese over the top and then sprinkle the parsley
    over everything. Cover the skillet and cook until
    set, about 10 minutes. Place the skillet in the
    oven under the broiler and toast the top for about
    2 minutes. Remove from the oven and let sit for a
    few minutes before serving.

ITALIAN WEDDING SOUP

Makes 4 Servings   Active Time: 30 Minutes   Total Time: 1 Hour and 15 Minutes

For the Meatballs

12 oz. ground chicken

⅓ cup panko bread crumbs

1 garlic clove, minced

2 tablespoons parsley, chopped

¼ cup Parmesan cheese, grated

1 tablespoon milk

1 egg, beaten

⅛ teaspoon fennel seeds

⅛ teaspoon red pepper flakes

½ teaspoon paprika

Salt and pepper, to taste

For the Soup

2 tablespoons extra virgin olive oil

1 onion, chopped

2 carrots, minced

1 celery stalk, minced

6 cups Chicken Stock
(see page 24)

¼ cup white wine

½ cup tubetini pasta

2 tablespoons dill, chopped

6 oz. baby spinach

Salt and pepper, to taste

Parmesan cheese, grated,
for garnish

1. Prepare the meatballs. Preheat oven to 350°F. In a bowl, add all the ingredients and mix with a fork until well-combined. Divide the mixture into 16 balls, roll with your hands until nice and round, and then place on a baking sheet.

2. Place the sheet in oven and bake for 20 to 25 minutes, until nicely browned and cooked through. Remove from oven and set aside.

3. Prepare the soup. In a medium saucepan, add the olive oil and cook over medium heat until warm. Add the onion, carrots, and celery and cook for 5 minutes, or until soft. Add the stock and the wine and bring to a boil. Reduce heat so that the soup simmers, add the pasta, and cook for 8 minutes.

4. Add the cooked meatballs and simmer for 5 minutes. Add the dill and the spinach and cook for 2 minutes, or until the spinach has wilted. Ladle into warm bowls, season with salt and pepper, and garnish with the Parmesan.

CHOCOLATE-COVERED STRAWBERRIES

Makes 20 to 30 Strawberries   Active Time: 10 Minutes
Total Time: 2 Hours and 10 Minutes

---

2 pints fresh strawberries

2 cups semi-sweet chocolate chips

6 graham crackers, crushed (optional)

1. Wash the strawberries and pat them dry. Place the chocolate chips in a microwave-safe bowl and microwave on high for 25 to 35 seconds. Remove from microwave and mix until smooth. Dip each strawberry into the chocolate halfway, or completely, whichever you prefer. If desired, roll chocolate-covered strawberries in graham cracker crumbs.

2. Line a baking sheet with parchment paper and place the strawberries on sheet. Place the strawberries in the refrigerator for at least 2 hours before serving.

Week 20

Thanks to a group of effortless preparations, this week is all about taking a step back and appreciating the miraculous warmth and life that the world is suddenly flooded with. Our favorites here are the Brown Derby—which is the rare whiskey cocktail that can work any time of day—and the Goat Cheese–Stuffed Peppadew Peppers, which are so sweet and tangy that you won't believe how little time they take to whip up.

Brown Derby

Goat Cheese–Stuffed
Peppadew Peppers

Nutty Stuffed Mushrooms

Steak and Pearl Onion Frittata

Greek Yogurt Dip

BROWN DERBY

2 oz. whiskey

4 oz. grapefruit juice

½ oz. honey

1 grapefruit slice, for garnish

1. Fill a cocktail shaker with ice and add the whiskey, grapefruit juice, and honey. Shake vigorously until thoroughly combined.

2. Add ice to a glass and strain the contents of the cocktail shaker into it. Garnish with the slice of grapefruit.

GOAT CHEESE–STUFFED PEPPADEW PEPPERS

Makes 4 to 6 Servings   Active Time: 5 Minutes
Total Time: 1 Hour

---

4 oz. spreadable goat cheese

6 oz. peppadew peppers

2 tablespoons extra virgin olive oil

4 tablespoons basil, chopped

Grilled bread or crackers, for serving

1. Stir the spreadable goat cheese. Then, spoon it into either a piping bag with a small round tip or a sandwich bag with a small hole cut in one corner. Drain the peppadew peppers, but don't rinse them.

2. Using the piping or sandwich bag, fill each pepper with goat cheese and place them on a plate. Once all the peppers are filled, drizzle olive oil on top and sprinkle with the basil. Serve with grilled bread or crackers.

NUTTY STUFFED MUSHROOMS

Makes 4 Servings   Active Time: 15 Minutes   Total Time: 35 Minutes

24 fresh cremini mushrooms, stemmed

4 scallions, chopped

6 basil leaves, torn

2 tablespoons pine nuts

¼ cup cheddar cheese

¼ cup olive oil

Salt and black pepper, to taste

1. Preheat your oven to 450°F and place the mushrooms in a 9 x 13–inch baking pan.

2. Combine the scallions, basil, and pine nuts in a mixing bowl and then stuff the mushrooms with the mixture. Drizzle with olive oil and then sprinkle the cheese over them. Season with salt and pepper and place in the oven.

3. Cook for 20 minutes, or until mushrooms become tender. Remove and let cool slightly before serving.

STEAK AND PEARL ONION FRITTATA

Makes 6 Servings   Active Time: 10 Minutes   Total Time: 25 Minutes

2 tablespoons olive oil

1 pound pearl onions

Salt and black pepper, to taste

12 large eggs

½ cup half-and-half

1 (7 to 8 oz.) strip steak, minced

4 tablespoons unsalted butter

2 tablespoons fresh parsley, chopped

2 cups Parmesan or Asiago cheese, shredded

1. Preheat oven to 400°F. Place a cast-iron skillet over medium-high heat and add the olive oil. Once the pan is hot, add the pearl onions, salt, and pepper and cook until onions are starting to caramelize, about 5 to 7 minutes.

2. While the onions are cooking, place the eggs, half-and-half, salt, and pepper in a bowl and whisk until combined. Add the steak to the pan with the onions and cook until the steak is cooked through, about 2 to 3 minutes. Add the butter and parsley and stir until the butter is melted. Sprinkle the cheese evenly over the onions and steak and then pour the egg mixture into the pan. The eggs should just cover everything. Place the skillet in the oven and cook for 8 minutes.

3. Turn the broiler on and cook for another 3 minutes, until the top of the frittata is brown. Remove from the oven and serve.

GREEK YOGURT DIP

Makes 1½ Cups   Active Time: 5 Minutes
Total Time: 15 Minutes

---

1 cup plain Greek yogurt

¼ cup honey

½ teaspoon nutmeg, grated

½ teaspoon sea salt

Selection of fruit, for serving

1. Place ingredients in a bowl and mix until well combined. Place in the refrigerator and let chill for 10 minutes.

2. Remove from the refrigerator and serve with a selection of your favorite fruits.

Week 21

Chances are you've been spending the entire
weekend prepping for Memorial Day, the
unofficial start of summer. Recognizing
that you need to unwind and don't have a lot
of time to prepare, we've curated a group of
simple, delicious recipes that will make it easy
to throw together a brunch that is up to your
typical standards. You'd do well to commit
Step 1 of the recipe for the Sofrito and Quinoa
Salad to memory. The resulting sauce—
Sofrito—is a versatile base that can elevate
a number of preparations.

Vineyard Splash

Sofrito and Quinoa Salad

Smoked Ginger Chicken Satay
with Almond Dipping Sauce

Salted Caramel Macaroons

VINEYARD SPLASH

4 oz. red grapes

Juice of 1 lime

Flesh from 3 slices of watermelon

1 part vodka

1 teaspoon sugar

Dash of club soda

1 handful of watermelon cubes, for garnish

1. Place the grapes, half the lime juice, and the watermelon in a blender and puree until smooth.

2. Fill a mason jar with your desired amount of ice. Add the vodka and remaining lime juice and then pour in the grape-and-watermelon puree. Add the sugar and stir until well combined.

3. Top with a dash of club soda and garnish with the watermelon cubes skewered on a cocktail pick.

SOFRITO AND QUINOA SALAD

Makes 4 to 6 Servings   Active Time: 15 Minutes   Total Time: 4 Hours and 15 Minutes

2 poblano peppers, seeded

1 white onion, peeled and quartered

1 red bell pepper, seeded

1 green bell pepper, seeded

3 plum tomatoes

2 garlic cloves, peeled

1 tablespoon cumin

2 tablespoons adobo seasoning

1½ cups quinoa, washed

Pumpkin seeds, toasted and salted, for garnish

1. Dice 1 of the poblanos, ½ of the onion, and ½ each of the bell peppers. Place these and the remaining ingredients, besides the quinoa and pumpkin seeds, in a blender or food processor and puree until smooth.

2. Add the puree and quinoa to a slow cooker and cook on low for 4 hours. Garnish with the pumpkin seeds before serving.

Tip: *You can purchase toasted pumpkin seeds at most grocery stores, but if you want to make them yourself, toss raw pumpkin seeds with a little canola oil and salt and bake at 325°F for 40 to 45 minutes.*

SMOKED GINGER CHICKEN SATAY WITH ALMOND DIPPING SAUCE

Makes 5 Servings   Active Time: 30 Minutes   Total Time: 2½ Hours

For the Ginger Chicken Satay

10 boneless, skinless chicken thighs, cut into small strips

2-inch piece of ginger, thinly sliced

1 large shallot, minced

3 garlic cloves, minced

1 teaspoon ground coriander

1 chili pepper of your choice, stemmed

2 teaspoons freshly ground black pepper

1 teaspoon sea salt

¼ cup olive oil

For the Grill

2 to 3 cups hickory chips

1 bag of bamboo skewers

For the Almond Dipping Sauce

½ cup almond butter

1½ cups coconut milk

Juice of 1 lime wedge

1 tablespoon fish sauce

½ teaspoon freshly ground black pepper

½ teaspoon sea salt

1. Prepare the Ginger Chicken Satay. Place all of the ingredients into a large sealable plastic bag and seal, making sure that marinade covers the chicken strips. Rub the marinade around the chicken in the bag and transfer to the refrigerator. Let marinate for 2 hours.

2. In a medium bowl, add the hickory chips and cover with water. Let soak for 1 hour.

3. Preheat your gas or charcoal grill to 400°F. Remove the chicken strips from the marinade and pierce with the bamboo skewers. Reserve the marinade and place alongside the grill with the chicken strips.

4. Prepare the Almond Dipping Sauce. Combine all ingredients in a small saucepan and bring to a boil over medium-high heat. Cook for about 3 to 4 minutes, or until the sauce turns golden brown. Remove from heat and cover with aluminum foil.

5. When the grill is ready, scatter the hickory chips over the coals or place them in a smoker box. Wait a few minutes for the smoke to build, and then place the skewered chicken strips over the smoke. Cover the grill, aligning the vent away from the coals so that the smoke rolls over the chicken strips. Cook for about 4 minutes on each side and then serve with the warm Almond Dipping Sauce.

SALTED CARAMEL MACAROONS

Makes 16 to 20 Macaroons   Active Time: 30 Minutes
Total Time: 2 Hours and 15 Minutes

6 tablespoons butter, melted

3 tablespoons milk

1 bag of soft caramels

4 cups shredded, sweetened coconut

1 teaspoon sea salt

4 oz. dark chocolate

1. Place the butter, milk, caramels, and salt in a small saucepan and cook over medium heat. Once the caramels and butter have melted, add the coconut and mix until the coconut is coated.

2. Line a baking sheet with parchment paper and place tablespoons of the caramel mixture onto the sheet. Let stand for 1 hour.

3. Place the chocolate in a microwave-safe bowl and microwave on high until chocolate is melted, about 15 to 30 seconds. Be careful not to overcook. Dip the bottom of the cooled macaroons into the melted chocolate and place them back on the baking sheet. Once all the macaroons have been dipped, use the rest of the chocolate to drizzle over the top. Place in the refrigerator for 30 to 45 minutes before serving.

Memorial Day

With summer on the horizon, it's time to capitalize on all those good vibes and put on a show. We're certain that your guests will find the fresh, light flavor and beautiful presentation of the Chilled Avocado Soup with Crab and Mango Salsa to be worth the price of admission. The Paloma Plus and the Mixed Bag sangria set the stage for this show-stopping soup, and presenting it at the same time as the Fig, Prosciutto, and Camembert Tart may send everyone over the edge. The Peach Crisp will bring them back, and probably keep them around for another round of drinks.

Paloma Plus

Mixed Bag

Virgin Baja Lemonade

Ham and Cheddar Quiche

Fig, Prosciutto, and Camembert Tart

Chilled Avocado Soup
with Crab and Mango Salsa

Peach Crisp

PALOMA PLUS

1 part tequila

Splash of grapefruit juice

Juice of 1 lime wedge

2 parts Fresca

1 grapefruit wedge, for garnish

1. Place the tequila, grapefruit juice, and lime juice in a glass filled with ice and stir.

2. Top with Fresca, stir, and garnish with the grapefruit wedge.

MIXED BAG

Makes 4 to 6 Servings

1½ cups frozen mixed berries, thawed

½ cup juice from thawing the berries

½ cup Simple Syrup (see page 32)

½ cup strawberry or blueberry vodka

1 (750 ml) bottle of sparkling wine, very cold

1. In a bowl, combine the thawed berries with the juice, syrup, and vodka. Cover and refrigerate for about 1 hour.

2. Divide the mixture between 4 to 6 glasses and top with the sparkling wine.

VIRGIN BAJA LEMONADE

5 parts lemonade

1 part coconut syrup

Splash of agave nectar

1 sprig of rosemary

1 lemon wheel, for garnish

1. Fill a cocktail shaker with ice, the liquid ingredients, and rosemary. Shake well.

2. Strain the resulting mixture into a highball glass filled with ice and garnish with the lemon wheel.

HAM AND CHEDDAR QUICHE

Makes 6 to 8 Servings   Active Time: 40 Minutes   Total Time: 1½ Hours

1 Baked Crust (see page 27)

2 tablespoons brown mustard

1 cup ham, cooked and diced

1 cup sharp cheddar cheese, shredded

1½ cups whole milk or half-and-half

1 teaspoon salt

1 teaspoon ground pepper

4 eggs, beaten

Paprika, to taste (optional)

1. Preheat the oven to 350° F. Place the crust in a 9" pie plate and use a pastry brush or the back of a spoon to spread the mustard on the bottom and sides. Sprinkle the ham pieces and shredded cheddar evenly over the bottom of the crust.

2. Add the dairy component, salt, and pepper to the beaten eggs and whisk to combine. Pour the egg mixture over the meat and cheese, shaking the plate gently to distribute evenly and settle the liquid. If desired, sprinkle the top with paprika. Put the quiche in the oven and bake for 35 to 40 minutes, or until the quiche is golden brown and the eggs are set. Remove and allow to sit for 10 minutes before slicing and serving.

FIG, PROSCIUTTO, AND CAMEMBERT TART

Makes 4 to 6 Servings   Active Time: 45 Minutes   Total Time: 1½ Hours

2 tablespoons olive oil

½ onion, thinly sliced

½ pound prosciutto, cut into
1-inch slices

1 Flaky Pastry Crust (see page 28)

1 tablespoon Dijon mustard

1 round of Camembert, at room
temperature

6 to 8 fresh figs, stemmed
and halved

3 tablespoons aged balsamic
vinegar

1 tablespoon honey

¼ cup arugula

1. Preheat the oven to 400°F. Place a medium skillet over medium heat. Add the olive oil and the onion. Cook and stir until the onion is lightly browned, about 3 minutes. Add the prosciutto slices to the skillet and cook, while stirring, for an additional minute. Remove the skillet from heat.

2. Place the crust on a baking sheet, spread the Dijon mustard evenly over the crust, and top with the onion-and-prosciutto mixture. Cut the Camembert into ¼-inch-thick wedges and place them over the onion mix. Then, place the fig halves on top of the cheese. In a small bowl, whisk the balsamic vinegar and honey together and drizzle the mixture over the tart.

3. Put the baking sheet in the oven and bake for 20 to 25 minutes until cheese is melted and figs are soft. Remove from the oven and let cool. Top with the arugula before serving.

CHILLED AVOCADO SOUP
WITH CRAB AND MANGO SALSA

Makes 6 Servings   Active Time: 25 Minutes   Total Time: 1 Hour and 45 Minutes

For the Crab and Mango Salsa

½ cup ripe mango, peeled and minced

½ cup red bell pepper, peeled, seeded, and minced

3 tablespoons red onion, minced

1 teaspoon chives, minced

1 teaspoon rice wine vinegar

2 tablespoons extra virgin olive oil

Salt, to taste

8 oz. peekytoe crab meat, cleaned, cooked, and free of shell

For the Soup

3 ripe avocados, peeled and diced

5 cups Vegetable Stock (see page 26)

Juice of 2 limes

1 teaspoon cumin

2 teaspoons salt

¼ teaspoon cayenne pepper

Crème fraîche, for garnish

Chives, for garnish

1. Prepare the salsa. In a bowl, add the mango, red bell pepper, red onion, chives, rice wine vinegar, and olive oil and stir gently until combined. Season with salt and chill in the refrigerator until ready to serve.

2. Prepare the soup. Place all ingredients in a food processor and puree. Strain through a fine sieve and chill in the refrigerator for a minimum of 1 hour.

3. Just before serving, use a ring cutter to make a tower out of the mango salsa. Top with the crab meat and place the tower on a chilled plate. Remove ring cutter.

4. Pour soup around the already-plated food. Place a dollop of crème fraîche on top and garnish with the chives.

PEACH CRISP

Makes 4 to 6 Servings   Active Time: 30 Minutes
Total Time: 1 Hour and 15 Minutes

5 or 6 peaches, pitted and sliced

¾ cup sugar

¾ cup flour, plus 1 or 2 tablespoons

¼ teaspoon salt

¼ cup dark brown sugar, firmly packed

8 tablespoons (1 stick) butter, chilled and cut into pieces

½ cup quick-cooking oats (not instant)

Whipped cream, for serving

1. Preheat the oven to 350°F. In a bowl, combine the peach slices with ¼ cup of the sugar and 1 or 2 tablespoons of the flour. The amount of flour you use will depend on how juicy the peaches are—more juice means more flour. Let the peaches sit in the bowl while you make the topping. If there's juice left in the bowl after sitting, add another tablespoon of flour.

2. Place the remaining sugar, remaining flour, the salt, and the brown sugar in a bowl and stir to combine. Add the butter and use a fork to combine into a crumbly mixture. Add the oats and stir.

3. Put the peaches in a cast-iron skillet and top with the oat mixture. Put the skillet in the oven and bake for about 1 hour, until the topping is golden and the peaches are bubbling. If it doesn't look crispy enough, turn the oven up to 375°F and continue to bake, checking every 5 minutes until it looks just right. Be careful not to burn the topping. Serve warm with fresh whipped cream.

Week 22

Yes, the Lavender Margarita, Basil, Chive, and Feta Bread, and the Curried Yogurt Soup are sure to dazzle the entire table, but the unsung hero of this menu is the Bacon and Zucchini Quiche. Bacon's rich, salty flavor brings out the best in zucchini, and will have you reconsidering your stance on this delicate squash. The Strawberries and Cream Trifle is there to soak up all this lusciousness and get you ready for a long nap in the sunshine.

Lavender Margarita

Basil, Chive, and Feta Bread

Curried Yogurt Soup

Bacon and Zucchini Quiche

Strawberries and Cream Trifle

LAVENDER MARGARITA

1 oz. lavender-infused simple syrup

2 oz. tequila

½ oz. orange liqueur (triple sec, Cointreau, or Grand Marnier)

1 oz. fresh lime juice

Sugar, for the rim

Splash of seltzer (optional)

1 sprig of lavender, for garnish (optional)

1 lemon wedge, for garnish (optional)

1. To make the infused syrup: See Simple Syrup recipe on page 32. When syrup is boiling, add 5 to 7 sprigs of lavender. After 1 minute, remove the saucepan from the heat and allow the lavender to cool in the syrup. When cool, strain the syrup into an airtight container.

2. Combine the syrup, tequila, orange liqueur, and lime juice in a cocktail shaker. Add ice and shake until well combined.

3. Wet the rim of a rocks glass and then dip it in the sugar. Fill glass with ice and strain the margarita into the glass. If desired, top with a bit of seltzer, and garnish with a lemon wedge or a sprig of fresh lavender.

BASIL, CHIVE, AND FETA BREAD

Makes 1 Loaf   Active Time: 10 Minutes   Total Time: 1 Hour

½ cup basil, chopped

½ cup chives, chopped

1 pat of unsalted butter

2 tablespoons sesame seeds

1¼ cups all-purpose flour

1 tablespoon baking powder

3 large organic eggs

¼ cup olive oil

½ cup plain yogurt, plus
2 tablespoons

½ teaspoon sea salt

½ teaspoon freshly ground
black pepper

7 oz. feta cheese

1. Preheat the oven to 350°F. Combine the basil and chives in a small bowl and set aside. Butter a 9 x 5–inch loaf pan and sprinkle half of the sesame seeds onto the bottom and sides, shaking the pan to coat.

2. Combine the flour and baking powder in a bowl. In a separate bowl, whisk together the eggs, oil, yogurt, salt, and pepper. Stir in the cheese and the herb mixture.

3. Fold the flour mixture into the egg mixture. Be careful not to overmix the batter; it is okay if a few lumps remain.

4. Pour the batter into the prepared pan. Level the surface with a spatula and sprinkle the remaining sesame seeds on top. Bake for 40 to 50 minutes until the top is golden and a knife inserted in the center comes out clean. Remove from the oven, allow to cool in the pan for a few minutes, and then run a knife around the pan to loosen. Transfer to a rack to cool completely.

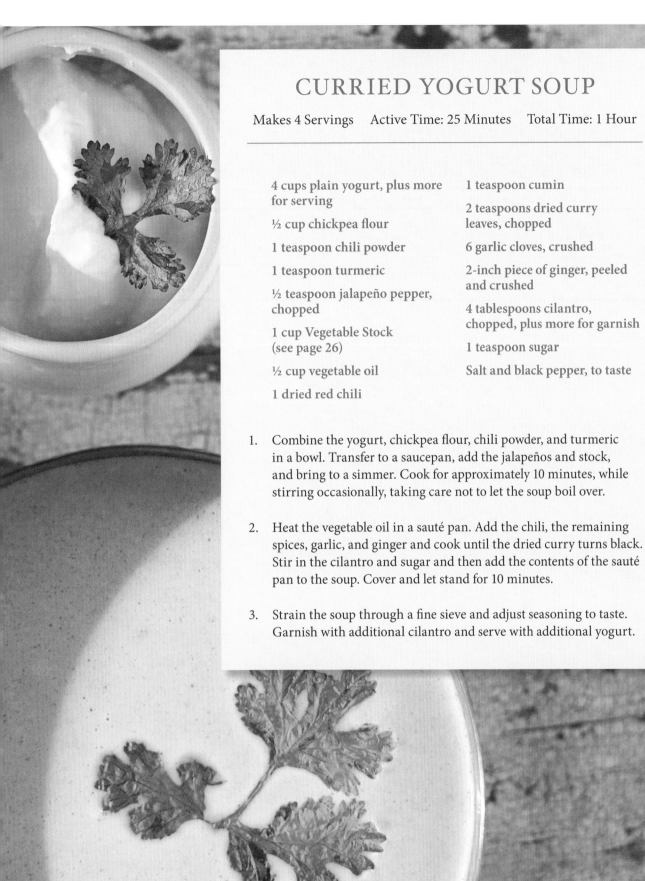

CURRIED YOGURT SOUP

Makes 4 Servings   Active Time: 25 Minutes   Total Time: 1 Hour

4 cups plain yogurt, plus more for serving

½ cup chickpea flour

1 teaspoon chili powder

1 teaspoon turmeric

½ teaspoon jalapeño pepper, chopped

1 cup Vegetable Stock (see page 26)

½ cup vegetable oil

1 dried red chili

1 teaspoon cumin

2 teaspoons dried curry leaves, chopped

6 garlic cloves, crushed

2-inch piece of ginger, peeled and crushed

4 tablespoons cilantro, chopped, plus more for garnish

1 teaspoon sugar

Salt and black pepper, to taste

1. Combine the yogurt, chickpea flour, chili powder, and turmeric in a bowl. Transfer to a saucepan, add the jalapeños and stock, and bring to a simmer. Cook for approximately 10 minutes, while stirring occasionally, taking care not to let the soup boil over.

2. Heat the vegetable oil in a sauté pan. Add the chili, the remaining spices, garlic, and ginger and cook until the dried curry turns black. Stir in the cilantro and sugar and then add the contents of the sauté pan to the soup. Cover and let stand for 10 minutes.

3. Strain the soup through a fine sieve and adjust seasoning to taste. Garnish with additional cilantro and serve with additional yogurt.

BACON AND ZUCCHINI QUICHE

Makes 6 to 8 Servings   Active Time: 45 Minutes   Total Time: 1½ Hours

---

1 Baked Crust (see page 27)

¾ pound thick-cut bacon, cut into pieces

1 small zucchini, cut into thin rounds

1 garlic clove, minced

3 to 5 oz. garlic-herb chèvre

1½ cups half-and-half

½ teaspoon salt

½ teaspoon freshly ground black pepper

4 eggs, beaten

1. Preheat the oven to 350°F and place the crust in a 9" pie plate. In a skillet, sauté the bacon pieces until just crispy, about 10 minutes. Transfer the pieces to a paper towel–lined plate to drain.

2. Add the zucchini pieces and garlic to the bacon fat, reduce the heat, and cook until the zucchini is just soft, about 10 minutes. Sprinkle the bacon pieces on the bottom of the crust and use a slotted spoon to put the zucchini over it. Dot the mixture with the garlic-herb chèvre.

3. In a medium bowl, add the half-and-half, salt, and pepper to the beaten eggs and whisk to combine. Pour the egg mixture over the other ingredients, shaking the plate gently to distribute evenly. Put the quiche in the oven and bake for 35 to 40 minutes or until the quiche is golden brown and the eggs are set. Remove from the oven and allow to sit for 10 minutes before slicing and serving.

STRAWBERRIES AND CREAM TRIFLE

Makes 4 to 6 Servings   Active Time: 45 Minutes
Total Time: 45 Minutes

4 pints strawberries

Juice of 1 lemon

3 tablespoons sugar

1 teaspoon cornstarch

1 quart whipping cream

1 tablespoon powdered sugar

1 teaspoon pure vanilla extract

12 oz. lemon curd, homemade
(see page 112) or store-bought

1 pound cake, sliced

1. Place the strawberries, lemon juice, sugar, and cornstarch in a medium saucepan and cook over medium heat until strawberries soften and begin to give up their juice, approximately 5 minutes. Remove from heat and let cool.

2. Place the whipping cream, powdered sugar, and vanilla extract in a bowl and whisk until soft peaks form. Very gently fold the lemon curd into the whipped cream.

3. Cover the bottom of a trifle dish with the lemon whipped cream. Place a layer of pound cake slices on top, and then scoop the strawberry mixture on top of the pound cake. Repeat until all the strawberries and pound cake have been used, giving you three or four layers. Top with remaining lemon whipped cream and place in refrigerator until ready to serve.

Week 23

First impressions are vital. But sometimes, it pays to save your best for last. The Chilled Cantaloupe and Ginger Soup with Champagne Espuma is a finale so grand that it almost doesn't matter what preceded it—almost. To get everyone ready for this fantastic finish, we have subtle, tantalizing dishes such as the Grilled Fruit and Feta Salad and Lemon Haddock with Basil Pesto.

Blue Fireflies

Cucumber-Cantaloupe Slush

Grilled Fruit and Feta Salad

Lemon Haddock
with Basil Pesto

Chilled Cantaloupe and Ginger Soup
with Champagne Espuma

BLUE FIREFLIES

3 Blue Curaçao ice cubes

1 part vodka

2 parts Sprite

Splash of fresh lime juice

1. Add three Blue Curaçao ice cubes to a highball glass.

2. Add vodka, Sprite, and fresh lime juice and stir together.

CUCUMBER-CANTALOUPE SLUSH

½ cucumber, peeled and sliced

¼ cup cantaloupe, cubed

3 parts club soda

1 cup ice

1 cucumber slice, for garnish

1. Place the cucumber and cantaloupe in a blender and puree until smooth.

2. Add the club soda and ice to the blender. Blend until the mixture achieves a slushy consistency.

3. Pour the mixture into a mason jar and garnish with the slice of cucumber.

GRILLED FRUIT AND FETA SALAD

Makes 4 Servings   Active Time: 15 Minutes   Total Time: 25 Minutes

1 small watermelon, cut into 1-inch-thick rounds

1 small, sweet onion, cut into ½-inch-thick rings

2 tablespoons olive oil

1 cup baby arugula

2 oz. feta cheese, crumbled

1 tablespoon balsamic vinegar

1 tablespoon red wine vinegar

Salt and black pepper, to taste

Mint leaves, chopped, for garnish

1. Preheat your grill to 500°F. Place the watermelon on the grill and cook until charred, about 2 to 3 minutes per side. Transfer the grilled watermelon to a cutting board, remove rind, and cut into cubes.

2. Brush the onion slices with half of the olive oil and place them on the grill. Grill until charred, about 5 to 6 minutes per side. Remove them from the heat and dice.

3. In a large bowl, place the arugula, feta, watermelon, and onion and toss to combine.

4. In a small bowl, combine the remaining olive oil, balsamic vinegar, red wine vinegar, and a pinch of salt. Drizzle this mixture over the salad and toss. Garnish with chopped mint leaves, season with salt and pepper, and serve.

LEMON HADDOCK WITH BASIL PESTO

Makes 4 Servings   Active Time: 25 Minutes   Total Time: 1 Hour

4 (8 oz.) haddock fillets

¼ cup olive oil

Sea salt and freshly ground black pepper, to taste

Juice of ½ lemon

Basil Pesto (see page 31)

1. Place the haddock fillets in a small baking pan, and then add the olive oil. Season the fillets with black pepper and sea salt, then with the lemon juice. Let rest at room temperature while preparing the grill.

2. Place a cast-iron skillet on your gas or charcoal grill 30 minutes before cooking and preheat to 450°F. Leave the grill covered while heating, as it will add a faint smoky flavor to the skillet.

3. When the grill is ready, place the fillets in the skillet and sear for about 5 minutes. Once the fillets have browned, turn and cook for 1 to 2 more minutes, until the fish is opaque through the center. Transfer the haddock fillets to a cutting board and let rest for 5 to 10 minutes. Serve with the pesto.

CHILLED CANTALOUPE AND GINGER SOUP WITH CHAMPAGNE ESPUMA

Makes 4 Servings   Active Time: 25 Minutes
Total Time: 2 Hours and 25 Minutes

For the Soup

2 cantaloupes, halved, flesh chopped into bite-sized pieces, shells reserved

2 teaspoons ginger, peeled and grated

2 tablespoons lemon juice

4 cups Champagne, chilled

¼ cup sugar

For the Champagne Espuma

1½ cups Champagne, chilled

1 tablespoon gelatin powder

1. Puree the melon, ginger, and lemon juice in a food processor and then pass through a fine sieve. Chill in the refrigerator for 2 hours.

2. Prepare the Champagne Espuma. Combine 1¼ cups Champagne and the gelatin powder. Place the remaining Champagne in a small saucepan, bring to a simmer over medium heat, and then remove from heat. Combine the contents of the saucepan and the gelatin mixture, strain, and pour into an iSi whipper. Place in fridge for 1 hour.

3. Just before serving, add the 4 cups of Champagne to the soup and whisk to combine. Add the sugar slowly, tasting as you go, making sure you have just enough to emphasize the melon's flavor. Pour into the reserved cantaloupe shells and serve with Champagne Espuma.

Note: *While an iSi whipper is not a kitchen essential, it's a good thing to have if you're going to be entertaining. If you don't have one, this soup is tasty enough to withstand the loss of the Champagne Espuma.*

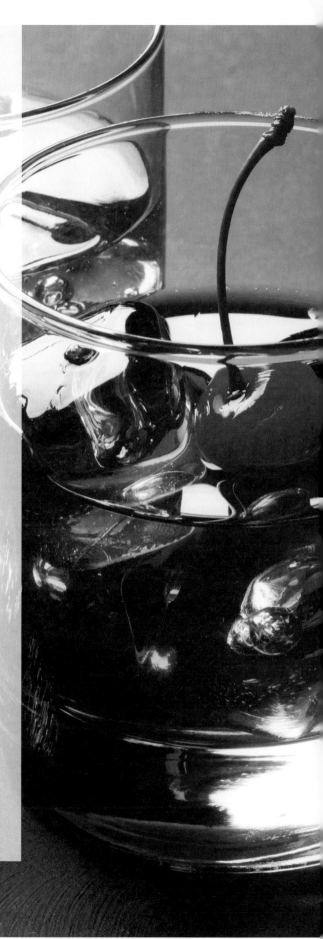

Week 24
Father's Day

Yes, Dad can be stuck in his ways, but when you roll out these seemingly simple dishes together, you may just be surprised at the memorable meal that results. Injecting a bit of smoke into a fresh salad is the ideal opening, and a dollop of savory Home-Style Baked Beans fits perfectly alongside the Strip Steaks with Mushrooms and Fingerling Potatoes. Taking his questionable style and fondness for facile jokes into account, it can be hard to believe that Dad always knows best. But after enjoying this spread of his favorites, you'll see that he does know a thing or two.

Old Fashioned

Grilled Romaine Salad

Home-Style Baked Beans

Strip Steaks with Mushrooms
and Fingerling Potatoes

Classic Vanilla Milkshake

OLD FASHIONED

**Splash of Simple Syrup
(see page 32)**

2 drops of bitters

1 maraschino cherry

2 oz. bourbon

1. Place the syrup, bitters, and maraschino cherry in a rocks glass.

2. Muddle together, fill the glass with ice, add bourbon, and gently stir.

GRILLED ROMAINE SALAD

Makes 4 Servings   Active Time: 5 Minutes   Total Time: 10 Minutes

---

1 head of romaine lettuce, leaves halved lengthwise

1 tablespoon olive oil, plus more for grill

1 tablespoon steak seasoning

2 tablespoons lemon juice

Parmesan cheese, for garnish

1. Place the romaine lettuce and olive oil in a bowl and toss to combine. Season with steak seasoning.

2. Preheat your grill to 400°F. Oil the grates lightly to prevent sticking. Place the lettuce on the grill cut side down and cook for about 5 minutes. The lettuce is done cooking when it becomes slightly wilted and lightly charred.

3. Remove from heat, drizzle with lemon juice, and sprinkle Parmesan cheese on top. Serve and enjoy.

HOME-STYLE BAKED BEANS

Makes 6 to 8 Servings   Active Time: 30 Minutes   Total Time: 1½ to 2 Hours

---

6 strips of thick-cut bacon

½ onion, diced

½ cup bell pepper, seeded and diced

1 teaspoon salt, plus more to taste

2 (15.5 oz.) cans of pinto beans, rinsed and drained

1 cup barbeque sauce

1 teaspoon Dijon mustard

2 tablespoons dark brown sugar

Fresh black pepper, to taste

1. Preheat the oven to 325°F. Warm a cast-iron skillet over medium heat and cook half the bacon pieces until they are just starting to brown, about 8 minutes. Transfer to a plate lined with paper towels to drain. Add the remaining pieces of bacon to the pan, raise the heat to medium-high, and cook until pieces are browned. Reduce the heat to medium, add the onion and pepper and cook, while stirring occasionally, until the vegetables soften, about 8 minutes.

2. Add the salt, beans, barbeque sauce, mustard, and brown sugar. Stir, season with additional salt and pepper, and cook until the liquid just starts to simmer.

3. Lay the partially cooked pieces of bacon on top and transfer the skillet to the oven. Bake for 1 hour. The bacon should be crisp and browned, and the sauce should be thick. Be careful not to overcook the beans, as they will start to dry out. Remove from the oven and allow to cool slightly before serving.

STRIP STEAKS WITH MUSHROOMS AND FINGERLING POTATOES

Makes 6 Servings   Active Time: 30 Minutes   Total Time: 1½ Hours

---

2 tablespoons kosher salt

½ teaspoon red pepper flakes

½ teaspoon ground black pepper

½ teaspoon fennel seeds

½ teaspoon mustard seeds

½ teaspoon coriander seeds

6 (7 oz.) strip steaks

2 pounds fingerling potatoes, halved lengthwise

2 tablespoons olive oil

¾ cup unsalted butter, at room temperature, cut into 7 chunks

6 sprigs of thyme, plus 2 tablespoons of leaves for garnish

1 large shallot, minced

2 pounds cremini mushrooms, cleaned and quartered

1 pound shiitake mushrooms, stemmed and thinly sliced

1 pound oyster mushrooms, thinly sliced

½ cup Cabernet Sauvignon

2 tablespoons light tamari

¼ cup Worcestershire sauce

2 tablespoons fish sauce

1. Preheat oven to 375°F. Place the salt, red pepper flakes, and ground black pepper in a bowl. Use a coffee grinder or a mortar and pestle to grind the fennel seeds, mustard seeds, and coriander seeds into a powder. Place the powder in the bowl with the salt, red pepper flakes, and ground black pepper and stir to combine. Place steaks on a plate and season liberally with the seasoning blend. Set the steaks aside and let stand for 1 hour.

2. Place the potatoes in a cast-iron skillet and cover with water. Cook over high heat until the potatoes are tender but not mushy. Drain and set aside. Wipe the skillet, add the olive oil, and warm over medium-high heat. Add the steaks to the pan, making sure you don't overcrowd. Cook steaks for 2 minutes, turn them over, and add 1 chunk of butter and 1 sprig of thyme for each steak. Cook steaks for 2 minutes, while spooning the butter over the steaks. Remove steaks and set aside. Discard the sprigs of thyme.

3. Add the shallot and the remaining chunk of butter to the pan. Cook for 1 minute and then add the cremini mushrooms. Cook for 5 minutes and then add the shiitake and oyster mushrooms. Cook for 3 more minutes and add the Cabernet Sauvignon. After 30 seconds, add the potatoes, tamari, Worcestershire sauce, and fish sauce. Stir until the mushrooms are evenly coated.

4. Return the steaks and their juices to the skillet. Place the skillet in the oven and cook for 3 minutes, until the steaks are warmed through. Remove the skillet from the oven and slice the steaks at a 45° angle every 2 inches. Scoop the potatoes and vegetables onto a plate, top with the sliced steak, sprinkle with the fresh thyme leaves, and serve.

CLASSIC VANILLA MILKSHAKE

Makes 4 Servings   Active Time: 5 Minutes   Total Time: 5 Minutes

2 pints vanilla ice cream

½ cup whole milk

½ teaspoon sea salt

2 teaspoons vanilla extract

Mint, for garnish (optional)

1. Place all ingredients in a blender and puree until combined. Pour into tall glasses and, if desired, garnish with mint.

Variation:

For a chocolate milkshake, use the same amount of chocolate ice cream or add 1 cup of chocolate syrup. If a malted milkshake is Dad's thing, add ½ cup of malted milk powder.

Summer

With all that warmth and sunshine, everyone knows that summer is the time to have fun. But the incredible excitement that the season fosters has a tendency to stretch us all too thin. In an attempt to keep you from getting sucked up in that frenzy, we've curated a series of menus that will make it easy to take a step back. And, thanks to a number of dishes that don't require the use of an oven or a stove, keeping your cool in your host role won't be a problem.

One of our favorite things about summer is the potential for a normal, low-key gathering to stretch out into the early evening and night, powered by the momentum that good people and beautiful weather can provide. With that in mind, we've arranged for a series of cocktails and dishes that provide the perfect launching pad for such excursions.

Week 25

Yes, we've been in the mind-set for a few weeks. But now that summer is officially here, we're ready to dive in headfirst. The Cool Summer ensures that you and your loved ones are in position to have exactly that. This delicious rum-and-citrus punch just may carry the gathering into the evening, the kind of impromptu celebration the summer is all about. You may wonder what Moussaka is doing amid summer classics such as Broccoli Salad and Strawberry-Rhubarb Crisp, but the cheesy egg crust and the lamb-eggplant-and-tomato sauce filling makes it one of the best twists ever put on the omelette.

Cool Summer

Crimson Lemonade

Broccoli Salad

Moussaka

Strawberry-Rhubarb Crisp

COOL SUMMER

Makes 4 to 6 Servings

30 mint leaves

Juice of 1½ limes

1 part white rum

2 parts lemonade

Lemon wheels, for garnish

Tear the mint leaves in half, place them at the bottom of a pitcher, add the lime juice, and muddle. Add ice, rum, and lemonade, stir, and garnish with the lemon wheels.

CRIMSON LEMONADE

1 cup lemonade

Splash of grenadine

Pour the lemonade into a mason jar filled with ice and top with the splash of grenadine.

BROCCOLI SALAD

Makes 6 to 8 Servings   Active Time: 15 Minutes
Total Time: 20 Minutes

1 head of broccoli, chopped into bite-sized pieces

6 to 8 slices of bacon, cooked and crumbled

½ cup red onion, minced

½ cup raisins

8 oz. sharp cheddar cheese, grated

1 cup mayonnaise

2 tablespoons white vinegar

¼ cup sugar

Salt and pepper, to taste

1. Place the broccoli, bacon, onion, raisins, and cheese in
    a large bowl.

2. Place the remaining ingredients in a medium bowl
    and stir until well combined. Add this mixture to the
    broccoli-and-bacon mixture and toss to coat. Season
    with salt and pepper before serving.

MOUSSAKA

Makes 4 to 6 Servings   Active Time: 1½ Hours   Total Time: 2 Hours

For the Filling

¼ cup salt, plus more to taste

4 cups cold water

1 large eggplant, ends trimmed and cubed

⅓ cup olive oil, plus 1 tablespoon

1 pound ground lamb

1 onion, diced

3 garlic cloves, minced

½ cup dry red wine

1 cup tomato sauce

2 tablespoons parsley, chopped

1 teaspoon dried oregano

½ teaspoon cinnamon

Black pepper, to taste

For the Crust

6 tablespoons butter

⅓ cup all-purpose flour

2½ cups milk

5 eggs, beaten

⅔ cup Parmesan cheese, grated

⅓ cup dill or parlsey, chopped

1. Preheat the oven to 350°F. Place the salt and water in a mixing bowl, add the eggplant, and stir. Cover the bowl with plastic wrap and let the eggplant soak for about 20 minutes. After soaking, drain in a colander and rinse the eggplant with cold water. Squeeze the cubes to remove as much water as possible, place them on a pile of paper towels, and blot them as dry as you can. Set the eggplant aside.

2. While the eggplant is soaking, heat a cast-iron skillet over medium-high heat. Add the tablespoon of olive oil and then add ground lamb. Cook until it is browned, about 4 minutes, and then transfer to a bowl.

3. Add a ¼ cup of the olive oil to the skillet and then add the cubes of eggplant. Cook, while stirring, until the eggplant starts to soften, about 5 minutes. Transfer to the bowl containing the lamb.

4. Add the remaining olive oil to the skillet. When it is warm, add the onion and garlic, and cook until the onion is translucent, about 3 minutes. Add the lamb and eggplant to the skillet, stir to combine, and then add the wine, tomato sauce, parsley, oregano, and cinnamon. Reduce the heat to low, season with salt and pepper, and simmer for about 15 minutes, while stirring occasionally.

5. Prepare the crust. Heat a skillet over medium heat and melt the butter. Reduce the heat slightly, add the flour, and stir to form a paste. Slowly add the milk while whisking to combine. Bring to a boil and remove the pan from the heat. Add about half of the mixture into the bowl of beaten eggs and stir briskly. Stir the tempered eggs into the mixture in the skillet, add the cheese and dill or parsley, and stir to combine.

6. Even out the top of the lamb-and-eggplant mixture in the cast-iron skillet and then top with the flour-egg-and-cheese mixture. Put the skillet in the oven and bake for 35 to 45 minutes, until the crust is set and golden brown. Remove from the oven and allow to rest for 5 minutes before serving.

STRAWBERRY-RHUBARB CRISP

Makes 4 Servings   Active Time: 30 Minutes
Total Time: 1 Hour

1½ cups rhubarb, cut into ½-inch pieces

1½ cups strawberries, sliced

2 tablespoons sugar

⅓ cup all-purpose flour, plus 2 teaspoons

4 tablespoons butter, chilled, cut into pieces

¼ cup dark brown sugar

¾ cup quick-cooking oats

Whipped cream, for serving

1. Preheat the oven to 450°F. In a bowl, combine the rhubarb pieces, strawberry slices, sugar, and the 2 teaspoons of flour. Toss to coat and then transfer to a cast-iron skillet.

2. In another bowl, use a fork to combine the butter and the brown sugar. Add the oats and remaining flour and use the fork to create a crumbly mixture. Sprinkle it over the mixture in the skillet.

3. Put the skillet in the oven and bake for about 30 minutes, or until the topping is golden and the rhubarb-and-strawberry mixture is bubbling. Serve warm with whipped cream.

Week 26

The crepe is no longer just a delicate pastry dosed with a dollop of something sugary. Savory versions have slowly been gaining steam for a while, and we believe it's time to take them into the mainstream. The Chicken and Mushroom Crepes, Sour Cream and Dill Scones, Peanut Butter and Banana Yogurt Bowl, and Raspberry Ice Cream Cake make for a light, flavorful meal that is easy to prepare—exactly what you want on the weekend before the 4th of July.

Bloody Mary

Sour Cream and Dill Scones

Peanut Butter and
Banana Yogurt Bowl

Chicken and Mushroom Crepes

Raspberry Ice Cream Cake

BLOODY MARY

Dash of Worcestershire sauce

Dash of lemon juice

1 part vodka

2 parts tomato juice

Garnish with anything your heart desires

1. Add the Worcestershire sauce and lemon juice to a pint glass, add ice, and then pour in the vodka and tomato juice.

2. Stir until thoroughly mixed and garnish with bacon, olives, lemon wedges, lime wedges, celery, pickles, or anything your heart desires.

SOUR CREAM AND DILL SCONES

Makes 4 to 6 Servings   Active Time: 30 Minutes   Total Time: 50 Minutes

2 cups all-purpose flour, plus more for dusting

1 teaspoon baking powder

½ teaspoon salt

1 teaspoon freshly ground black pepper

4 tablespoons butter, chilled and cut into small pieces

¾ cup sour cream

1 tablespoon dill, minced

1 egg, beaten with a little milk

1. Preheat the oven to 400°F and position a rack in the middle. In a large bowl, whisk together the flour, baking powder, salt, and pepper. Add the butter pieces and mix with a fork until a crumbly dough forms. Stir in the sour cream and dill, taking care not to overmix.

2. With flour on your hands, transfer the dough to a lightly floured surface. Form the dough into a circle about ½-inch thick. With a long knife or a water glass, cut the dough into 6 to 8 circles.

3. Butter a cake pan, and put the scones in a circle in it, leaving some space between the pieces. Brush with the beaten egg and bake for 20 to 25 minutes, or until golden.

PEANUT BUTTER AND BANANA YOGURT BOWL

Makes 4 Servings   Active Time: 10 Minutes   Total Time: 10 Minutes

4 cups nonfat Greek yogurt

½ cup unsalted peanut butter

3 bananas

3 tablespoons chia seeds, plus more for garnish

4 cups baby spinach

4 tablespoons unsweetened coconut flakes, for garnish

4 tablespoons peanuts, crushed, for garnish

1. Place all of the ingredients, besides the garnishes, in a food processor. Puree until smooth.

2. Top with the garnishes and serve.

CHICKEN AND MUSHROOM CREPES

Makes 16 Crepes   Active Time: 1 Hour   Total Time: 6 Hours

For the Crepes

4 tablespoons butter

⅛ teaspoon salt

1 cup whole milk

3 eggs, beaten

⅞ cup flour

For the Filling

4 tablespoons butter

1 pound mushrooms, stemmed and chopped

1 to 2 cups cooked chicken, diced

1 (14 oz.) can of cream of mushroom soup

2 tablespoons Madeira or vermouth

⅓ cup milk

2 tablespoons parsley, chopped

Salt and black pepper, to taste

1. Heat the skillet over low heat and melt 2 tablespoons of the butter very slowly. Add the salt and milk to the beaten eggs and whisk together until well combined. Whisk in the flour and then add the melted butter. Keep whisking until the batter is smooth and there are no lumps. Cover the bowl with plastic wrap or a clean dish towel and let it rest in a cool, dark place for 3 to 4 hours.

2. While the crepe batter is settling, prepare the filling. Place a skillet over medium heat and add the butter. Add the mushroom pieces and cook, while stirring, until softened and lightly browned, about 5 to 8 minutes. Add the chicken, cream of mushroom soup, Madeira or vermouth, and the milk, stir to combine, and cook for about 3 minutes. Stir in the parsley, season with salt and pepper, and transfer the mixture to a bowl. Cover and refrigerate until ready to prepare the crepes.

3. When the crepe batter is ready, you'll need a spatula that won't scratch the surface of the skillet. Have that and a ladle ready by the stove. Heat the skillet over medium-high heat and melt a slice of the remaining 2 tablespoons of butter in it. Stir the crepe batter. When the skillet is hot but not smoking (the butter should not brown), use the ladle to scoop about ¼ cup of batter into the skillet. When the batter hits the pan, tilt it gently to spread the batter evenly over the bottom. When the bottom is covered, cook for just over 1 minute, and then flip the crepe over and cook the other side for about 30 seconds. Tilt the skillet over a plate to slide the crepe out.

4. You should be able to make several crepes per slice of butter, but gauge how dry the pan is: if you think it needs butter, add some. If the pan gets too hot and the butter browns, wipe it out with a paper towel and start over. Continue making the crepes until all the batter is used up. As they cool on the plate, put pieces of waxed paper between them to keep them from sticking together.

5. Preheat the oven to 350°F. Lightly grease a 9 x 13–inch baking dish. Working with one crepe at a time, put a generous scoop of the filling in the middle and fold the crepe up around the filling. Place the crepe in the baking dish so that the seam faces down. When the baking dish is filled with stuffed crepes, cover the dish with foil and bake for about 30 minutes until the filling is bubbling and hot. Remove from the oven, remove the foil, and let cool for a few minutes before serving.

RASPBERRY ICE CREAM CAKE

Makes 8 to 10 Servings   Active Time: 20 Minutes
Total Time: 1 Hour and 20 Minutes

1 large package of ladyfingers

1 quart vanilla ice cream

1 jar of raspberry preserves

1 quart raspberry ice cream

1 pint fresh raspberries, for serving (optional)

Whipped cream, for serving (optional)

1. Line the bottom of a 9" springform pan with the ladyfingers. Spread a layer of vanilla ice cream on top. Spread a thin layer of raspberry preserves on top of the vanilla ice cream and then add a layer of raspberry ice cream. Add another layer of raspberry preserves and raspberry ice cream, top with ladyfingers, and repeat until you reach the top of the pan.

2. Place the pan in the freezer for at least 1 hour. When ready to serve, whipped cream or additional raspberries make lovely additions.

4th of July

The sun is blazing, the air is thick with smoke and the sounds of firecrackers—it's got to be the 4th. It's the high-water mark of the summer, and we've planned accordingly. With the Capescrew and the Stars & Stripes sangria, your drinks have those who want to relax and those feeling particularly patriotic covered. Not that you have to worry too much about keeping everyone happy with the meal you've got in store. Both simple and stunning, the flavors present in the Goat Cheese and Brussels Sprouts Slaw and Chimichurri Strip Steak are sure to have your guests saluting you. Yes, it's a lot of food, but, considering the fortune of living in such a great country, there's a lot to celebrate.

Capescrew

Stars & Stripes

Virgin Apple Pie

Goat Cheese and Brussels Sprouts Slaw

Strawberry-Mint Salad

Chimichurri Strip Steak

Red, White, and Blue Bread Pudding

Light Strawberry-Blueberry Trifle

CAPESCREW

1 part vodka

Splash of triple sec

1 part orange juice

1 part cranberry juice

1 orange wheel, for garnish

1. Fill a highball glass with ice and add the vodka, triple sec, orange juice, and cranberry juice.

2. Stir until thoroughly mixed and garnish with the orange wheel.

STARS & STRIPES

Makes 4 to 6 Servings

1 (750 ml) bottle of sweet white wine

½ cup blueberries, frozen

½ cup blackberries, frozen

½ cup raspberries, frozen

½ cup vodka

1 cup berry seltzer

1 apple, peeled and chopped, for garnish (optional)

1. Combine all of the sangria ingredients except the seltzer in a large pitcher or container. Cover and refrigerate for 4 or more hours.

2. After removing the mixture from the refrigerator, add ice and seltzer. Garnish with apple pieces, if desired, stir, and serve.

VIRGIN APPLE PIE

3 parts apple cider

1 part cream soda

Dash of cinnamon

Dollop of whipped cream, for garnish

1. Add the apple cider and cream soda to your glass.

2. Top with a dash of cinnamon and then stir until thoroughly mixed. Garnish with the whipped cream.

GOAT CHEESE AND BRUSSELS SPROUTS SLAW

Makes 4 to 6 Servings   Active Time: 15 Minutes   Total Time: 15 Minutes

1 cup milk

2 tablespoons white vinegar

¾ cup mayonnaise

¼ cup nonfat Greek yogurt

1½ tablespoons Pasilla pepper seeds, ground

1 cup goat cheese, crumbled

1 tablespoon black pepper, coarsely ground

Pinch of kosher salt

Juice of ½ lime

1 tablespoon Thai basil, minced

2 pounds Brussels sprouts, shaved

¼ pound parsnips, peeled and grated

1. Place everything except the Brussels sprouts and parsnips in a large bowl and whisk until combined. Reserve half of the dressing for drizzling.

2. Add the Brussels sprouts and parsnips to the bowl and toss to coat. Refrigerate until ready to serve and serve with reserved dressing.

STRAWBERRY-MINT SALAD

Makes 4 Servings   Active Time: 15 Minutes   Total Time: 15 Minutes

4 cups fresh strawberries, sliced

Juice of 1 lime

¼ cup fresh mint, torn

Honey, to taste

1. Place the strawberries in a large bowl. Drizzle with the lime juice and sprinkle the mint over the strawberries.

2. Drizzle with the honey and serve.

CHIMICHURRI STRIP STEAK

Makes 4 Servings Active Time: 20 Minutes Total Time: 24 Hours

For the Chimichurri Sauce

2 tablespoons fresh oregano

4 tablespoons extra virgin olive oil

2 cups fresh parsley

1½ cups fresh cilantro

1 small white or yellow onion, chopped

2 scallions

1 jalapeño pepper (seeds removed if you don't want the extra heat)

¼ tablespoon salt

¼ tablespoon black pepper

¼ tablespoon onion powder

¼ tablespoon garlic powder

1 tablespoon sugar

⅓ cup water

For the Steaks

4 (5 to 6 oz.) strip steaks

1 tablespoon salt, plus more to taste

1 tablespoon olive oil

2 tablespoons beef tallow

Black pepper, to taste

1. Prepare the Chimichurri Sauce. Place all of the ingredients in a blender and puree until smooth. Transfer half of the Chimichurri Sauce and the steaks to a container and let them marinate in the refrigerator overnight. Refrigerate the other half of the sauce in a separate container.

2. Preheat oven to 375°F. Remove the steaks from the marinade and season both sides with salt. Place the olive oil and beef tallow in a cast-iron skillet and warm over medium-high heat. Add the steaks and cook for 2 minutes on each side. Add 3 tablespoons of the reserved sauce, season with pepper, and place the skillet in the oven for 5 minutes.

3. Remove the pan from the oven, divide between serving plates, and top with the remaining Chimichurri Sauce.

RED, WHITE, AND BLUE BREAD PUDDING

Makes 4 to 6 Servings   Active Time: 45 Minutes   Total Time: 2 Hours

4 tablespoons butter

4 cups day-old bread, cubed

1 cup fresh or frozen blueberries

1 gallon strawberry ice cream, softened

2 eggs, beaten

1. Place a cast-iron skillet over low heat and melt the butter. Add the bread pieces to the skillet and distribute evenly. Sprinkle the blueberries over the bread pieces.

2. Add the ice cream to the beaten eggs and stir just enough to combine. Pour the mixture over the bread in the skillet and shake gently to distribute the liquid evenly. Remove from heat, cover with aluminum foil, and allow the mixture to rest for about 30 minutes.

3. Preheat the oven to 350°F. Place the skillet in the oven and bake for 40 to 45 minutes until the cream mixture is set and it is slightly brown around the edges. Remove from the oven and allow to cool for 5 to 10 minutes before inverting the bread pudding onto a serving dish.

LIGHT STRAWBERRY-BLUEBERRY TRIFLE

Makes 8 to 10 Servings   Active Time: 20 Minutes   Total Time: 20 Minutes

¼ cup water

2 tablespoons granulated sugar

2 tablespoons fresh lemon juice

2 (8 oz.) packages of cream cheese

1 cup powdered sugar

2 cups heavy cream

1 teaspoon pure vanilla extract

¼ teaspoon sea salt

1 angel food cake, sliced

1 pound fresh strawberries, sliced

1 pound fresh blueberries

1. Place the water, granulated sugar, and lemon juice in a saucepan and cook until sugar dissolves. Remove pan from heat and let cool.

2. Place the cream cheese and powdered sugar in the bowl of an electric mixer and beat until light and fluffy. Slowly add the heavy cream to the bowl and beat until well combined. Add the vanilla extract and salt and beat until combined.

3. Place the slices of angel food cake in a layer at the bottom of a trifle dish. Pour roughly one-third of the lemon syrup over the cake. Spread approximately one-third of the cream cheese mixture on top of this. Place half of the strawberry slices on top and top with layers of cake, syrup, and cream cheese mixture. Sprinkle half of the blueberries on top and top with layers of cake, syrup, and cream cheese mixture. Decorate the top with the remaining fruit before serving.

Week 27

A bevy of brunch classics—the Screwdriver, Caprese Salad, and Key Lime Chiffon Pie—help you set the stage for innovative showstoppers like the Chilled Honeydew Melon Soup with Crispy Proscuitto di Parma and Chia Seed Pudding with Baker's Chocolate and Cherries. All in all, it's a spread that's sure to dazzle anyone who's coming past.

Screwdriver

Chilled Honeydew Melon Soup with
Crispy Proscuitto di Parma

Caprese Salad

Chia Seed Pudding with
Baker's Chocolate and Cherries

Key Lime Chiffon Pie

SCREWDRIVER

1 part vodka

2 parts orange juice

Pomegranate juice, for the rim

1 orange slice, for garnish

1. Fill a glass with ice. Add the vodka and top off with orange juice.

2. Dab your finger with a bit of pomegranate juice and rub it along the rim of the glass. Garnish with the slice of orange.

CHILLED HONEYDEW MELON SOUP
WITH CRISPY PROSCIUTTO DI PARMA

Makes 4 Servings   Active Time: 15 Minutes   Total Time: 30 Minutes

1 honeydew melon, peeled, halved, and seeded

1 tablespoon lemon juice

8 slices of prosciutto

2 cups dry white wine, chilled

2 tablespoons sugar

Fresh grapes, for garnish

Lemon zest, for garnish

1. Puree the melon and lemon juice in a food processor and then strain through a fine sieve. Chill in the refrigerator for 20 minutes.

2. Preheat oven to 375°F. Line a baking sheet with parchment paper and place the slices of prosciutto on the sheet. Place the sheet in the oven and bake for 5 to 10 minutes, or until the prosciutto is crispy. Remove the sheet from the oven and place prosciutto on a paper towel to drain.

3. Just before serving, add the chilled white wine, whisk until combined, and then add the sugar. Ladle into chilled bowls, top with the prosciutto, and garnish with fresh grapes and lemon zest.

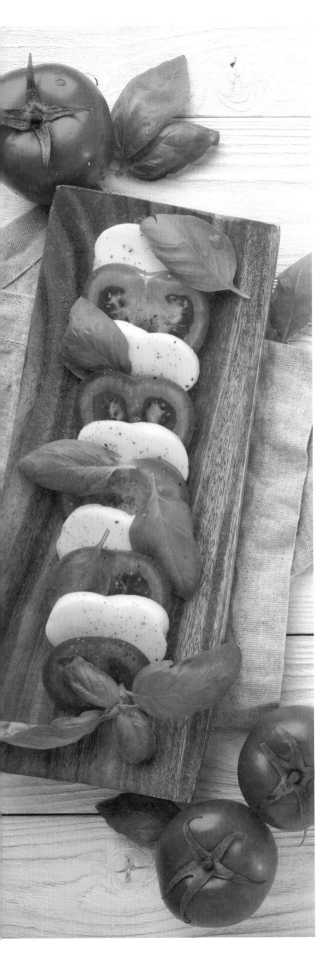

CAPRESE SALAD

Makes 4 to 6 Servings   Active Time: 10 Minutes
Total Time: 10 Minutes

---

4 beefsteak tomatoes, sliced into ½-inch-thick pieces

1 package of fresh mozzarella cheese, sliced into
¼-inch-thick pieces

½ cup basil leaves

1 tablespoon extra virgin olive oil

1 tablespoon balsamic vinegar

Sea salt and freshly ground black pepper, to taste

1. Place the tomatoes on a platter and then layer the
   mozzarella and basil leaves on top.

2. In a small glass, combine the extra virgin olive oil and
   balsamic vinegar. Drizzle it over the tomato towers,
   and season with salt and pepper.

CHIA SEED PUDDING WITH BAKER'S CHOCOLATE AND CHERRIES

Makes 4 Servings   Active Time: 5 to 10 Minutes
Total Time: 12 Hours

1½ cups lite coconut milk

½ cup nonfat Greek yogurt

1 cup sweet dark cherries, fresh or frozen

½ cup chia seeds

1 oz. Baker's Unsweetened Chocolate

2 tablespoons honey

Pinch of salt

1. Place all of the ingredients in a blender and blend until it reaches the desired consistency.

2. Let the pudding set up in the refrigerator overnight to give the chia seeds time to soften and let all of the flavors meld together.

   Tip: Baker's Unsweetened Chocolate is 100% cocoa with no dairy or sugar added. If you are looking for a slightly sweeter version of this pudding, try using a chocolate with between 85% to 95% cocoa content.

KEY LIME CHIFFON PIE

Makes 6 to 8 Servings   Active Time: 30 Minutes   Total Time: 2 Hours

1 Graham Cracker Crust (see page 29)

2 cups heavy cream

¼ cup sugar

⅓ cup fresh lime juice

1 tablespoon unflavored gelatin

½ cup sweetened condensed milk

Whipped cream, for garnish

Lime zest and/or lime wheels, for garnish

1. Place the crust in a 9" pie plate. In a large bowl, beat the cream until peaks start to form. Add the sugar and beat until stiff peaks begin to form.

2. Place the lime juice and gelatin in a small saucepan and stir until the gelatin has dissolved. Cook over medium heat until the mixture starts to thicken, about 3 to 5 minutes. Remove the pan from heat and allow to cool slightly. Stir in the condensed milk and then fold this mixture into the cream mixture.

3. Pour the filling into the crust, cover with plastic wrap, and chill in the refrigerator until set, about 45 minutes. Garnish with whipped cream and lime zest and/or lime wheels.

Week 28

It's starting to heat up, and we're doing all we can to keep you cool. With only one dish that needs to be cooked, you'll be able to keep the sweat off your brow while whipping together this delicious meal. Kefta is great on its own, but dip it into the refreshing Tzatziki and you'll wonder why you've been restricting yourself to hamburgers and ketchup for so long. The Golden Gazpacho with Parsley Oil and Classic Summer Fruit Salad ensure that you'll remain light on your feet and keep you from getting zapped by the heat.

Watermelon Margarita

Virgin Strawberry Daiquiri

Kefta

Tzatziki

Golden Gazpacho
with Parsley Oil

Classic Summer Fruit Salad

WATERMELON MARGARITA

1½ oz. watermelon, cubed

2 oz. tequila

1 oz. fresh lime juice

½ oz. Simple Syrup (see page 32)

1 oz. triple sec

1 lime wedge, for the rim

Sea salt, for the rim

1. Place the watermelon in a blender or food processor and blend until smooth.

2. Fill a cocktail shaker with ice and add the watermelon puree, tequila, lime juice, Simple Syrup, and triple sec, and shake vigorously until well combined.

3. Rub the lime wedge around the rim of a rocks glass and then dip the rim in sea salt. Fill the glass to the top with ice and strain the margarita into the glass. Garnish with the lime wedge.

VIRGIN STRAWBERRY DAIQUIRI

2 oz. lemon-lime soda

½ oz. orange juice

¼ oz. Simple Syrup (see page 32)

Juice of ½ lime

½ cup strawberries, hulled

1 cup ice

1 handful of sliced strawberries, for garnish

1. Add all ingredients to a blender and blend until smooth. Make sure that all ice and strawberries have been sufficiently blended; it may take a few blending cycles.

2. Pour the blended cocktails into a cocktail or Hurricane glass. Garnish with the slices of strawberry.

KEFTA

Makes 4 to 6 Servings
Active Time: 30 to 35 Minutes
Total Time: 50 Minutes

1 pound ground beef
(85% lean recommended)

1 pound ground lamb

½ cup white onion, minced

2 garlic cloves, roasted and mashed

Zest of 1 lemon

1 cup parsley, washed and minced

2 tablespoons mint, chopped

1 teaspoon cinnamon

2 tablespoons cumin

1 tablespoon paprika

1 teaspoon ground coriander

Salt and black pepper, to taste

6 wooden skewers

¼ cup olive oil

1. In a mixing bowl, add all of the edible
    ingredients except for the olive oil and stir
    until well combined. Cook a small bit of the
    mixture as a test and taste. Adjust seasoning
    as necessary. Then form the mixture into
    18 ovals. Place three meatballs on each
    skewer. Add the olive oil to a Dutch oven
    and warm over medium-high heat. Working
    in batches, add three skewers to the pot and
    sear the Kefta for 2 minutes on each side.

2. Return all of the skewers to the pot, cover,
    and remove it from heat. Let stand for 10
    minutes so the Kefta get cooked through.
    When the Kefta are cooked through, remove
    the skewers and serve.

TZATZIKI

Makes 1½ Cups   Active Time: 15 Minutes   Total Time: 15 Minutes

1 cup plain Greek yogurt

1 cucumber, seeded and grated

2 garlic cloves, minced

1 teaspoon lemon zest

1 tablespoon fresh lemon juice

2 tablespoons dill, chopped

Salt and black pepper, to taste

Cucumber spears, for serving

Pita bread, sliced, for serving

Place all ingredients in a small bowl and whisk until the mixture is well combined. Serve with cucumber spears and slices of pita bread.

GOLDEN GAZPACHO WITH PARSLEY OIL

Makes 4 to 6 Servings   Active Time: 1 Hour   Total Time: 16 Hours

For the Soup

4 tomatoes, chopped

½ red onion, peeled and chopped

½ cucumber, chopped

1 red bell pepper, seeded
and chopped

1 celery stalk, chopped

1 cup crusty bread, chopped

2 tablespoons parsley, leaves
removed and chopped

2 tablespoons chives, chopped

1 garlic clove, minced

¼ cup red wine vinegar

2 tablespoons extra virgin olive oil

1 teaspoon lemon juice

1 teaspoon sugar

2 teaspoons Tabasco

1 teaspoon Worcestershire sauce

2 cups tomato juice

Salt and black pepper, to taste

For the Parsley Oil

1 cup parsley, chopped

1 cup baby spinach

1 cup vegetable oil

1. Prepare the soup. Combine all ingredients in a large bowl, cover, and place in refrigerator to marinate overnight.

2. Transfer the soup to a food processor and puree to desired consistency. Chill in refrigerator for 1 hour.

3. Prepare the Parsley Oil. In a small saucepan, bring 4 cups of water to boil. Add the parsley leaves and spinach, cook for 1 minute, drain, and submerge in ice water. Remove from ice water and squeeze out any excess water.

4. In a food processor, add the parsley, spinach, and vegetable oil, and puree for 3 to 4 minutes. Strain through a cheesecloth, discard the solids, and set aside.

5. When ready to serve, remove the soup from the refrigerator, season to taste, and top with the Parsley Oil.

CLASSIC SUMMER
FRUIT SALAD

Makes 8 to 10 Servings   Active Time: 5 Minutes
Total Time: 25 Minutes

5 fresh mint leaves, minced

¼ cup fresh orange juice

1 teaspoon honey

1 pint strawberries, halved

1 pint blueberries

1 pint raspberries

2 cups seedless grapes, halved

1. Add mint, orange juice, and honey to a bowl, stir
   to combine, and set aside.

2. In a separate bowl, combine the strawberries,
   blueberries, raspberries, and grapes. Add
   dressing and toss to coat. Place in refrigerator
   and chill for 20 minutes before serving.

Week 29

For years, Italians have been sitting around small chestnut tables soaking up the brutal sun without a care in the world. What's their secret? How can we all learn to stay so cool and relaxed on oppressively hot days? Whip up a platter of Dill Pickle Arancini and a few Caprese Chicken Sandwiches, and you're on your way to understanding. The Lemon Squares aren't especially Italian, but they're so refreshing they'll keep you in that relaxed, untroubled frame of mind.

Sea Breeze

Dill Pickle Arancini

Caprese Chicken Sandwiches

Lemon Squares

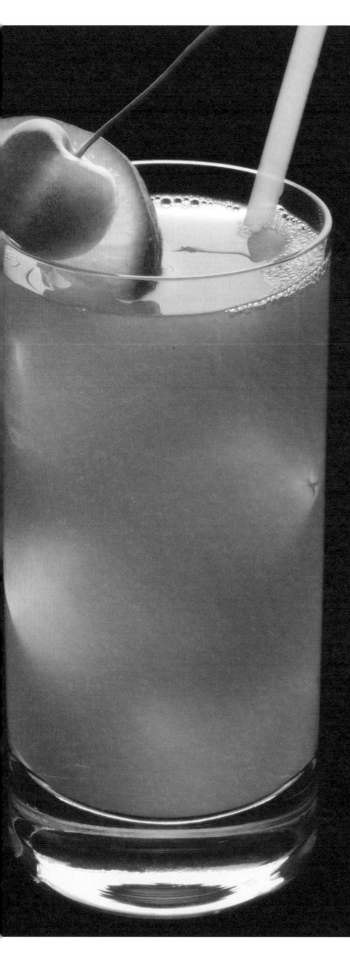

SEA BREEZE

Juice of ½ lime
1 part vodka
2 parts cranberry juice
1 part grapefruit juice
1 lime wedge, for garnish
1 cherry, for garnish

1. Fill a highball glass with ice and add the lime juice, vodka, cranberry juice, and grapefruit juice.

2. Stir until thoroughly mixed and garnish with the lime wedge and cherry.

DILL PICKLE ARANCINI

Makes 8 to 10 Servings   Active Time: 30 Minutes   Total Time: 1½ Hours

8 cups Chicken Stock (see page 24)

8 tablespoons (1 stick) butter

2 cups Arborio rice

1 small white onion, minced

1 cup white wine

1½ cups Havarti with dill, grated

1½ cups dill pickles, chopped

Salt and black pepper, to taste

4 cups canola or vegetable oil

6 large eggs, beaten

5 cups panko bread crumbs

Cajun Remoulade (see page 40)

1. Bring the Chicken Stock to a simmer in a large saucepan. In a separate pot, melt the butter over high heat. Once the butter is bubbling, add the rice and onion and cook until the onion is translucent, about 4 minutes. Deglaze the pot with the white wine and reduce until the wine has almost completely evaporated. Then, reduce the heat to medium-high and begin adding the hot chicken stock, ¼ cup at a time, stirring frequently until incorporated and reduced slightly. Continue this process until all the liquid has been added and the rice is tender.

2. Turn off the heat, add the Havarti and pickles, and season with salt and pepper. Pour the mixture onto a baking sheet and let cool.

3. Place the oil in a Dutch oven and cook over medium heat until it reaches 350°F. When the rice mixture is cool, form it into golf ball–sized spheres. Dip it into in the beaten eggs and then the bread crumbs. Place the balls in the oil and cook until warmed through and golden brown. Serve with Cajun Remoulade.

CAPRESE CHICKEN SANDWICHES

Makes 6 Servings   Active Time: 20 Minutes   Total Time: 35 Minutes

8 tablespoons extra virgin olive oil

2 teaspoons fresh parsley, minced

Juice of 1 lemon

Salt and black pepper, to taste

4 boneless, skinless chicken breasts

2 baguettes, halved lengthwise

10 to 12 medium tomatoes, sliced

8 oz. fresh mozzarella, cut into ¼-inch-thick rounds

¼ cup basil leaves

Balsamic vinegar, to taste (optional)

Basil Pesto (see page 31)

1. Combine 4 tablespoons of the olive oil, parsley, lemon juice, salt, and pepper in a large mixing bowl. Add the chicken breasts and toss until coated. Set aside and let come to room temperature.

2. Preheat your gas or charcoal grill to 450°F. When the grill is ready, place the chicken breasts on the grill, season with salt and pepper, and cook for 3 to 4 minutes. Turn the chicken over and cook for 3 minutes, or until grill marks form. If using a charcoal grill, bank the coals on one side. If using a gas grill, turn off the burners on one side. Place the chicken breasts on the side with indirect heat, cover the grill, and cook until the chicken has an internal temperature of 165°F. Remove from the grill, slice thinly, and set aside.

3. Drizzle the remaining olive oil over the cut sides of the bread halves. Place them on the grill and cook until lightly browned.

4. Cut the halves of bread into three pieces. Place 3 to 4 pieces of chicken, a few tomato slices, and 2 to 3 slices of mozzarella on each piece. Preheat the broiler to the oven and place the sandwiches on a baking sheet. Place in the oven and broil until the cheese is melted.

5. If using, drizzle with balsamic vinegar. Top with Basil Pesto. Serve open-faced or form into sandwiches.

LEMON SQUARES

Makes 12 to 16 Squares   Active Time: 15 Minutes
Total Time: 1 Hour

---

8 tablespoons (1 stick) butter

⅓ cup confectioners' sugar

1 cup all-purpose flour, plus 2 tablespoons

Pinch of salt

2 large eggs, at room temperature

1 cup granulated sugar

⅓ cup fresh lemon juice

1 tablespoon lemon zest

1. Preheat the oven to 350°F and grease the bottom and sides of an 8 x 8–inch baking pan. Place the butter, ¼ cup of the confectioners' sugar, the 1 cup of flour, and salt in a mixing bowl and stir until combined. Press mixture into the baking pan and bake for 20 minutes, or until it is set and lightly browned. Remove from oven and set aside.

2. Place the eggs, granulated sugar, remaining flour, lemon juice, and lemon zest in a mixing bowl and beat with an electric mixer on medium until well combined. Pour mixture over the crust and bake for 20 minutes, or until barely browned. The custard should still be soft. Let the pan cool on a wire rack, then dust with the remaining confectioners' sugar and cut into bars.

Week 30

A dish beloved by grandmothers and the world's finest chefs, Ratatouille is nutritious, rich, and quite fun to prepare. You can easily make it vegetarian, but we think that the grilled sweet Italian sausage is essential. It's also very versatile, so don't be afraid to experiment—you can even serve it cold if it's one of those weeks where the thermometer is threatening to bubble over. Follow it up with the delicious Chilled Blueberry and Yogurt Soup and your loved ones may be suggesting you open a restaurant.

Vodka Sunrise

Virgin Piña Colada

Mushroom, Spinach, and Leek Galette

Ratatouille

Chilled Blueberry and Yogurt Soup

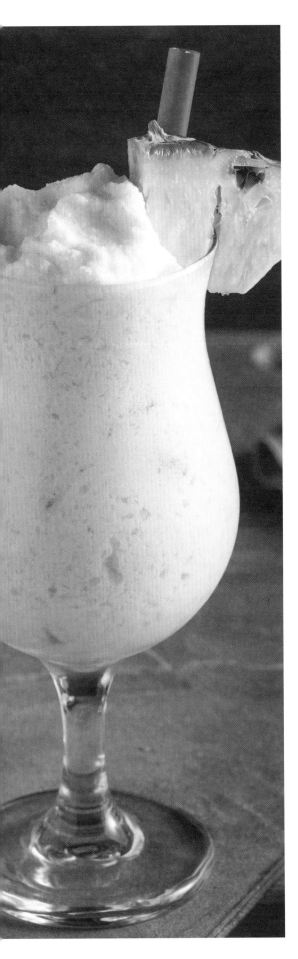

VODKA SUNRISE

1 part vodka

Dash of lemon juice

2 parts orange juice

Splash of grenadine

1 maraschino cherry, for garnish

1 orange slice, for garnish

1. Add ice to a glass and pour in the vodka and lemon juice. Mix together.

2. Add orange juice to fill, then top with a splash of grenadine. Rather than stirring, allow the grenadine to slowly filter down through the orange juice and vodka.

3. Garnish with the maraschino cherry and orange slice.

VIRGIN PIÑA COLADA

1 part coconut cream

3 parts pineapple juice

1 cup ice

1 pineapple chunk, for garnish

1. Add coconut cream, pineapple juice, and ice to the blender and blend until smooth.

2. Pour into a Hurricane glass and garnish with the pineapple chunk.

MUSHROOM, SPINACH, AND LEEK GALETTE

Makes 4 to 6 Servings   Active Time: 30 Minutes   Total Time: 1½ Hours

1 Flaky Pastry Crust (see page 28)

4 tablespoons butter

2 leeks, white and light green parts only, washed and thinly sliced

1½ cups mushrooms, sliced

4 cups baby spinach

½ cup Parmesan cheese, grated

1 tablespoon half-and-half

1. Preheat the oven to 375°F and place the crust in a greased 9" pie plate. Melt 2 tablespoons of the butter in a skillet over medium heat, and then add the leeks. Cook, while stirring, until the leeks soften, about 2 minutes. Add the remaining butter and the mushrooms and cook over low heat, while stirring occasionally, until the mushrooms are soft and the leeks are caramelized, about 10 minutes.

2. Raise the heat to medium and add the baby spinach, stirring as the leaves wilt. When wilted, remove the skillet from heat.

3. Place the vegetable mixture in the center of the crust. Fold the extra crust over the filling so that it covers about 1 inch. Sprinkle with Parmesan cheese and brush the top of the crust with the half-and-half. Put the galette in the oven and bake for 20 to 30 minutes until the crust is golden brown.

RATATOUILLE

Makes 4 Servings   Active Time: 40 Minutes   Total Time: 2 Hours

⅓ cup olive oil, plus more
as needed

6 garlic cloves, minced

1 medium eggplant, cut into
bite-sized cubes

2 red bell peppers, seeded
and diced

4 tomatoes, concasse
(see page 21) and chopped

2 zucchini, cut into rounds

1 pound sweet Italian sausage,
grilled and sliced into rounds

Salt and black pepper, to taste

1. Heat half the olive oil in a Dutch oven or deep skillet over medium-high heat. Add the garlic and eggplant and cook, while stirring, until pieces are coated with oil and softened, about 2 minutes.

2. Reduce the heat to medium and add the peppers and remaining oil, while stirring. Cover and cook for 15 minutes while stirring occasionally. If the mixture seems too dry, add a little more olive oil.

3. Once the eggplant and peppers are tender, add the tomatoes, zucchini, and sausage, and stir to combine. Remove the lid and cook, while stirring occasionally, until the eggplant and peppers are soft, and the tomatoes are wilted. Remove from the heat, season with salt and pepper, and let sit for at least 1 hour. Reheat before serving.

CHILLED BLUEBERRY AND YOGURT SOUP

Makes 4 Servings   Active Time: 5 Minutes
Total Time: 30 Minutes

2 cups blueberries, plus more for garnish

4 cups plain Greek yogurt

1 cup orange juice

1 cup Champagne

1 vanilla bean, scraped

1 teaspoon cinnamon

Sugar, to taste

1. Place all ingredients except sugar in a food processor and gently pulse until combined.

2. Season with sugar to taste and place in the refrigerator for 15 minutes.

3. Serve in chilled bowls, or champagne flutes, with additional blueberries.

Week 31

There's no shortage of zucchini kicking around in the summer, but there always seems to be a dearth of preparations in which the vegetable can shine. These Grilled Zucchini Nachos are an antidote to that issue, and set the stage beautifully for the Grilled Salmon with Honey-Soy Baste. The classic combination of sweet and salty sits beautifully on the mild salmon. After a series of modern-leaning preparations, take it all the way back with some Ambrosia and watch the nostalgia well up in the eyes of your guests.

Peach Tree Iced Tea

Grilled Zucchini Nachos

Grilled Salmon
with Honey-Soy Baste

Ambrosia

PEACH TREE
ICED TEA

6 mint leaves

1 part peach schnapps

1 part vodka

2 parts iced tea

1. Tear the mint leaves in half and place them at the bottom of a glass.

2. Add the peach schnapps, muddle, and then add the ice.

3. Add the vodka and iced tea and stir until thoroughly mixed.

GRILLED ZUCCHINI NACHOS

Makes 4 Servings   Active Time: 10 Minutes
Total Time: 20 Minutes

2 medium zucchini, sliced into ¼-inch-thick rounds

¼ cup olive oil

Salt and black pepper, to taste

1 cup cheddar cheese, shredded

1 (14 oz.) can of black beans, rinsed and drained

1 large tomato, chopped

1 large avocado, seeded and chopped

2 scallions, chopped

¼ cup cilantro, chopped

Juice from 1 lime wedge

1. Preheat your gas or charcoal grill to 450°F. Place the zucchini in a medium bowl, add the olive oil, and toss. Season with salt and pepper.

2. Place the zucchini on the grill and cook until tender, about 4 to 5 minutes. Sprinkle the cheese over the zucchini and continue cooking until the cheese is slightly melted.

3. Place cooked chips on a large platter and top with the black beans, tomato, avocado, scallions, cilantro, and a squeeze of lime juice.

GRILLED SALMON
WITH HONEY-SOY BASTE

Makes 6 Servings   Active Time: 20 Minutes   Total Time: 2½ Hours

---

For the Honey-Soy Baste

¾ cup Dijon mustard

¾ cup soy sauce

¾ cup honey

8 garlic cloves, minced

1 cup olive oil

1 tablespoon sesame seeds

For the Salmon

1 large salmon fillet, cut into
6 rectangular slices

2 tablespoons sea salt

2 tablespoons freshly ground black pepper

6 lemon wedges, for serving

1. Prepare the Honey-Soy Baste. In a bowl, combine all of the ingredients and let rest for 1 hour.

2. Place the salmon in a baking dish and season both sides with salt and pepper. Add 1 cup of the Honey-Soy Baste to the dish and let marinate for 1 hour in the refrigerator.

3. Preheat your gas or charcoal grill to 450°F. If you are using a charcoal grill, place the coals on one side of the grill to differentiate the heat. If you are using a gas grill, don't turn on one of the burners. When the grill is hot, place the salmon skin side down over indirect heat and cook, while basting every 3 minutes, for about 13 to 15 minutes, until the fillets are juicy and the meat is flaky. Carefully remove the salmon from the grill and serve with lemon wedges.

AMBROSIA

Makes 6 to 8 Servings   Active Time: 20 Minutes
Total Time: 3 Hours and 20 Minutes

½ cup heavy cream

1 tablespoon sugar

½ cup sour cream

¼ teaspoon nutmeg, grated

3 cups mini-marshmallows

6 clementines, segmented

1 cup pineapple, cubed

1 cup shredded coconut

1 cup pecans, toasted and chopped

¾ cup maraschino cherries

1. Place the cream and sugar in a bowl and whisk
   until stiff peaks begin to form. Whisk in the sour
   cream and nutmeg.

2. Add the mini-marshmallows, clementines,
   pineapple, coconut, pecans, and cherries to the
   bowl. Cover and let chill for a minimum of 3 hours
   before serving.

Week 32

Simple, bold preparations will keep your head up during the dog days. The combination of Champagne and tequila is criminally underutilized, as you'll see after a Tequila Sparkler or two. A refreshing, tangy Watermelon and Goat Cheese Salad sets up the star of the show, the Coffee Prime Rib. The bold flavor of coffee on a juicy, perfectly prepared prime rib is nothing short of heavenly. And if you're smart, you'll have some extra mint-infused mango on hand to meet the inevitable demands of your awestruck guests.

Tequila Sparkler

Cherry-Almond Water

Watermelon and Goat Cheese Salad

Coffee Prime Rib

Coconut and Tapioca Soup
with Mint-Infused Mango

TEQUILA SPARKLER

1 part tequila

Splash of lime juice

3 parts Champagne

1 lime wedge, for garnish

Pour tequila and lime juice into a champagne flute. Top with Champagne and garnish with the lime wedge.

CHERRY-ALMOND WATER

Makes 8 Servings

1 cup sweet cherries, pitted and halved

½ teaspoon pure almond extract

8 cups cold, filtered water

1. Place the cherries and almond extract in a pitcher or jar and cover with the water.

2. Let sit for 1 to 2 hours at room temperature for a quick infusion, or refrigerate for anywhere from 4 hours to overnight. Serve chilled.

WATERMELON AND GOAT CHEESE SALAD

Makes 4 Servings   Active Time: 5 Minutes   Total Time: 15 Minutes

1 seedless watermelon, cut into 1-inch-thick slices

2 tablespoons olive oil, plus more as needed

2 teaspoons lime juice

Pinch of salt

1 pint strawberries, thinly sliced

1 cucumber, sliced

1 cup goat cheese, crumbled

1. Preheat your gas or charcoal grill to 500°F. Brush both sides of the watermelon slices with the olive oil. When the grill is ready, place the slices on the grill and cook on each side for about 4 minutes. Remove, let cool, and then cut the flesh into chunks.

2. Place the 2 tablespoons of olive oil, lime juice, and salt in a large bowl and stir to combine. Add the strawberries, cucumber, and watermelon and toss to coat. Sprinkle the goat cheese on top before serving.

COFFEE PRIME RIB

Makes 6 to 8 Servings   Active Time: 1 Hour   Total Time: 4 Hours

1 (6-rib) rib roast

2 tablespoons black peppercorns, crushed

2 tablespoons fresh sea salt

¼ cup coffee, finely ground

3 tablespoons thyme, minced

2 tablespoons dark brown sugar

2 teaspoons ground mustard

1 teaspoon smoked paprika

3 tablespoons extra virgin olive oil

1. Remove the rib roast from the refrigerator 1 hour before cooking and let stand at room temperature. Preheat the oven to 450°F.

2. Place the pepper, salt, coffee, thyme, brown sugar, mustard, and paprika in a bowl and stir to combine.

3. When the rib roast has come to room temperature, rub the olive oil all over it. Rub the coffee mixture over the exterior and underneath the fat cap. Transfer the roast to a large rack set in a roasting pan. Then transfer the pan to the oven and sear for about 15 minutes.

4. Reduce the heat to 325°F and cook for 2½ to 3 hours, until a thermometer registers 125°F for medium-rare. During the roasting process, the crust of the rib roast may begin to brown—if that is the case, gently cover the rib roast with a sheet of aluminum foil in order to help retain moisture.

5. Remove the rib roast from the oven, transfer to a large cutting board, and let stand for about 10 minutes before carving.

COCONUT AND TAPIOCA SOUP WITH MINT-INFUSED MANGO

Makes 4 to 6 Servings   Active Time: 30 Minutes   Total Time: 2 Hours and 40 Minutes

For the Mint-Infused Mango

½ cup water

½ cup white wine

½ cup sugar

Zest of 1 Lime

2 mint sprigs, leaves removed and chopped

1 cup mango, cubed

For the Soup

5 cups milk, plus more as needed

½ cup sugar

1 vanilla bean, halved and scraped

1 cup small tapioca pearls

1 (14 oz.) can of coconut milk

Mint leaves, for garnish

Coconut Tuile (see recipe), for garnish

1. Prepare the Mint-Infused Mango. In a small saucepan, add the water, white wine, sugar, and lime zest and bring to a boil. Remove from heat, add the mint sprigs, and cover. Let stand until cool. Once cool, transfer to a bowl with the mango and let chill in refrigerator for at least 2 hours.

2. Prepare the soup. In a large saucepan, add the milk, sugar, vanilla seeds, and vanilla pod and bring to a boil. Reduce heat so that the soup simmers and add the tapioca pearls. Cook for 10 minutes, or until the tapioca pearls are soft. Remove the pan from heat, add the coconut milk, and let stand until cool. Serve with the Mint-Infused Mango and garnish with mint leaves and the Coconut Tuile.

Coconut Tuile

⅓ cup shredded, unsweetened coconut

¼ cup powdered sugar

1 tablespoon flour

1 tablespoon butter, melted

1 egg white

1. In a mixing bowl, add the coconut, powdered sugar, and flour and whisk to combine. In a separate bowl, add the melted butter and the egg white and whisk vigorously until combined.

2. Add the coconut mixture to the butter-and-egg mixture and combine. Chill in refrigerator for 2 hours.

3. Preheat oven to 350°F. Spread the chilled tuile on a greased baking sheet. Place in the oven and cook for 8 minutes, or until golden brown.

Week 33

Everyone loves tacos, so there's no reason to keep people waiting until dinner to enjoy this beloved dish. Alongside all your favorite fixings and the Spicy Shrimp Polenta, you and your guests will be too busy stuffing your faces to mind the few beads of sweat on your brow. Close out the meal with the Frozen Chocolate-Covered Bananas, and we're betting you'll be blown away by how accessible all that deliciousness was.

Sweet Peach

Spicy Shrimp Polenta

Breakfast Tacos

Frozen Chocolate-Covered Bananas

SWEET PEACH

Makes 4 to 6 Servings

1 (750 ml) bottle of dry white wine

2 peaches, pitted and cut into bite-sized pieces

½ cup blueberries, frozen

1 cup peach nectar

¼ cup peach schnapps

2 cups seltzer

1. Combine all of the ingredients, except the seltzer, in a large pitcher or container. Cover and refrigerate for at least 4 hours.

2. After removing the mixture from the refrigerator, add ice and seltzer. Stir and serve.

SPICY SHRIMP POLENTA

Makes 4 to 6 Servings   Active Time: 30 Minutes   Start to Finish: 1 Hour

3 tablespoons canola oil

½ pound small shrimp, peeled, deveined, and halved

1 cup polenta

3 cups water

1 teaspoon horseradish

1 teaspoon red pepper flakes

Salt and freshly ground black pepper, to taste

Sprigs of cilantro, for garnish

1. Preheat the oven to 400°F. Place the canola oil in a cast-iron skillet and warm over medium-high heat. When hot but not smoking, add the shrimp. Cook the shrimp until just pink, about 3 to 5 minutes. Remove the pan from heat and use a slotted spoon to transfer the shrimp to a paper towel–lined plate.

2. In a medium saucepan, add the polenta and water, and whisk to combine. Heat over medium heat and bring to a boil, whisking constantly to prevent lumps from forming. When bubbling, reduce the heat to low and simmer for 3 minutes, or until smooth. Remove saucepan from heat, and stir in the horseradish and pepper flakes. Season with salt and pepper and then stir in the shrimp.

3. Pour the polenta into the skillet and smooth the surface with the back of a wooden spoon. Put the skillet in the oven and bake for about 30 minutes, until the polenta is lightly golden and coming away from the edge of the pan. Remove, allow to cool for 5 to 10 minutes, and then invert the polenta cake onto a platter. Allow to cool to room temperature before cutting into wedges. Garnish each wedge with a sprig of cilantro.

BREAKFAST TACOS

Makes 6 Servings   Active Time: 30 Minutes   Total Time: 40 Minutes

---

2 tablespoons cooking oil

8 eggs

1 tablespoon chili powder

1 tablespoon cumin

½ tablespoon adobo seasoning

1 tablespoon dried oregano

2 tablespoons cilantro, chopped

Salt, to taste

6 corn tortillas, warmed

Salsa, for serving

Guacamole
(see page 60), for serving

1. Heat the oil in a cast-iron skillet over medium heat. In a separate bowl, combine the eggs, spices, and cilantro.

2. Add the egg mixture to the skillet and scramble until eggs are cooked through. Season with salt and serve with warm tortillas, salsa, guacamole, and other fixings of your choice.

Tip: *Some other great toppings for these tacos are hot sauce, Cotija or goat cheese, shredded cheddar, and additional cilantro. Don't hesitate to add your own favorites to the mix.*

FROZEN CHOCOLATE-COVERED BANANAS

Makes 4 Servings   Active Time: 10 Minutes
Total Time: 1 Hour and 10 Minutes

---

4 bananas, not too ripe

1 pound semi-sweet chocolate

1½ tablespoons butter, softened

⅓ cup salted peanuts, chopped

⅓ cup rainbow sprinkles

⅓ cup shredded coconut

1. Cut the bananas into thirds and insert a popsicle stick into each piece. About two-thirds of the stick should be in the banana.

2. Place chocolate in a microwave-safe bowl and microwave for 12-second intervals, removing to stir each time. When the chocolate is almost completely melted, stir in the softened butter. The mixture should look glossy.

3. Dip bananas in chocolate and spoon chocolate over fruit so that the bananas are completely covered. Roll the chocolate-covered banana into your preferred combination of peanuts, sprinkles, and/or coconut.

4. Place bananas on a wax paper–lined baking sheet and chill in the refrigerator or freezer for 1 hour before serving.

Week 34

We did what we could, but the summer heat finally got the best of you. Well, the Whalen Smash, Grilled Peach Salad, and Shrimp Cocktail will keep you and your house cool. And while you'll have to briefly brave the grill while preparing the Korean Chicken Thighs, your sacrifice will be more than worth it—especially since you've got the Watermelon and Cherry Soup to cool you off.

Whalen Smash

Virgin Margarita

Grilled Peach Salad

Shrimp Cocktail

Korean Chicken Thighs

Watermelon and Cherry Soup

WHALEN SMASH

½ lemon, cut into thirds

4 mint leaves

3 parts bourbon

1 part ginger beer

1 lemon or lime slice, for garnish (optional)

1. Squeeze the lemon wedges into a rocks glass and then drop the spent wedges into the glass.

2. Add the mint leaves, muddle, and add ice as desired.

3. Add the bourbon, top with ginger beer, and stir. If desired, garnish with a slice of lemon or lime (or both).

VIRGIN MARGARITA

1 lime wedge, for the rim

Salt, for the rim

1 part lemon juice

1 part lime juice

1 part orange juice

1 part Simple Syrup (see page 32)

1. Rub the lime wedge along the rim of a margarita coupe and dip it into the salt.

2. Add the lemon juice, lime juice, orange juice, and syrup to a cocktail shaker filled with ice and shake until combined.

3. Place ice in your margarita coupe and strain the contents of the cocktail shaker into it. Garnish with the lime wedge.

GRILLED PEACH SALAD

Makes 4 Servings   Active Time: 5 Minutes   Total Time: 20 Minutes

3 peaches, pitted and halved

2 tablespoons olive oil, plus more as needed

2 bell peppers, sliced

1 tablespoon honey

4 cups baby arugula

3 tablespoons slivered almonds

½ tablespoon lemon juice

1. Preheat your gas or charcoal grill to 500°F. When the grill is ready, brush the cut side of the peaches with olive oil and then place them on the grill, cut side down. Brush the slices of pepper with olive oil and place them on the grill. Grill the peaches for about 2 to 3 minutes, or until they become caramelized. Flip, cook for 2 minutes, and remove from the grill. Grill the bell peppers for about 8 minutes while flipping them over once. Transfer to a plate.

2. When cool enough to handle, dice the peaches and peppers, transfer them to a large bowl with the 2 tablespoons of olive oil, honey, arugula, and slivered almonds, and toss to coat. Drizzle the lemon juice over the top before serving.

SHRIMP COCKTAIL

Makes 10 to 12 Servings   Active Time: 10 Minutes   Total Time: 1 Hour and 10 Minutes

2 pounds precooked shrimp

2 cups tomato sauce

1 to 2 tablespoons fresh
horseradish

1 teaspoon Dijon mustard

¼ small lemon, juiced

Sea salt and freshly ground black
pepper, to taste

Lemon wedges, for serving

1. Arrange the shrimp on a large platter and place in the refrigerator.
   Chill for at least 1 hour before serving.

2. In a medium bowl, combine the remaining ingredients. Place the bowl
   in the refrigerator and chill for about 30 minutes.

3. Place the bowl of cocktail sauce and the wedges of lemon in the center
   of the shrimp platter and serve.

KOREAN CHICKEN THIGHS

Makes 4 to 6 Servings   Active Time: 20 Minutes   Total Time: 16 Hours

1 lemongrass stalk, tender part only (the bottom half)

2 garlic cloves, peeled

1 tablespoon fresh ginger, peeled

1 scallion

¼ cup brown sugar

2 tablespoons chili paste

1 tablespoon sesame oil

1 tablespoon rice vinegar

2 tablespoons fish sauce

1 tablespoon black pepper

4 to 6 skin-on, bone-in chicken thighs (if you plan on chopping the chicken, you can go with boneless)

1. Place all of the ingredients, except the chicken thighs, in a blender and puree until combined. Transfer the marinade to a container or plastic bag, place the chicken thighs in the marinade, and place in the refrigerator overnight.

2. Preheat your gas or charcoal grill to 450°F. When the grill is ready, reserve the marinade, place the chicken thighs on the grill, and sear for 5 to 7 minutes.

3. Place a cast-iron skillet on the grill, add the reserved marinade, and transfer the seared chicken thighs to the skillet. Cook for about 15 to 2 minutes, until the centers of the chicken thighs reach 165°F.

WATERMELON AND CHERRY SOUP

Makes 4 Servings   Active Time: 20 Minutes   Total Time: 16 Hours

2½ cups watermelon, peeled and cubed

1 tablespoon kirsch

Zest and juice of 1 lime

½ vanilla bean, seeds scraped and pod reserved

¾ cup cherries, pitted

1 cup Riesling

1 cup Champagne

1. Combine 1 cup of the watermelon, the kirsch, lime zest, lime juice, vanilla bean seeds, and the vanilla pod in a bowl and chill in the refrigerator for 1 hour. Transfer to a baking sheet and freeze overnight.

2. Add the remaining watermelon, cherries, and Riesling to a food processor and puree until smooth. Strain through a fine sieve and chill in the refrigerator until ready to serve.

3. Remove the baking tray from the freezer and cut the mixture into cubes. Add these cubes and the Champagne to the puree and serve.

Week 35

The effervescence of the Bright Ruby is certain to get everyone's week off to an auspicious start. Follow that lovely feeling up with savory steaks and a zesty tart, and everyone at the table will be grounded enough to channel that energy into something special.

Bright Ruby

Marinated Tri-Tip Steaks

Tomato, Goat Cheese, and Basil Tart

Lemon Cake

BRIGHT RUBY

1 part gin

Dash of triple sec

2 parts grapefruit juice

2 parts club soda

Dash of grenadine

1 orange slice, for garnish

1. Fill a cocktail shaker with ice and add the gin, triple sec, and grapefruit juice. Shake until well combined.

2. Fill a highball glass with ice and strain the contents of the cocktail shaker into it. Top with club soda and the grenadine, and garnish with the slice of orange.

MARINATED
TRI-TIP STEAKS

Makes 4 Servings   Active Time: 45 Minutes
Total Time: 16 Hours

2 cups red wine, plus more as needed

2 tablespoons red wine vinegar

2 garlic cloves, crushed

2 sprigs of rosemary, leaves removed and minced

2 sprigs of thyme, leaves removed and minced

½ small white onion, minced

1 teaspoon fresh lemon juice

½ teaspoon dried oregano

Sea salt and black pepper, to taste

1 tri-tip roast, about 1½ inches thick and 2 to 2½ pounds

1. Place all of the ingredients except for the roast in a large resealable plastic bag and let stand for 20 minutes. Place the roast in the bag so that it is completely submerged. If needed, add more wine. Place in the refrigerator and let marinate overnight.

2. Remove the bag containing the marinated roast 1 hour before you are going to grill it and let stand at room temperature.

3. Preheat your gas or charcoal grill to 450°F while preparing one section for indirect heat. When the grill is ready, remove the roast from the marinade and grill over direct heat for about 5 minutes per side. Then, move the roast over indirect heat, cover the grill, and cook for another 20 to 30 minutes, flipping the roast over every 5 minutes.

4. Remove the roast from the grill and transfer to a large cutting board. Let stand for 10 minutes and then cut into thin slices.

TOMATO, GOAT CHEESE, AND BASIL TART

Makes 4 to 6 Servings   Active Time: 30 Minutes   Total Time: 1½ Hours

1 Flaky Pastry Crust (see page 28)

1½ pounds tomatoes, seeded and sliced into ¼-inch-thick pieces

1 tablespoon kosher salt, plus more to taste

2 tablespoons olive oil, plus more for drizzling

1 Vidalia onion, thinly sliced

Freshly ground black pepper, to taste

1 cup goat cheese, crumbled

½ cup feta cheese, crumbled

8 to 10 basil leaves, shredded

1. Preheat the oven to 350°F. Roll the crust out to 9" and place it in a greased 9" pie plate. Place the tomato slices on a paper towel–lined plate and sprinkle with the salt. Let stand for 15 minutes and then turn the slices over.

2. In a skillet, add the olive oil and warm over medium heat. Add the onion and cook, while stirring, until the onion is lightly browned, about 3 minutes. Season with salt and pepper, and then transfer to a bowl.

3. Spread the onion over the bottom of the crust and dot with the goat cheese. Cover with the tomato slices, sprinkle with the feta, and drizzle with additional olive oil.

4. Put the tart in the oven and bake for 20 minutes. Increase the heat to 400°F and bake for an additional 10 minutes until the top of the tart is toasted. Remove from oven and sprinkle with the basil.

LEMON CAKE

Makes 6 to 8 Servings   Active Time: 40 Minutes
Total Time: 1½ Hours

¾ cup sugar

Zest of 2 lemons

6 tablespoons butter, cut into small pieces

2 eggs

1 cup flour

1 teaspoon baking powder

½ cup milk

Confectioners' sugar, for dusting

1. Preheat the oven to 350°F and grease a 9" cake pan. In a large bowl, combine the sugar and lemon zest. Add the butter and beat until the mixture is light and fluffy. Add the eggs one at a time, stirring and combining thoroughly after each addition.

2. Place the flour and baking powder in a measuring cup and stir to combine. Alternately add the flour mixture and the milk to the butter-and-sugar mixture and stir until thoroughly combined.

3. Transfer the batter to the cake pan, place it in the oven, and bake for 30 to 35 minutes, until the top is golden and a toothpick inserted in the center comes out clean. Remove and let cool before dusting with the confectioners' sugar and cutting into wedges.

Labor Day

It's that time of year when the world is about to regain its sanity. But you've got a little bit of time left to focus on good times, so we're going to go all out. Everyone loves Chicken & Waffles, but having to go out and wait in line for an hour to get it can make it seem out of reach. Whipping some up in your own kitchen and allowing people to enjoy it on the comfortable confines of your porch is sure to open people's eyes to what's possible. The dishes orbiting this special treat are simple, flavorful, and able to be enjoyed throughout the day, as the mood strikes. Sure, it's Labor Day, but you don't want to work any more than you have to.

Creamsicle

Peachy Keen

Black Bean Hummus

Stuffed Tomatoes

Fried Chicken & Waffles

Tropical Fruit Salad

Cheesecake-Filled Strawberries

CREAMSICLE

1 part orange juice

1 part vodka

1 part heavy cream

Splash of triple sec

1 orange slice, for garnish

1. Add the liquid ingredients to a mixing glass filled with ice and stir.

2. Strain into a rocks glass filled with ice and garnish with the orange slice.

PEACHY KEEN

Makes 4 to 6 Servings

1 cup peaches, cut into bite-sized pieces

1 cup blueberries, frozen

¼ cup peach schnapps

1 (750 ml) bottle of sparkling wine, very cold

1. In a bowl, add the peach pieces, blueberries, and schnapps and stir to combine.

2. Ladle 2 spoonfuls of fruit into each glass. Top each glass with sparkling wine. Repeat as desired with any remaining fruit and wine, making sure to keep the wine chilled.

BLACK BEAN HUMMUS

Makes 1 Cup   Active Time: 10 Minutes
Total Time: 10 Minutes

½ (14 oz.) can of black beans

1 tablespoon tahini

3 tablespoons fresh lime juice

3 tablespoons extra virgin olive oil

½ teaspoon sea salt

¼ tablespoon freshly ground black pepper

¼ teaspoon Tabasco

¼ teaspoon anchovy paste

Cilantro leaves, chopped, for garnish

Pita bread, for serving

Assorted vegetables, for serving

1. Place all ingredients in a food processor and blend until desired consistency is achieved. If too thick, add a tablespoon of water. If too thin, add more black beans.

2. Garnish with cilantro and serve with warm pita bread and an assortment of vegetables.

STUFFED TOMATOES

Makes 6 Servings   Active Time: 1 Hour
Total Time: 2 Hours

6 ripe, large tomatoes

Salt and pepper, to taste

1 pound Italian sausage, casings removed

1 onion, diced

4 garlic cloves, minced

8 white mushrooms, stemmed and diced

½ green bell pepper, seeded and diced

2 cups plain bread crumbs

2 tablespoons dried sage

1 cup Parmesan cheese, grated

1. Preheat the oven to 375°F and grease a 9 x 9–inch baking pan. Cut off the tops of the tomatoes and use a small paring knife to scoop out the insides. Once hollowed out, season with salt and turn upside down on a paper towel–lined plate. Let stand for about 30 minutes.

2. Heat a skillet over medium-high heat and cook the sausage, breaking it up with a wooden spoon as it cooks. Cook until there is no pink showing in the meat. Transfer to a large bowl, and add the onion and garlic to the skillet. Cook until the onion is translucent, about 4 minutes. Add the mushrooms and pepper and cook over medium heat, while stirring, until vegetables are soft, about 10 minutes.

3. Transfer the mushroom mixture to the bowl containing the sausage and stir to combine. Then add the bread crumbs, sage, and Parmesan. Season with salt and pepper, and stir.

4. Position the tomatoes in the baking pan and divide the filling between them. Cover the pan with aluminum foil and put it in the oven. Bake for about 30 minutes, remove the foil, and continue baking for another 10 to 15 minutes until cooked through. Serve hot.

FRIED CHICKEN & WAFFLES

Makes 6 Servings   Active Time: 1 Hour
Total Time: 1½ Hours

6 chicken pieces

¼ cup flour

Salt and black pepper, to taste

1 cup milk

1 tablespoon white vinegar

2 eggs, lightly beaten

1½ cups cornflakes, finely crushed

½ cup plain bread crumbs

1 teaspoon paprika

1 cup vegetable oil

Maple syrup, for serving

1. Preheat the oven to 400°F. Place a cast-iron skillet in the oven as it warms and rinse and dry the chicken pieces.

2. In a shallow bowl or cake pan, add the flour, season with salt and pepper, and whisk to combine. Add the milk and the vinegar, and let the combination sit for 10 minutes. When ready, add the milk mixture to the bowl with the beaten eggs. In another large bowl, combine the cornflakes, bread crumbs, paprika, and 2 tablespoons of the vegetable oil.

3. Dip the chicken pieces into the seasoned flour, then the milk mixture, then the bread crumb mixture, being sure to coat all over. When coated, put the pieces on a plate, cover with plastic wrap, and refrigerate for about 15 minutes.

4. Put on oven mitts, remove the skillet from the oven, and carefully put the remaining oil in it. Heat it on low until the oil is 350°F. Add the cold chicken pieces and turn in the hot oil until both sides are coated.

5. Put the skillet back in the oven and bake for about 30 minutes, turning the pieces over after 15 minutes. The chicken is done when the juices run clear. Serve with the Belgian Waffles and maple syrup.

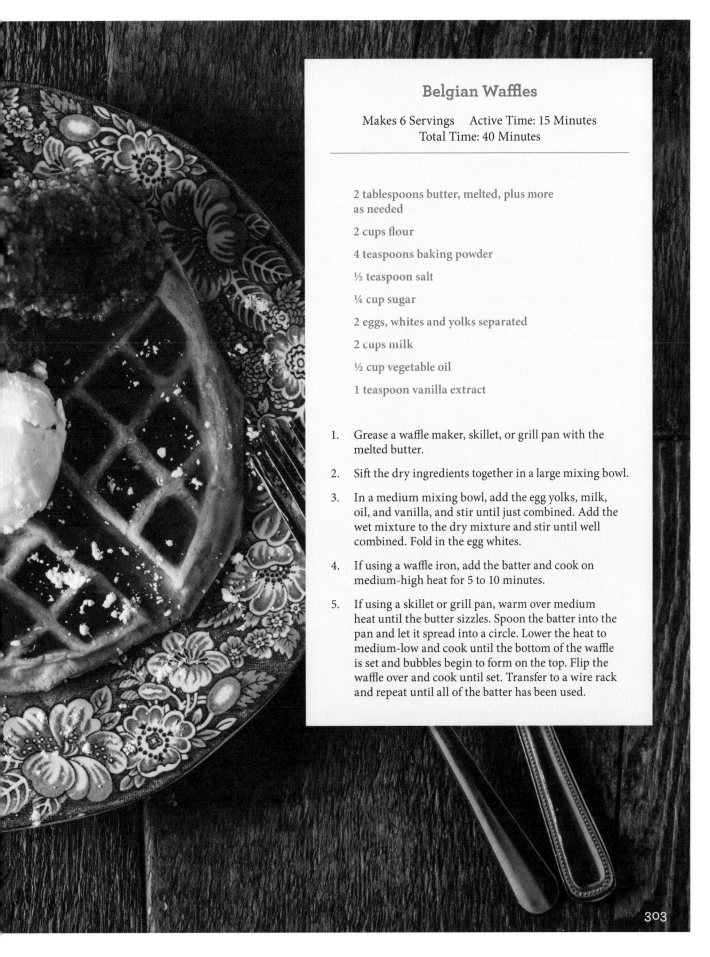

Belgian Waffles

Makes 6 Servings   Active Time: 15 Minutes
Total Time: 40 Minutes

---

2 tablespoons butter, melted, plus more
as needed

2 cups flour

4 teaspoons baking powder

½ teaspoon salt

¼ cup sugar

2 eggs, whites and yolks separated

2 cups milk

½ cup vegetable oil

1 teaspoon vanilla extract

1. Grease a waffle maker, skillet, or grill pan with the
   melted butter.

2. Sift the dry ingredients together in a large mixing bowl.

3. In a medium mixing bowl, add the egg yolks, milk,
   oil, and vanilla, and stir until just combined. Add the
   wet mixture to the dry mixture and stir until well
   combined. Fold in the egg whites.

4. If using a waffle iron, add the batter and cook on
   medium-high heat for 5 to 10 minutes.

5. If using a skillet or grill pan, warm over medium
   heat until the butter sizzles. Spoon the batter into the
   pan and let it spread into a circle. Lower the heat to
   medium-low and cook until the bottom of the waffle
   is set and bubbles begin to form on the top. Flip the
   waffle over and cook until set. Transfer to a wire rack
   and repeat until all of the batter has been used.

TROPICAL FRUIT SALAD

Makes 10 to 12 Servings   Active Time: 10 Minutes
Total Time: 10 Minutes

Zest and juice of 1 lime

¼ cup fresh mint, chopped

1 tablespoon honey

4 kiwis, peeled and sliced

1 pineapple, peeled and cubed

1 mango, peeled and cubed

1 cup strawberries, sliced

2 cups seedless grapes (red or green), halved

1 cup blueberries

1. Combine lime zest, lime juice, mint, and honey in a small bowl and set aside.

2. Combine the fruit in large bowl, add the dressing, and toss to coat.

CHEESECAKE-FILLED STRAWBERRIES

Makes 20 to 25 Strawberries   Active Time: 25 Minutes   Total Time: 1 Hour and 25 Minutes

⅓ cup heavy cream

8 oz. cream cheese

½ cup powdered sugar

1 teaspoon pure vanilla extract

¼ teaspoon salt

2 pints fresh strawberries, stemmed and cored

Walnuts, chopped, for garnish

1. Beat the heavy cream until soft peaks form. Add the cream cheese, sugar, vanilla, and salt and beat until light and fluffy. Transfer the mixture into a plastic bag or a piping bag.

2. If using a plastic bag, cut a small opening in one of the bottom corners and squeeze the mixture into the cavities you made in the strawberries. You want the filling to form a mound on top of the strawberries without overflowing. Stick the walnut pieces into the cream cheese, and then place in the refrigerator for 1 hour before serving.

Week 36

This particular pho is ready so quickly that you won't be able to believe the flavor. Combined with the Mint-Cilantro Chutney and the Pan-Seared Rice Cakes you've got a meal that will quickly erase the chill that suddenly entered the morning air. By the time the day has warmed up, the Chocolate, Peanut Butter, and Banana Milkshake will be there, providing both refreshment and classic breakfast flavors.

Raspberry Fizz

Watermelon-Lime Refresher

Pan-Seared Rice Cakes

Mint-Cilantro Chutney

Fast Pho

Chocolate, Peanut Butter,
and Banana Milkshake

RASPBERRY FIZZ

3 parts Champagne

1 part raspberry liqueur

3 raspberries, for garnish

1. Pour the Champagne into a champagne flute and top with raspberry liqueur.

2. Drop some fresh raspberries into the drink for garnish.

WATERMELON-LIME REFRESHER

Makes 4 Servings

6 cups watermelon, seeded and cubed

4 oz. Simple Syrup (see page 32)

Juice of 4 limes

4 cups ice

Lime wheels, for garnish

1. Add the watermelon, syrup, and lime juice to a blender along with the ice (1 cup per serving). Puree until smoothie-like in consistency.

2. Pour into your mason jar and garnish with a lime wheel.

PAN-SEARED RICE CAKES

Makes 4 Servings   Active Time: 30 Minutes   Total Time: 1½ Hours

---

1 cup water

½ cup Arborio rice

1 teaspoon oregano, chopped

¼ teaspoon Tabasco

Salt, to taste

4 tablespoons butter

1. In a small saucepan, add the water and rice and bring to a boil. Cover, reduce heat to low, and simmer for 10 minutes. Remove lid and stir frequently.

2. Add the oregano, Tabasco, and salt. Lay down a sheet of plastic wrap on a cutting board. Spoon the rice onto the plastic and then roll into a 12-inch log. Cut this in half, transfer to the refrigerator, and chill for 1 hour.

3. Remove from the refrigerator and cut the logs into 8 slices. In a nonstick skillet, add the butter and cook over medium heat until melted. Add the rice cakes and cook for 2 to 3 minutes on each side, or until golden brown.

MINT-CILANTRO CHUTNEY

Makes 1 Cup   Active Time: 5 Minutes
Total Time: 5 Minutes

---

1 cup cilantro, packed

½ cup fresh mint leaves, packed

¼ cup white onion, chopped

3 tablespoons water

½ tablespoon fresh lime juice

½ teaspoon serrano pepper, chopped

½ teaspoon sugar

Salt, to taste

Place all ingredients in a blender and puree.
Take care not to over-puree the mixture.
You want the chutney to have some texture.

FAST PHO

Makes 4 Servings   Active Time: 15 Minutes
Total Time: 30 Minutes

---

2 tablespoons vegetable oil

1 small yellow onion, peeled and chopped

1-inch piece of ginger, unpeeled

2 cinnamon sticks

3 star anise

2 cardamom pods, seeds removed and chopped

1 cup cilantro

5 whole cloves

1 tablespoon coriander seeds

1 tablespoon fennel seeds

6 cups Beef Stock (see page 25)

1 tablespoon black peppercorns

1 tablespoon fish sauce

1 tablespoon hoisin

1 teaspoon Sriracha

3 oz. rice noodles

1 pound strip steak, grilled and thinly sliced (optional)

1 jalapeño pepper, sliced, for garnish

Bean sprouts, for garnish

Lime wedges, for garnish

Thai basil, for garnish

1. In a medium saucepan, add the oil and cook over medium heat until warm. Add the onion and ginger, and cook for 5 minutes, or until soft.

2. Meanwhile, in a sauté pan, add the spices and cook over medium heat for 2 to 3 minutes, until they become nice and fragrant. Add to the saucepan. Add the stock and peppercorns and bring to a boil. Reduce heat so that the broth simmers and cook for 10 minutes.

3. Strain the soup into a fresh clean pot. Season with fish sauce, hoisin, and Sriracha and return to a simmer.

4. Place the rice noodles in a bowl and cover with boiling water. Leave to soak for 4 minutes, or according to manufacturer's instructions.

5. Combine rice noodles and soup in warm bowls. Top with strip steak, if desired, and garnish with the jalapeño, bean sprouts, lime wedges, and Thai basil.

CHOCOLATE, PEANUT BUTTER, AND BANANA MILKSHAKE

Makes 4 Servings   Active Time: 5 Minutes   Total Time: 5 Minutes

2 pints chocolate ice cream

4 bananas, peeled and frozen

1 cup creamy peanut butter

½ cup whole milk

6 tablespoons chocolate syrup

½ teaspoon sea salt

Place the ingredients in a blender and puree until well combined. Pour into tall glasses and serve with a straw.

Week 37

The lightness and lusciousness in this collection is what's going to jump to the fore, but don't lose sight of the perfect balance of flavors. The Bourbon Sweet Tea and the Corn Fritters provide sweetness that is complemented beautifully by the bitterness of the Fennel Seed Yogurt and the fresh, delicate qualities of the Crab Quiche. There's enough diversity in this menu that you'll walk away feeling like you sat through three meals, only you'll actually be able to function.

Bourbon Sweet Tea

Corn Fritters

Fennel Seed Yogurt

Crab Quiche

Almond Coffee Cake

BOURBON SWEET TEA

Makes 4 to 6 Servings

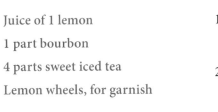

Juice of 1 lemon

1 part bourbon

4 parts sweet iced tea

Lemon wheels, for garnish

1. Add the lemon juice and the spent lemon halves to a pitcher.

2. Add ice, and then pour in the bourbon and sweet tea.

3. Stir until thoroughly mixed, ladle into pint glasses filled with ice, and garnish with the lemon wheels.

CORN FRITTERS

Makes 4 to 6 Servings   Active Time: 15 Minutes   Total Time: 30 Minutes

2 cups vegetable oil

½ cup cornmeal

3 tablespoons all-purpose flour, plus 1½ teaspoons

4½ tablespoons sugar

¾ teaspoon salt

¼ teaspoon baking powder

⅛ teaspoon baking soda

⅛ teaspoon cayenne pepper

¼ cup buttermilk

1 egg, beaten

2 tablespoons jalapeño pepper, seeded and chopped

¾ cup Fontina cheese, grated

1. Place the oil in a Dutch oven and heat to 320°F. Add the cornmeal, flour, sugar, salt, baking powder, baking soda, and cayenne pepper to a small bowl and whisk until combined. In a separate bowl, add the buttermilk, egg, and jalapeño and whisk to combine.

2. Combine the buttermilk mixture and the dry mixture, add the cheese, and stir until combined.

3. Drop spoonfuls of the batter into the hot oil and fry until golden brown. Remove from oil with a slotted spoon and transfer to a paper towel–lined plate to drain.

FENNEL SEED YOGURT

Makes 4 Servings   Active Time: 5 Minutes
Total Time: 5 Minutes

1 cup Greek yogurt

2 tablespoons Pernod

1 teaspoon ground fennel seed

Combine the ingredients in a bowl. Place in refrigerator and chill until ready to serve.

CRAB QUICHE

Makes 6 to 8 Servings   Active Time: 40 Minutes   Total Time: 1½ Hours

1 Flaky Pastry Crust (see page 28)

3 tablespoons unsalted butter

2 tablespoons scallions, greens only, thinly sliced

1 cup mushrooms, sliced

2 cups half-and-half

2 tablespoons dry vermouth

½ teaspoon salt

¼ teaspoon cayenne pepper

4 eggs, beaten

1 pound lump crab meat

1. Preheat the oven to 350°F and place the crust in a greased 9" pie plate. Place a skillet over medium heat and melt the butter. Add the scallions and mushrooms, and cook for about 5 minutes, or until scallions are tender.

2. Add the half-and-half, vermouth, salt, and cayenne pepper to the bowl containing the eggs and whisk to combine. Stir the scallion-and-mushroom mixture and the crab meat into the egg mixture. Pour this mixture into the crust, shaking the plate gently to distribute evenly.

3. Put the quiche in the oven and bake for about 40 minutes, or until the quiche is golden brown and a knife inserted into the center comes out clean. Remove from the oven and allow to sit for 20 minutes before slicing and serving.

ALMOND COFFEE CAKE

Makes 6 to 8 Servings   Active Time: 1½ Hours   Total Time: 2 Hours

For the Cake

1¾ cups all-purpose flour

⅔ cup sugar

½ teaspoon baking soda

¼ teaspoon salt

8 tablespoons (1 stick) butter, softened

2 eggs

1 teaspoon almond extract

½ cup buttermilk

For the Topping

½ cup sugar

½ cup dark brown sugar

½ teaspoon ginger

¼ teaspoon salt

¾ cup unsalted butter, melted

½ cup dried organic coconut

1. Preheat the oven to 325°F and grease a 9" cake pan.

2. Prepare the cake. Whisk the flour, sugar, baking soda, and salt together in a large bowl. Add the butter and beat with an electric mixer until well combined. In a small bowl, whisk together the eggs, almond extract, and buttermilk. Pour this into the dry mixture and beat on high speed until the batter is light and fluffy. Pour the batter into the cake pan.

3. Prepare the topping. Whisk the sugars, ginger, and salt together in a bowl. Add the melted butter and stir to combine. Then add the coconut and stir until a crumbly mixture forms.

4. Dot the cake with the topping and place it in the oven. Bake for 45 minutes, until a knife inserted in the center comes out clean. Remove and allow to cool for 10 minutes before serving.

Fall

Fall is a time to slow down and reflect on the good times had in the recent past and the celebrations to come. Since there is a greater tendency to take it easy when autumn arrives, and the crisp air and vibrant leaves frame each day in splendor, it is the perfect season to spoil your loved ones with a string of decadent brunches. Don't worry about going overboard—a full stomach is all the more reason to get out in the glorious light and go for a long walk.

But fall is also a time when a tightly bunched group of holidays and the increasingly dwindling sunlight can wear us down. If you get going in the season and feel like that's going to be the case, these menus provide some shelter from the storm. Filling enough to reduce your load in the kitchen and enjoyable enough to keep you at the table, laughing, talking, and recharging for what lies ahead.

Week 38

Summer has a way of lingering in the mind, and this menu is a nod to that unwillingness to let go. Wait until the sun has gotten high in the sky to break out this spread, which is actually capable of providing closure. The Avocado and Goat Cheese Toast is one of those simple wonders that you'll almost feel guilty accepting everyone's praise for. While it's delicious as is, crumbling a little bacon on top takes it up a notch.

Caribbean Cranberry Twist

Lime Rickey

Bite-Sized Zucchini Pizzas

Avocado and Goat Cheese Toast

Chilled Cherry Soup
with Brioche French Toast

CARIBBEAN CRANBERRY TWIST

1 part coconut rum

1 part orange juice

1 part cranberry juice

Splash of triple sec

1 orange slice, for garnish

1. Fill a highball glass with ice and add the rum, orange juice, and cranberry juice. Stir until thoroughly mixed.

2. Top with the splash of triple sec and garnish with the orange slice.

LIME RICKEY

1 part Simple Syrup (see page 32)

Juice of 1 lime

4 parts club soda

1 lime wedge, for garnish

1. Place the Simple Syrup and lime juice in a mason jar and stir.

2. Top with the club soda and garnish with the lime wedge.

BITE-SIZED ZUCCHINI PIZZAS

Makes 4 Servings   Active Time: 20 Minutes   Total Time: 25 Minutes

½ cup butter, melted

2 garlic cloves, minced

1 large zucchini, cut into rounds

½ cup mozzarella cheese

15 oz. tomato sauce

1. Preheat your gas or charcoal grill to medium heat. In a small bowl, combine the melted butter and garlic and set aside.

2. When the grill is about 400°F, place the zucchini on the grill and cook for about 2 minutes. Flip the slices over and brush with the butter-and-garlic mixture. Cook for about 3 minutes, flip over, and brush this side with the mixture. Cook for 3 more minutes.

3. Divide the mozzarella and sauce between the slices of zucchini and cook until the cheese is slightly melted.

AVOCADO AND GOAT CHEESE TOAST

Makes 4 Servings   Active Time: 5 Minutes   Total Time: 10 Minutes

1 cup balsamic vinegar

2 avocados, halved and pitted

2 teaspoons lemon juice

Salt and black pepper, to taste

4 slices of bread

1 cup arugula

3 tomatoes, sliced

2 oz. goat cheese

¼ cup basil leaves, chopped

1. Preheat your gas or charcoal grill to medium heat. Place the balsamic vinegar in a small saucepan and bring to a boil. Cook until the mixture becomes syrupy, about 10 minutes. Set aside

2. Place the avocados on the grill, flesh side down. Cook until grill marks appear, about 3 to 4 minutes. Remove from heat and scoop the flesh into a small bowl.

3. Add the lemon juice, season with salt and pepper, and mash the ingredients until the mixture is combined but slightly chunky.

4. Place the bread on the grill until it is browned, about 1 minute on each side.

5. Spread the avocado mixture between the slices of bread. Top with arugula, tomato slices, goat cheese, and basil. Drizzle with the balsamic glaze and serve.

Variation:
Top the toast with chopped bacon or poached eggs
to make it even tastier.

CHILLED CHERRY SOUP
WITH BRIOCHE FRENCH TOAST

Makes 4 to 6 Servings   Active Time: 30 Minutes   Total Time: 1 Hour and 40 Minutes

---

1 cup water

1 cup Riesling

¼ cup sugar

1 vanilla bean, scraped

2 cinnamon sticks

¼ cup lemon juice

2½ pounds red cherries, pitted

¼ cup kirsch

2 teaspoons lemon zest

½ cup sour cream, plus more for garnish

Mint leaves, shredded, for garnish

1. In a large saucepan, combine the water, Riesling, sugar, vanilla bean, cinnamon stick, and lemon juice. Bring to a boil, reduce heat so that the soup simmers, and cook for 5 minutes. Turn off the heat and let stand for 30 minutes.

2. Strain the mixture through a fine sieve. Reserve 12 cherries for garnish and put the rest in a saucepan. Cover with the strained liquid from the large saucepan and bring to a boil. Reduce heat so that the soup simmers and cook for 5 minutes.

3. Transfer the soup to a food processor and puree. Strain through a fine sieve, add the kirsch and lemon zest, and chill.

4. Once chilled, whisk in the sour cream. Pour into 4 chilled bowls, garnish with sour cream, fresh mint, and the reserved cherries, and serve with the Brioche French Toast.

Brioche French Toast

4 slices of brioche, cut ¼-inch thick

1 tablespoon sugar

½ teaspoon cinnamon

¼ teaspoon nutmeg

1 tablespoon all-purpose flour

2 large eggs

½ cup heavy cream

1 teaspoon vanilla extract

1. Slice the bread a few hours in advance and leave uncovered.

2. Whisk together the sugar, cinnamon, nutmeg, and flour in a bowl. In a separate bowl, whisk together the eggs, cream, and vanilla extract. Add the wet ingredients to the dry and whisk to combine.

3. Divide the batter between 4 saucers and soak the bread for 2 minutes on each side, until the mixture is absorbed, but not too soggy.

4. Warm a nonstick pan over medium heat. Add the bread to the pan and cook for 2 to 3 minutes on each side, until golden brown.

Week 39

While summer is the season everyone looks forward to, fall is quietly everyone's favorite. The magnificence of autumn always catches us unaware, framing the world in a comforting, golden light that it makes it shine like at no other time. To go with the crisp air, we've selected an Alabama Slammer, which may just get you up and tossing the pigskin around. After you work up an appetite doing that, sit down to a table freighted with a Quiche with Sautéed Leeks, Apple-Rutabaga Soup with Pork Belly, and a stunning French Apple Tart, and those longings for summer will be replaced by an appreciation for the lovely present you've found yourself in.

Alabama Slammer

Quiche with Sautéed Leeks

Apple-Rutabaga Soup
with Pork Belly

French Apple Tart

ALABAMA SLAMMER

¾ oz. peach liqueur

¾ oz. amaretto

¾ oz. sloe gin

¾ oz. vodka

6 oz. orange juice

Dash of grenadine

1 orange slice, for garnish

1 maraschino cherry, for garnish

1. Fill a mason jar or Hurricane glass with ice and then add all of the alcoholic ingredients.

2. Top with the orange juice and grenadine and stir until thoroughly combined. Garnish with the slice of orange and maraschino cherry.

QUICHE WITH SAUTÉED LEEKS

Makes 6 to 8 Servings   Active Time: 30 Minutes
Total Time: 1½ Hours

---

1 Flaky Pastry Crust (see page 28)

3 large leeks, white and light green parts only, thinly sliced

2 tablespoons olive oil

1 cup whole milk or half-and-half

½ to ¾ cup Swiss or Gruyère cheese, shredded

4 eggs, beaten

Salt and pepper, to taste

1. Place the crust in a 9" pie plate or cast-iron skillet. Place the sliced leeks in a colander and rinse thoroughly to remove any sand or grit. Pat dry. In a skillet, heat the olive oil over medium-high heat. Add the leeks and cook, while stirring, for 1 to 2 minutes. Lower the heat and cook, while stirring often, until the leeks become tender and golden, about 10 to 15 minutes.

2. Add the milk or half-and-half and cheese to the beaten eggs and whisk to combine. Season with salt and pepper. Spread the sautéed leeks over the crust and then pour the egg mixture over the leeks, shaking gently to distribute evenly.

3. Put the quiche in the oven and bake for about 40 minutes or until it is puffy and golden brown. Remove from the oven and allow to sit for 10 minutes before slicing and serving.

APPLE-RUTABAGA SOUP WITH PORK BELLY

Makes 6 Servings   Active Time: 25 Minutes   Total Time: 26 Hours

---

¼ cup butter

1 cup onion, chopped

1 cup Granny Smith apples, peeled, cored, and chopped

1 cup rutabaga, peeled and chopped

1 cup butternut squash, peeled and chopped

1 cup carrots, peeled and chopped

1 cup sweet potato, peeled and chopped

4 cups Vegetable Stock (see page 26)

3 cups heavy cream

Salt and cayenne pepper, to taste

Rosemary, for garnish

1. In a large saucepan, add the butter and cook over medium heat until melted. Add the onion, apples, rutabaga, butternut squash, carrots, and sweet potato and cook for 10 minutes, or until vegetables are soft.

2. Add the stock and bring to a boil. Reduce heat so that the soup simmers and cook for 20 minutes, or until vegetables are cooked through.

3. Transfer the soup to a food processor, puree until smooth, and strain through a fine sieve.

4. Return soup to pan and bring to a simmer. Add heavy cream and season with salt and cayenne pepper.

5. Ladle into bowls, serve with the Pork Belly, and garnish with rosemary.

Pork Belly

1½ pounds pork belly

6 cups water

1 teaspoon fennel seeds

2 star anise

1 cinnamon stick

1 teaspoon black peppercorns

6 cloves

1 bay leaf

¼ cup salt

1. Place the pork belly fat side up and score a crisscross pattern on the pork belly with a sharp knife. The cut should be approximately ¼-inch deep.

2. In a medium saucepan, add the water, fennel seeds, star anise, cinnamon stick, peppercorns, cloves, bay leaf, and salt. Bring to a boil, remove from heat, and let cool. When cool, place the pork belly and the contents of the saucepan in a roasting pan. Place in refrigerator and marinate for 24 hours.

3. Preheat oven to 450°F. Rinse the marinated pork belly and set on a rack in a baking tray, fat side up. Place tray in oven and cook for 30 minutes. Lower temperature to 275°F and cook for 1 hour, until it is tender, but not mushy. Remove tray from the oven, cut the pork belly into 6 pieces, and serve with the Apple-Rutabaga Soup.

FRENCH APPLE TART

Makes 6 to 8 Servings   Active Time: 1 Hour   Total Time: 3 to 16 Hours

---

1 cup all-purpose flour, plus more for dusting

½ teaspoon salt

1½ cups sugar, plus 1 tablespoon

2¾ cups unsalted butter, cut into small pieces

3 tablespoons ice water

8 to 10 apples, peeled, cored, and sliced

1. To make the pastry, whisk together the flour, salt, and the 1 tablespoon of sugar in a large bowl. Using your fingers, work 6 tablespoons of the butter into the flour mixture until you have coarse clumps. Sprinkle the ice water over the mixture and continue to work it with your hands until the dough just holds together. Shape it into a ball, wrap it in plastic wrap, and refrigerate it for at least 1 hour, or overnight.

2. Distribute the remaining pieces of butter evenly over the bottom of a cast-iron skillet. Sprinkle the remaining sugar evenly over the bottom of the skillet. Place the apple slices in a circular pattern, starting at the edge of the pan and working in. The slices should overlap and face the same direction. Place either 1 or 2 slices in the center when finished working around the outside. As the tart bakes, the slices will slide down a bit.

3. Place the skillet on the stove and turn the heat to medium-high. Cook the apples in the pan, uncovered, until the sugar and butter start to caramelize, about 35 minutes. While they're cooking, spoon some of the juices over the apples (but don't overdo it).

4. Preheat the oven to 400°F and position a rack in the center. Take the chilled dough out of the refrigerator and, working on a lightly floured surface, roll it out into a circle just big enough to cover the skillet. Gently drape the pastry over the apples, tucking it in around the sides. Put the skillet in the oven and bake for about 25 minutes, until the pastry is golden brown.

5. Remove the skillet from the oven and allow to cool for about 5 minutes. Find a plate that is an inch or 2 larger than the top of the skillet and place it over the top. You will be inverting the tart onto the plate. Be sure to use oven mitts or secure pot holders, as the skillet will be hot. Holding the plate tightly against the top of the skillet, turn the skillet over so the plate is now on the bottom. If some of the apples are stuck to the bottom, gently remove them and place them on the tart. Allow to cool a few more minutes before serving.

Week 40

The Steak Frites is undoubtedly the preparation that has you excited this week. And while you're far from misguided to feel that way, don't overlook the Quinoa and Black Bean Salad, which is the key to the meal. Delicious in its own right, it provides you with the perfect foundation to enjoy the decadent combination on the horizon.

Tequila Sunrise

Virgin 75

Quinoa and Black Bean Salad

Steak Frites

Apple Cider Doughnut Cake

TEQUILA SUNRISE

1 part tequila

Dash of lemon juice

2 parts orange juice

Splash of grenadine

1 maraschino cherry, for garnish

1 orange slice, for garnish

1. Place ice in a highball glass and then add the tequila and the lemon juice.

2. Add orange juice to fill and top with a splash of grenadine. Don't stir the drink. Instead, allow the grenadine to slowly filter down through the orange juice and tequila. Garnish with a maraschino cherry and an orange slice.

VIRGIN 75

1 sugar cube

1 part lemon juice

4 parts ginger ale

1 lemon twist, for garnish

1. Place a sugar cube at the bottom of a champagne flute.

2. Add the lemon juice and then slowly add the ginger ale. Garnish with the twist of lemon.

QUINOA AND BLACK BEAN SALAD

Makes 4 to 6 Servings   Active Time: 25 Minutes
Total Time: 16 Hours

1 pound black beans

1 cup quinoa

2 cups water

1 cup Salsa Verde
(see page 56)

4 tomatillos, husked, rinsed, and diced

2 Fresno chilies, thinly sliced

1 yellow bell pepper, seeded and diced

1 cup baby spinach

1 tablespoon kosher salt

1 tablespoon cumin

1 tablespoon garlic powder

1 tablespoon dried oregano

1. In a bowl, cover the beans with water and soak overnight.

2. Thoroughly wash the quinoa in a fine mesh strainer to remove the outer layer. In a medium saucepan, add the water and bring to a boil. Add the quinoa. Reduce heat to low, cover, and cook for 15 minutes. Remove lid and fluff with a fork, then transfer to a large salad bowl.

3. Drain and rinse the beans. Place them in the same saucepan used for the quinoa. Cover with fresh water and cook over medium heat until the beans are fork tender but still have a little texture. Stir occasionally to keep the beans from sticking to the pan. Cook for about 70 minutes.

4. While the beans are cooking, add the remaining ingredients to the quinoa, stir to combine, and place the salad bowl in the refrigerator until the beans are done cooking. Drain and rinse beans with cold water until cool. Add to salad bowl, stir to combine, and serve.

Tip: If you do not have time to soak beans overnight or you just want a quick fix, you can use the same amount of canned beans. Make sure to rinse the canned beans thoroughly before cooking, and use the low-sodium variety to maintain the salt balance in the recipe.

STEAK FRITES

Makes 4 Servings   Active Time: 30 Minutes
Total Time: 2 Hours

3 cups peanut or vegetable oil

1 pound Yukon Gold potatoes, peeled, washed, and cut into thin strips

Salt and pepper, to taste

6 tablespoons unsalted butter

4 small steaks (sirloin or rib eye are the best choices), about 1-inch thick

Fresh parsley, for garnish

1. Preheat the oven to 200°F. Prepare everything ahead of time so you can cook the steaks immediately after the frites. If you wait too long, the frites will get soft. Line a baking sheet with paper towels (for the frites when they're cooked). Put the steaks on a plate in the refrigerator (keep them cold until ready to go in the pan). Make sure your potato strips are clean and dry.

2. Place the oil in a Dutch oven and add the potatoes. Heat the oil over medium-high heat (be careful of splattering). As the oil gets hotter, the potatoes will get limp and just start to brown (about 15 minutes). At this point, start turning them with tongs to get all of the sides crispy and browned. Cook for another 5 minutes or so.

3. Transfer the frites to the baking sheet and sprinkle with salt. Cover with paper towels and place the sheet in the oven.

4. Drain the oil from the skillet into a glass measuring cup. Return the Dutch oven to the stove and add the butter. Take the steaks out of the fridge. When the butter is hot but not smoking, put the steaks in the skillet. Sear them over the high heat for a minute per side, and then reduce the heat to medium. Sprinkle with salt and pepper and cook, while turning them every few minutes, for about 8 minutes. The steaks will be somewhat rare and juicy inside.

5. Transfer the steaks to plates, pile the frites beside them, and garnish with parsley.

APPLE CIDER DOUGHNUT CAKE

Makes 8 to 10 Servings   Active Time: 20 Minutes   Total Time: 1 Hour and 40 Minutes

For the Cake

2 cups all-purpose flour, plus more for dusting

¾ cup olive oil

1¾ cups sugar

3 eggs, at room temperature

2 teaspoons pure vanilla extract

¾ cup yogurt

1 cup apple cider

1 cup whole wheat flour

1½ teaspoons baking powder

1½ teaspoons cinnamon

½ teaspoon baking soda

¾ teaspoon salt

For the Topping

4 tablespoons butter, melted

¼ cup confectioners' sugar

1 teaspoon cinnamon

1. Preheat the oven to 350°F. Liberally grease a Bundt pan and lightly flour it, tapping out the excess to create a thin, even coat. In a large mixing bowl, combine the olive oil and sugar. Whisk in 1 egg at a time. When the eggs are fully incorporated, add the vanilla extract, yogurt, and apple cider. In a separate bowl, combine the flours, baking powder, cinnamon, baking soda, and salt.

2. Add the dry mixture to the wet mixture and stir until just combined. Transfer the batter to the prepared Bundt pan and bake for 45 to 50 minutes, or until a toothpick inserted into the middle comes out mostly clean. Remove from oven, and allow to rest for 30 minutes. Turn onto a wire cooling rack and let cool completely.

3. When the cake is still slightly warm, brush the top with the melted butter. Sprinkle the confectioners' sugar and cinnamon on top.

Week 41

Now that the leaves are approaching their peak color, the time is ripe for the sweet, nutty flavors available in pumpkin spice. The Pumpkin Pie Tea Latte is here to answer that call, and will keep you plenty warm while you enjoy the beautiful Chilled Corn Soup with Garlic Custard. Flank those bowls with Hummus and Pita Bread, and you've got a meal that manages to rise to the level of the day. It will be a challenge to keep your wits about you after all that deliciousness, but don't forget to warn everyone that the cherries in the Cherry Clafoutis still have their pits.

Pumpkin Pie Tea Latte

Hummus

Pita Bread

Chilled Corn Soup
with Garlic Custard

Cherry Clafoutis

PUMPKIN PIE TEA LATTE

4 parts hot black tea

1 part Baileys Irish Cream

1 part milk, frothed

Dash of pumpkin pie spice

Fill a mug about two-thirds of way with hot black tea. Add Baileys Irish Cream and stir together. Top with the frothed milk and the dash of pumpkin pie spice.

HUMMUS

Makes 1⅓ Cups   Active Time: 15 Minutes   Total Time: 15 Minutes

---

1 (14 oz.) can of chickpeas

3 tablespoons extra virgin olive oil

3 tablespoons tahini

1½ tablespoons lemon juice, plus more as needed

1 small garlic clove, roughly chopped

1 teaspoon salt

½ teaspoon finely ground black pepper

1. Drain the chickpeas and reserve the liquid. If time allows, remove the skins from each of the chickpeas. This will make your hummus much smoother.

2. Place the chickpeas, olive oil, tahini, lemon juice, garlic, salt, and pepper in a food processor.

3. Puree the hummus until it is very smooth, about 5 to 10 minutes. Scrape down the sides of the bowl as needed to integrate any large chunks.

4. Taste and adjust seasoning. If your hummus is stiffer than you'd like, add 2 to 3 tablespoons of the reserved chickpea liquid and blend until desired consistency is achieved.

Hummus Variations:

For even tastier and more authentic hummus, soak dried chickpeas overnight and cook them for 1 hour. You can also dress it up with any of the following options: add 1 to 3 teaspoons of spices like cumin, sumac, harissa, or smoked paprika; drizzle a little pomegranate molasses on top; blend in 1 cup of roasted eggplant, zucchini, bell peppers, or garlic; fold in ¾ cup of chopped green or black olives; for a nutty hummus, blend in some lightly toasted walnuts, almonds, or pine nuts; or add ¼ cup of chopped preserved lemons.

PITA BREAD

Makes 16 Pitas   Active Time: 1 Hour   Total Time: 2 Hours

2¼ teaspoons active dry yeast

2½ cups water (110 to 115°F)

3 cups all-purpose flour, plus more for dusting

2 tablespoons olive oil

1 tablespoon salt

3 cups whole wheat flour

Butter, for greasing

1. Combine the yeast and the water in a bowl. Let sit for about 10 minutes until foamy.

2. Add the yeast mixture to a large bowl. Add the all-purpose flour and stir until a stiff dough forms. Cover and let the dough rise for about 1 hour.

3. Add 1 tablespoon of the oil and salt to the dough and then stir in the whole wheat flour in ½-cup increments. Stir until the dough is soft. Turn out onto a lightly floured surface and knead it until it is smooth and elastic, about 10 minutes.

4. Coat the bottom and sides of a large mixing bowl (ceramic is best) with butter. Place the ball of dough in the bowl, cover loosely with plastic wrap, place in a naturally warm, draft-free location, and let it rise until doubled in size, about 45 minutes to 1 hour.

5. On a lightly floured surface, punch down the dough and cut into 16 pieces. Put the pieces on a baking sheet and cover with a dish towel while working with individual pieces. Roll out the pieces with a rolling pin until they are approximately 7" in diameter. Stack them between sheets of plastic wrap.

6. Heat a cast-iron skillet over high heat and add the remaining olive oil. Working with one pita at a time, cook for about 20 seconds on one side, then flip and cook for a minute on the other side, until bubbles form. Turn again and cook until the pita puffs up, another minute or so. Store the cooked pitas under a tea towel until ready to serve.

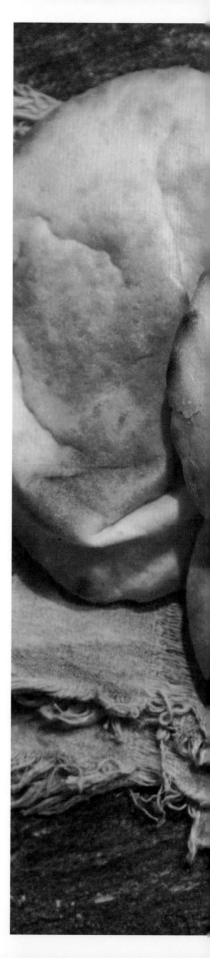

CHILLED CORN SOUP WITH GARLIC CUSTARD

Makes 4 Servings   Active Time: 30 Minutes   Total Time: 2 Hours and 15 Minutes

8 ears of sweet corn

10 cups water

1 bay leaf

12 sprigs of thyme

6 black peppercorns

2 onions, peeled and chopped

2 tablespoons butter

4 garlic cloves, minced

2 tablespoons lemon juice

Salt and pepper, to taste

Cilantro, for garnish

1. Remove the kernels from the ears of corn. Place the water, corn cobs, bay leaf, thyme, peppercorns, and 1 of the chopped onions in a stockpot and bring to a boil. Reduce the heat so that the stock simmers and cook for 1 hour.

2. Strain through a fine sieve, discard the solids, and reserve the stock. In a medium saucepan, melt the butter. Add the remaining onion and the garlic and cook over medium heat for 5 minutes, or until soft. Add the corn kernels, while reserving 2 tablespoons for garnish, and reduce the heat to low. Cook for 5 minutes.

3. Transfer the corn mixture to a food processor and combine with 4 cups of the corn stock. Puree, adding more stock if necessary to produce a creamy consistency. Season with lemon juice, salt, and pepper. Chill in refrigerator for at least 1 hour.

4. Place the Garlic Custard, reserved corn kernels, and cilantro leaves in the middle of chilled bowls. Pour the soup around the center and serve.

Garlic Custard

1 tablespoon butter

3 garlic cloves, minced

1 cup heavy cream

½ teaspoon salt

2 medium eggs

Yolk from 1 medium egg

1½ teaspoons chives, chopped

Black pepper, to taste

1. Preheat the oven to 325°F. Grease four 4 oz. ramekins and place them on a baking tray. In a small saucepan, melt the butter. Add the garlic and cook over low heat for 5 minutes, or until soft. Add the cream and the salt. Increase heat to medium and bring to a simmer. Remove from heat, let stand for 10 minutes, and strain through a fine sieve.

2. Place the eggs and the egg yolk in a medium-sized bowl and whisk until combined. Add the chives and whisk until combined.

3. Add the garlic mixture and whisk until combined. Season with additional salt and pepper, divide the mixture between the ramekins, and place the tray in the oven. Before closing the door, pour enough hot water on the baking tray to go halfway up the ramekins. Cook for 18 minutes, or until the custard is firm and a knife comes out clean when inserted.

4. Remove the tray from the oven and chill the custard in the refrigerator for 1 hour. When ready to serve, use a knife to remove the custard from the ramekins.

CHERRY CLAFOUTIS

Makes 4 to 6 Servings   Active Time: 20 Minutes
Total Time: 45 Minutes

8 tablespoons (1 stick) butter, melted

1 cup sugar, plus 2 teaspoons

⅔ cup flour

½ teaspoon salt

1 teaspoon pure vanilla extract

3 eggs, beaten

1 cup milk

3 cups ripe cherries (pits in)

Confectioners' sugar, for topping

1. Preheat the oven to 400°F. In a large bowl, combine 6
    tablespoons of the butter, ½ cup of the sugar, flour, salt,
    vanilla, eggs, and milk until all ingredients are blended
    and smooth. Set aside.

2. Put the remaining butter in a cast-iron skillet and put it
    in the oven to warm up.

3. Transfer the skillet to the stovetop. Put ½ cup of the
    sugar in the skillet and shake it so it distributes evenly.
    Add the cherries. Pour the batter over the cherries,
    sprinkle with the remaining sugar, and put the skillet
    back in the oven. Bake for about 30 minutes, or until the
    topping is golden brown and set in the center.

4. Remove from the oven, sprinkle with confectioners'
    sugar, and serve warm.

*Note: There is some debate about whether the pits
should be removed from the cherries before baking,
but even Julia Child left them in, on the belief that
they add flavor.*

Week 42

The delicious Blackened Pear sangria will have you wondering why you and everyone else consistently overlooks this delicious fruit. Follow up this tasty revelation with some meaty and yet light Portobello Mozzarella Caps and the impossibly creamy and savory Mashed Potato, Bacon, and Scallion Pizza, and your guests will be in complete awe of your abilities.

Blackened Pear

Portobello Mozzarella Caps

Mashed Potato, Bacon,
and Scallion Pizza

Sour Cream, Pear,
and Walnut Pie

BLACKENED PEAR

Makes 4 to 6 Servings

For the Black Pepper Simple Syrup

1½ cups water

1 cup sugar

1 tablespoon black peppercorns

1 tablespoon coarsely ground black pepper

For the Sangria

1 cup pear pieces from a 15 oz. can

¼ cup juice from the can of pears

12 blackberries, plus more for garnish

1 (750 ml) bottle of sparkling wine, very cold

1. Prepare the simple syrup. In a small saucepan, combine the water, sugar, whole black peppercorns, and coarsely ground black pepper. Bring the mixture to a boil over medium heat and stir to dissolve the sugar. Once it's at a boil, reduce the heat to low and let the syrup simmer for 15 to 20 minutes. Remove from heat and let cool. Strain the cooled syrup into an airtight glass container and refrigerate. The syrup will keep, refrigerated, for about 3 weeks.

2. In a bowl, combine the pear pieces, juice from the pears, blackberries, and ¼ cup of black pepper simple syrup. Cover and refrigerate for about an hour.

3. Divide the fruits and juices between 4 to 6 glasses. Top each glass with sparkling wine and garnish with additional blackberries.

PORTOBELLO MOZZARELLA CAPS

Makes 4 Servings   Active Time: 15 Minutes   Total Time: 45 Minutes

1 (8 oz.) bottle of Italian dressing

4 portobello mushroom caps

2 bell peppers, sliced

2 tablespoons olive oil

10 oz. fresh mozzarella

½ teaspoon dried oregano

6 basil leaves, torn

1. Fill a large resealable bag with the salad dressing, add the mushroom caps, and let sit for 15 minutes. Preheat your gas or charcoal grill to medium-high heat.

2. When the grill is about 450°F, brush the sliced bell peppers with the olive oil and place on the grill. Place the marinated mushroom caps on the grill. Cook, while turning occasionally, until tender. This will take 7 to 10 minutes for the mushrooms and 4 to 5 minutes for the peppers. Remove the peppers from the grill and cut into small chunks.

3. Place the mushroom caps top side up and top with mozzarella. Cook until the cheese starts to melt, about 3 minutes. Remove from heat, top with the peppers, oregano, and basil, and serve.

MASHED POTATO, BACON, AND SCALLION PIZZA

Makes 4 to 6 Servings   Active Time: 25 Minutes   Total Time: 45 Minutes

1 ball of pizza dough, stretched into a 10-inch round

2 tablespoons olive oil

Salt and black pepper, to taste

2 tablespoons Asiago cheese, grated

¾ cup mashed potatoes

1½ cups mozzarella, grated

Heavy cream, to taste

½ cup bacon, cooked and chopped

½ cup scallions, chopped

1 tablespoon of parsley, rosemary, and thyme mixture

1. Preheat your oven to 550°F. Brush the dough with the olive oil. Season with pepper and sprinkle the Asiago over the dough. Spread the mashed potatoes over the dough and then top with the mozzarella.

2. Drizzle generously with the cream and top with the bacon, scallions, and herb mixture. Season with salt and place in the oven. Cook, while rotating the pizza halfway through, until golden brown, about 15 to 20 minutes.

SOUR CREAM, PEAR, AND WALNUT PIE

Makes 6 to 8 Servings   Active Time: 1 Hour
Total Time: 2 Hours

---

1 Flaky Pastry Crust (see page 28)

1¼ cups sour cream

¾ cup granulated sugar

¾ cup flour

¼ teaspoon salt, plus ⅛ teaspoon

2 teaspoons pure vanilla extract

1 egg

4 to 5 cups ripe pears, peeled, cored, and sliced; or 2 (15 oz.) cans of pear slices in unsweetened syrup, drained

½ cup walnuts, chopped

3 tablespoons 100% natural maple syrup (preferably Grade B dark)

¼ cup light brown sugar, packed

½ teaspoon ground cardamom

3 tablespoons cold butter, cut into slivers

1. Place the crust in a greased 9" pie plate. Preheat the oven to 400°F. In a large bowl, whisk together the sour cream, sugar, ¼ cup of the flour, ¼ teaspoon salt, vanilla, and egg until combined. Stir in the pear slices. Transfer the fruit mixture into the crust.

2. In a separate bowl, combine the remaining flour, the remaining salt, the walnuts, maple syrup, brown sugar, and cardamom. Add the butter slivers and work with a fork or pastry blender to form a crumbly dough. Chill in refrigerator until ready to use.

3. Put the pie in the oven and bake for 15 minutes, then reduce the oven temperature to 350°F and bake for another 30 minutes. Remove pie from oven, take topping out of the refrigerator, and sprinkle it over the pie. Bake for another 20 to 25 minutes until topping is golden brown. Remove from the oven and allow to cool before serving.

Week 43

The smooth, luxurious Black Velvet will soothe whatever fears the goblins and ghouls patrolling your neighborhood have stirred up. Since we know you're going to dip into the candy at some point today, we're trying to keep the midday meal as light as possible. Then again, once you get a bowl of the beautiful, luxurious Chocolate & Coconut Soup with Brûléed Bananas in front of you, all that candy may seem pretty low-rent.

Black Velvet

Non Island Iced Tea

Sweet Potato Pancakes

Vegetable Frittata

Chocolate & Coconut Soup
with Brûléed Bananas

BLACK VELVET

1 part Champagne

1 part Guinness or other stout

1. Fill a champagne flute approximately halfway with Champagne.

2. Float the Guinness on top of the Champagne by slowly and carefully pouring it over the back of a spoon. The result should be a bright layer of Champagne beneath a layer of dark, opaque beer.

NON ISLAND ICED TEA

1 part unsweetened iced tea

1 part lemonade

1 part cola

1 lime slice, for garnish

Place all of the ingredients in a highball glass filled with ice. Stir until mixed and garnish with a lime slice.

SWEET POTATO PANCAKES

Makes 6 to 8 Servings   Active Time: 1 Hour
Total Time: 1½ Hours

6 large sweet potatoes, washed and peeled

1 large onion

3 eggs, beaten

½ cup matzo meal

½ teaspoon sugar

Salt and black pepper, to taste

1 cup canola oil

1. Finely chop the sweet potatoes and place them in a colander in the sink. Grate the onion or use a knife to dice very finely. Put the onion in a bowl. Squeeze as much liquid out of the sweet potatoes as possible. Combine the potatoes and onion and begin processing in a food processor or blender to turn the mixture into a rough puree. Don't overblend or chop, as the mixture will get too starchy.

2. Squeeze the puree through a fine sieve to remove excess liquid and then let the mixture sit and drain on its own for about 20 to 30 minutes.

3. Place the puree in a large bowl and add the eggs, matzo meal, and sugar. Stir to combine and season with salt and pepper.

4. Heat a cast-iron skillet over medium-high heat and add the oil. Be careful making the pancakes, as the oil can splatter. Take spoonfuls of the sweet potato mixture and place them in the oil. Cook for about 3 minutes a side. The pancakes should be golden brown on the outside and cooked through on the inside. You may need to adjust the temperature of the oil to get the right cooking temperature, especially if you have more than 3 pancakes in the skillet at one time. When cooked, transfer the pancakes to a paper towel–lined plate.

VEGETABLE FRITTATA

Makes 4 Servings   Active Time: 20 Minutes   Total Time: 40 Minutes

3 tablespoons butter

½ onion, minced

2 garlic cloves, minced

2 carrots, sliced thin

½ small zucchini, sliced thin

½ red pepper, seeded and sliced thin

⅓ cup parsley, minced

6 eggs, beaten

Salt and pepper, to taste

1 teaspoon red pepper flakes
(optional)

1. Preheat the broiler to low.

2. Place a cast-iron skillet over medium-high heat. Melt the butter in the skillet. Add the onion and garlic and cook, stirring, until the onion is translucent, about 3 minutes. Add the carrots and zucchini slices, lower the heat to medium, and cook, while stirring occasionally, until softened, about 5 minutes. Add the red pepper and continue to cook, for about 5 minutes.

3. Add the parsley, and then pour the eggs over the vegetables. Shake the skillet to distribute evenly. Season with salt and pepper. Sprinkle with red pepper flakes, if desired. Cover and cook until eggs are set, about 10 minutes. Put the skillet in the oven and cook for a few minutes to "toast" the top. Remove from the oven and let sit for a few minutes before serving.

CHOCOLATE & COCONUT SOUP WITH BRÛLÉED BANANAS

Makes 4 Servings   Active Time: 25 Minutes
Total Time: 45 Minutes

For the Soup

2 cups milk

1 (14 oz.) can of coconut milk

1 cup heavy cream

1 vanilla bean, scraped

12 oz. 60% dark chocolate

½ fresh coconut

¾ cup sugar

½ cup water

For the Brûléed Bananas

2 bananas

Sugar, for dipping

1. Prepare the soup. In a medium saucepan, add milk, coconut milk, cream, vanilla bean pod, and vanilla seeds and bring to a simmer. Turn off the heat and let stand for 20 minutes.

2. Preheat the oven to 350°F. Remove the outer shell of the coconut and use a spoon to remove the meat. Slice coconut meat very thinly and set aside. In a small saucepan, add the sugar and water, and bring to a boil. Remove from heat and let stand until cool. Once the syrup is cool, dip the coconut slices into the syrup and place on a parchment-lined baking sheet. Place tray in oven and bake for 8 minutes, or until the coconut is golden brown. Remove and set aside.

3. Prepare the Brûléed Bananas. Peel and cut your bananas along the bias. Dip the angled piece into the sugar and then use a kitchen torch to caramelize the sugar. Set aside.

4. After 20 minutes, remove the vanilla pod from the soup and return to a simmer. Turn off heat, add chocolate, and whisk until the chocolate is melted. Pass soup through a fine sieve. Serve in hot bowls with the Brûléed Bananas and candied coconut.

Week 44

Meaty, versatile, and nutritious, eggplant was built to carry a brunch. The Eggplant Parmesan is a meal onto itself, but everyone will be happy to see a bowl of the wonderfully light, lemony Avgolemono with Orzo Salad beside it. This Greek classic will transport you from the frost that greeted you this morning to a small inn on the Mediterranean. Finish up with the sweet and savory Baked Apples Farcie and everyone will be ready to meet the fast-approaching holiday rush head-on.

Bloody Maria Express

Eggplant Parmesan

Avgolemono with Orzo Salad

Baked Apples Farcie

BLOODY MARIA
EXPRESS

Dash of Worcestershire sauce

Dash of lemon juice

1 part tequila

2 parts tomato juice

Anything your heart desires, for garnish

1. Place the Worcestershire sauce and lemon juice in a pint glass, and add ice.

2. Pour in the tequila and tomato juice and stir until thoroughly mixed.

3. Garnish with anything you want—lemon, lime, cilantro, olives, or even bacon.

EGGPLANT PARMESAN

Makes 4 Servings   Active Time: 20 Minutes
Total Time: 1 Hour

1 large eggplant, cut into ¼-inch slices

Salt, to taste

2 tablespoons olive oil

1 cup Italian bread crumbs

2 tablespoons Parmesan cheese, grated

1 egg, beaten

½ cup tomato sauce

2 garlic cloves, minced

1 cup mozzarella cheese, shredded

1. Preheat the oven to 350°F. Put the slices of eggplant in a
    single layer on paper towels, sprinkle salt over them, and
    let rest for about 15 minutes. Turn the slices over, sprinkle
    with salt, and let sit for another 15 minutes.

2. Rinse the eggplant and dry with paper towels.

3. Drizzle the oil over a baking sheet. In a shallow bowl,
    combine the bread crumbs and Parmesan cheese. Put
    the beaten egg in another shallow bowl. Dip the slices of
    eggplant in egg, then the bread crumb mixture, coating
    both sides. Transfer the eggplant to a baking sheet.

4. Place the sheet in the oven and cook for about 10 minutes.
    Turn the slices of eggplant over and bake another 10
    minutes. Remove the sheet from the oven and set aside.

5. Put a layer of tomato sauce in a baking dish and stir in the
    garlic. Lay the eggplant slices in the sauce, layering to fit.
    Top with the shredded mozzarella.

6. Put the dish in the oven and bake for about 30 minutes,
    until the sauce is bubbling and the cheese is golden brown.
    Remove, let cool for about 10 minutes, and serve.

AVGOLEMONO WITH ORZO SALAD

Makes 4 Servings   Active Time: 45 Minutes   Total Time: 1 Hour and 15 Minutes

6 cups Chicken Stock
(see page 24)

2 bone-in, skin-on chicken thighs

1 cup orzo

3 eggs

1 tablespoon lemon juice

1 tablespoon cold water

Salt and black pepper, to taste

Parsley, chopped, for garnish

Lemon slices, for garnish

1. Pour the stock into a large saucepan and bring to a boil. Reduce the heat so that the broth simmers. Add the chicken thighs and cook for 20 minutes.

2. Remove the chicken thighs and set aside. Add the orzo and cook for 5 minutes. Meanwhile, remove the meat from the chicken thighs, discard the skin and bones, and chop the meat into bite-sized pieces.

3. Strain the orzo from the broth and set aside. Return the broth to the pan and bring to a simmer. Place the eggs in a mixing bowl and beat until frothy. Add the lemon juice and cold water and whisk to combine. Add approximately ½ cup of the stock to bowl and stir constantly.

4. Add another cup of hot stock to the egg mixture and then add the tempered eggs to the saucepan. Be careful not to let the stock boil once you add the eggs, otherwise it will curdle.

5. Add half of the cooked orzo and the chicken to the saucepan. Season with salt and pepper and ladle into warmed bowls. Garnish with parsley and lemon slices and serve with the Orzo Salad.

Orzo Salad

½ cup orzo, cooked

¼ cup feta cheese, crumbled

¼ cup red bell pepper, chopped

3 tablespoons yellow bell pepper, chopped

3 tablespoons Kalamata olives, chopped

1 scallion, sliced

1 teaspoon capers, drained and chopped

1 teaspoon garlic, minced

1 teaspoon parsley, leaves removed and chopped

1 tablespoon pine nuts, toasted and chopped

2 teaspoons lemon juice

1 teaspoon white wine vinegar

1 teaspoon Dijon mustard

½ teaspoon cumin

3 tablespoons extra virgin olive oil

Salt and black pepper, to taste

1. In a medium-sized mixing bowl, add the orzo, feta cheese, bell pepper, Kalamata olives, scallions, capers, garlic, parsley, and pine nuts and stir until combined.

2. In a small bowl, add the lemon juice, vinegar, mustard, and cumin and stir until combined. Gradually whisk in the olive oil and then add the dressing to the orzo mixture. Toss to blend, season with salt and pepper, and serve.

BAKED APPLES FARCIE

Makes 6 Servings   Active Time: 30 to 40 Minutes
Total Time: 1½ Hours

---

6 Pink Lady apples

2 tablespoons olive oil, plus more for rubbing

Salt and black pepper, to taste

8 oz. pork sausage, casing removed

4 fresh sage leaves

2 small shallots, diced

2 tablespoons Calvados

½ cup garlic bread crumbs

2 tablespoons heavy cream (optional)

2 oz. goat cheese, cut into 6 rounds

1. Preheat the oven to 350°F. Slice the tops off of the apples and set aside. Use a paring knife to cut a circle in the apples' flesh and then scoop out the center. Make sure to leave a ½-inch-thick wall inside the apple.

2. Rub the apples inside and out with olive oil and season with salt and pepper. Set aside.

3. In a large skillet, add the olive oil and warm over medium-high heat. Crumble the pork sausage into the pan and then add the sage and shallots. Cook for 2 minutes. Splash with Calvados and cook for another 2 minutes until the alcohol has cooked off. Season to taste, remove from heat, and let cool for 10 minutes.

4. In a large mixing bowl, add the bread crumbs, the cooked sausage mixture, and the cooking juices. If using, add the cream and toss to combine.

5. Fill each apple with 1 teaspoon of the sausage-and-bread crumb mixture. Next, add the slices of goat cheese. Fill each apple over its brim with the remaining sausage-and-bread crumb mixture and place in baking dish. Carefully balance the top of each apple on the mixture. Place in the oven and bake for 40 to 45 minutes, until the apples are tender.

Week 45

With the rich and beautiful Lamb and Sweet Potato Hash and the airy, earthy Broccoli and Cheddar Quiche, this spread is one that people are sure to speed through. Luckily, you've got the simple, luscious sweetness of the Pear and Cinnamon Bread Pudding to slow things down and keep everyone at the table for a little bit longer.

Irish Rose

Citrus-Rosemary Water

Lamb and Sweet Potato Hash

Broccoli and Cheddar Quiche

Pear and Cinnamon
Bread Pudding

IRISH ROSE

2 parts Irish whiskey

3 parts lemon-lime soda

Juice of 1 lemon wedge

Juice of 1 lime wedge

1 part grenadine

1 lime wedge, for garnish

1. Fill a mason jar with ice and then add the whiskey and lemon-lime soda.

2. Add the lemon juice and lime juice, top with grenadine, and stir until thoroughly mixed. Garnish with the lime wedge.

Variation:

Don't have grenadine? Substitute some cherry soda for the grenadine and lemon-lime soda.

CITRUS-ROSEMARY WATER

Makes 8 Servings

1 orange, thinly sliced

½ grapefruit, thinly sliced

1 sprig of rosemary

8 cups cold, filtered water

1. Place the orange, grapefruit, and rosemary in a pitcher or jar and cover with water.

2. Let sit for 1 to 2 hours at room temperature for a quick infusion, or refrigerate for anywhere from 4 hours to overnight.

LAMB AND SWEET POTATO HASH

Makes 4 to 6 Servings   Active Time: 20 Minutes   Total Time: 13 to 17 Hours

For the Marinade

4 garlic cloves, pureed

3 sprigs of oregano, minced

¼ cup Dijon mustard

¼ cup Cabernet Sauvignon

1 tablespoon kosher salt

1 tablespoon black pepper

For the Lamb and Sweet Potato Hash

1½ pounds leg of lamb, butterflied

4 tablespoons butter, clarified

2 cups water

1 pound sweet potatoes, peeled and minced

2 poblano peppers, diced

2 yellow onions, minced

1 tablespoon garlic, minced

1 tablespoon cumin

1 tablespoon kosher salt, plus more for seasoning

1 tablespoon fresh oregano, chopped

Black pepper, to taste

1. Prepare the marinade. Combine all of the ingredients for the marinade in a small bowl and then transfer to a 1-gallon resealable bag. Place the lamb in the bag, squeeze all of the air out, and place in the refrigerator for 12 to 16 hours.

2. Preheat oven to 350°F. Place a cast-iron skillet over medium-high heat and add half of the clarified butter. Remove the lamb from the bag, place in the skillet, and sear for 5 minutes on each side.

3. Add the water to the skillet, place it in the oven, and cook for 20 minutes, or until the center of the lamb reaches 140°F. Remove the skillet from the oven, set the lamb aside, and drain the liquid from the skillet. Let the lamb sit for 15 minutes, and then mince.

4. Place the sweet potatoes in a Dutch oven, cover with water, bring to a boil, and cook over medium-high heat for about 15 minutes, until they are just tender. Be careful not to overcook them, as you don't want to end up with mashed potatoes. Drain the potatoes and set aside.

5. Add the remaining clarified butter, the poblano peppers, onions, garlic, and cumin to the skillet and cook over medium heat until all of the vegetables are soft, about 10 minutes. Return the potatoes and the lamb to the skillet. Add the salt and cook for another 15 minutes. When ready to serve, add the oregano and season with black pepper.

BROCCOLI AND CHEDDAR QUICHE

Makes 6 to 8 Servings   Active Time: 45 Minutes   Total Time: 1½ Hours

1 Flaky Pastry Crust (see page 28)

3 cups broccoli florets and stems

1 teaspoon Dijon mustard

1¼ cups cheddar cheese, shredded

1 cup half-and-half

1 teaspoon salt

½ teaspoon ground black pepper

6 eggs, beaten

½ cup Parmesan cheese, grated

1. Place the crust in a greased 9" pie plate and preheat the oven to 350°F. In a saucepan, steam the broccoli pieces until cooked but still crisp, about 15 minutes. Drain, rinse with cold water, and set aside to dry.

2. Brush the mustard over the crust. Next, sprinkle about ¼ cup of the cheddar cheese over the crust and place the broccoli pieces on top.

3. Add the half-and-half, salt, and pepper to the beaten eggs and whisk to combine. Add the remaining cheddar cheese and stir until well combined. Pour the egg mixture over the broccoli pieces, shaking gently to distribute evenly. Sprinkle the Parmesan over everything.

4. Put the quiche in the oven and bake for 35 to 40 minutes or until the quiche is puffy and golden brown. Remove from the oven and allow to sit for 10 minutes before slicing and serving.

PEAR AND CINNAMON BREAD PUDDING

Makes 4 Servings   Active Time: 20 Minutes   Total Time: 55 Minutes

6 cups stale bread, torn into small pieces

2 tablespoons unsalted butter, melted

4 eggs, beaten

1¾ cups milk

¾ cup sugar

2 teaspoons cinnamon

1 teaspoon pure vanilla extract

3 pears, peeled and sliced

Caramel Sauce (see page 94)

1. Preheat oven to 350°F. Place the bread pieces in a greased 9 x 9–inch baking dish. Combine the butter, eggs, milk, sugar, cinnamon, and vanilla in a mixing bowl, and then pour the mixture over the bread.

2. Push the mixture down with a fork and make sure to soak all of the bread. Top with the pear slices and bake for 40 to 45 minutes until the top is brown. Remove from the oven, top with the Caramel Sauce, and serve.

Week 46

The Cider 75 is a more accessible take on the classic French 75, and its crispness makes it the perfect salve for those who are already overwhelmed by the holiday onslaught. The Savory Scones are a great vehicle for some Whipped Herb Butter (see page 33), and the combination of nutty quinoa and tart citrus in the salad will awaken everyone's taste buds. Once these delicious treats have set the stage, a comforting bowl of Clam Chowder arrives to steal the show.

Cider 75

Savory Scones

Citrus and Quinoa Salad

Mel's Clam Chowder

Chocolate Cheesecake Tart

CIDER 75

1 sugar cube
1 part apple brandy
2 parts dry hard cider
1 lemon twist, for garnish

Place a sugar cube at the bottom of a champagne flute. Add the apple brandy and top with the hard cider. Garnish with a twist of lemon.

SAVORY SCONES

Makes 4 to 6 Servings   Active Time: 30 Minutes   Total Time: 50 Minutes

---

2 cups all-purpose flour, plus more for dusting

1 teaspoon baking powder

½ teaspoon salt

1 teaspoon freshly ground black pepper

½ teaspoon dry mustard

4 tablespoons butter, chilled and cut into small pieces

½ cup sharp cheddar cheese, grated

½ cup milk

1 egg, beaten with a little milk

1. Preheat the oven to 400°F and position a rack in the middle of the oven. In a large bowl, whisk together the flour, baking powder, salt, pepper, and dry mustard. Add the butter pieces and mix with an electric mixer until just blended, or mix with a fork so that the dough is somewhat crumbly. Stir in the cheese and milk, being careful not to overmix.

2. With flour on your hands, transfer the dough to a lightly floured surface. Form the dough into a circle about ½-inch thick. With a long knife, cut the dough into 6 to 8 wedges. Put the scone wedges in a round, greased cake pan, while making sure to leave some space between the pieces.

3. Brush with the beaten egg and bake for 20 to 25 minutes, or until golden.

CITRUS AND QUINOA SALAD

Makes 6 Servings   Active Time: 30 Minutes   Total Time: 45 Minutes

For the Salad

1½ cups quinoa, washed

3 cups water

1 teaspoon kosher salt

½ pound carrots, peeled and julienned

1 shallot, peeled, halved lengthwise, and cut into thin half-moons

½ cup dried cranberries

½ cup walnuts, crushed

Zest and segments of 2 blood oranges (reserve the membranes and juice for the dressing)

For the Dressing

Reserved membranes and juice from 2 blood oranges

Juice of 1 lime

¼ cup rice vinegar

½ cup canola oil

¼ cup honey

1 tablespoon kosher salt

1. Place the quinoa, water, and salt in a medium saucepan and bring to a boil. Once the quinoa starts to boil, reduce the heat to medium or medium-low and simmer until the quinoa has absorbed all of the water. Remove the pan from heat and cover for 5 to 10 minutes. Remove the cover, fluff with a fork, and let cool.

2. Place the carrots, shallot, cranberries, walnuts, blood orange zest, blood orange segments, and the quinoa in a salad bowl and stir until combined. Set aside.

3. Prepare the dressing. Place the ingredients for the dressing in a blender and puree until smooth.

4. Serve the salad with the dressing on the side.

Tip: *If you want the quinoa to cool as evenly as possible, line a baking sheet with parchment paper and pour the quinoa onto it in an even layer. Once it's cool, just fold up the paper and transfer the quinoa wherever you want it.*

MEL'S CLAM CHOWDER

Makes 6 Servings   Active Time: 30 Minutes
Total Time: 1½ Hours

½ pound bacon, minced

2 tablespoons fresh thyme, chopped

4 cups celery, washed and minced

4 medium Spanish onions, peeled and minced

4 tablespoons unsalted butter

6 garlic cloves, minced

⅓ cup flour, plus 1 tablespoon

1½ pounds creamer potatoes, minced

2 cups of Bar Harbor Pure Clam Juice

2 tablespoons Worcestershire sauce

3 dashes of Tabasco

2 cups heavy cream

6 (6½ oz.) cans of Bar Harbor Whole Maine
Cherrystone Clams, with juice

Salt and pepper, to taste

1. Place the bacon in a Dutch oven and cook over
    medium-high heat until it is crispy. Stir the
    bacon occasionally as it cooks. Drain the fat
    from the pan and add the thyme, celery, onions,
    butter, and garlic. Reduce the heat to medium
    and cook until the onions are translucent. Add
    the flour and stir until all the vegetables are
    coated. Cook for 10 minutes, while frequently
    stirring and scraping the bottom of the pan to
    keep anything from burning.

2. Add the potatoes and clam juice, and cook until
    potatoes are tender, about 20 minutes. Add the
    Worcestershire sauce and Tabasco, stir, and then
    add the cream. Cook until the chowder is just
    thick enough to coat a spoon. Add the clams,
    season with salt and pepper, and cook until
    heated through, about 10 minutes.

CHOCOLATE CHEESECAKE TART

Makes 6 to 8 Servings   Active Time: 40 Minutes   Total Time: 1½ Hours

8 to 10 Oreo cookies, filling scraped off

1 tablespoon unsweetened cocoa powder

2 tablespoons Kahlúa

8 tablespoons (1 stick) unsalted butter, melted

2 (8 oz.) packages of cream cheese, softened

1 cup sugar

1 tablespoon cocoa powder

½ teaspoon pure vanilla extract

2 eggs

Chocolate shavings, for topping (optional)

1. Preheat the oven to 350°F. Place the cookies in a food processor or blender and pulse until they are crumbs. If you don't have a food processor, you can also put the cookies in a resealable plastic bag and use a rolling pin to crush them.

2. Put the crumbs in a bowl and add the unsweetened cocoa powder and the Kahlúa. Stir in 6 tablespoons of the butter. Place the other 2 tablespoons of the butter in a cast-iron skillet. Press the cookie crumb mixture into the skillet, extending the crust about halfway up the side. Place in the oven and bake until the crust is firm, about 10 minutes. Remove the skillet from the oven and allow to cool. Reduce oven temperature to 325°F.

3. In a large bowl, add the cream cheese, sugar, cocoa powder, vanilla, and eggs and stir until thoroughly combined. Scrape the mixture into the cooled crust, put the skillet in the oven, and bake for 40 to 60 minutes, until set. Remove the skillet from the oven, allow to cool, and refrigerate for 1 hour before serving. If desired, top with chocolate shavings.

Week 47

A definitive chill has entered the air, and while the first few snowflakes are always magical, anything more than a dusting tends to jangle the nerves. But after a Hot Buttered Rum, you're well on your way to soothing them. Follow with the Apple and Pork Stew and some Chocolate and Walnut Fudge and you'll have plenty of perspective once the snow really starts to fly.

Hot Buttered Rum

Sparkling Grapefruit and
Rosemary Water

Mujadara

Apple and Pork Stew

Chocolate and Walnut Fudge

HOT BUTTERED RUM

Small pat of butter

1 teaspoon brown sugar

Dash of cinnamon

Dash of nutmeg

Dash of orange zest

Splash of pure vanilla extract

6 oz. water

2 oz. dark rum

Dash of allspice

1 cinnamon stick, for garnish

1. Muddle the butter, brown sugar, cinnamon, nutmeg, and orange zest in the bottom of a mug. When the ingredients are thoroughly combined, add the vanilla.

2. Bring the water to boil in kettle or small saucepan. Add the rum and hot water to the jar. Add the dash of allspice, stir until combined, and garnish with a cinnamon stick.

SPARKLING GRAPEFRUIT AND ROSEMARY WATER

Makes 4 Servings

Rosemary-infused simple syrup, to taste

2 cups grapefruit juice

2 cups sparkling water

Sprigs of rosemary, for garnish

1. Prepare the Simple Syrup as directed on page 32. When the sugar is dissolved, remove from heat, add 5 sprigs of rosemary, and let cool. When cool, strain the syrup into a container and store in the refrigerator for up to 3 weeks.

2. Combine the grapefruit juice and sparkling water in a pitcher filled with ice. Add the rosemary syrup, stir, and pour over ice. Garnish with the sprigs of rosemary and serve.

MUJADARA

Makes 6 to 8 Servings   Active Time: 10 Minutes   Total Time: 35 Minutes

1 cup brown or green lentils

2 leeks, white and light green parts only

¼ cup extra virgin olive oil

2 garlic cloves, minced

¾ cup long-grain rice

1½ teaspoons ground cumin

½ teaspoon ground allspice

¼ teaspoon cayenne pepper

4¼ cups water

2 teaspoons salt, plus more as needed

1 bay leaf

1 cinnamon stick

4 cups Swiss chard or kale, trimmed and chopped

Salt and pepper, to taste

1. Place the lentils in a large bowl and cover with warm tap water. Halve the leeks lengthwise, run them under warm water to remove any dirt, and then thinly slice them. Pat the leeks dry with paper towels.

2. Heat the olive oil in a Dutch oven over medium-high heat. Add the leeks and cook for 5 to 10 minutes, while stirring occasionally, until they are crispy and golden brown. Transfer half of the leeks to a bowl and set aside. Add the garlic and rice to the pot and cook for about 2 minutes before adding the cumin, allspice, and cayenne.

3. Drain the lentils and add them to the pot. Add the water, salt, bay leaf, and cinnamon stick and bring the mixture to a simmer. Cover and cook over low heat for 15 minutes.

4. Add the greens, cover the pot, and cook for 5 minutes, until the rice and lentils are tender and the greens are wilted. Remove from heat and let stand, covered, for 5 minutes. Garnish with the reserved leeks and season with salt and pepper before serving.

APPLE AND PORK STEW

Makes 4 to 6 Servings   Active Time: 20 Minutes   Total Time: 1 Hour and 15 Minutes

---

1½ pounds pork shoulder, cubed

⅓ cup all-purpose flour

2 tablespoons vegetable oil

2 tablespoons butter

2 onions, diced

4 garlic cloves, minced

1 tablespoon thyme, leaves removed and chopped

1 tablespoon rosemary, leaves removed and chopped

2 potatoes, peeled and chopped into ½-inch cubes

1 cup red wine

6 cups Veal Stock (see page 26)

2 Granny Smith apples, peeled, cored, and chopped

Salt and pepper, to taste

1. In a mixing bowl, add the pork and flour, and toss until the pork is coated. In a large saucepan, add the oil and cook over medium-high heat until warm. Add the pork and cook for 5 minutes, or until evenly browned. Remove the meat from the pan and set aside.

2. Reduce the heat to medium and add the butter. Add the onions and garlic and cook for 5 minutes, or until soft. Add the herbs and potatoes, and cook for 5 minutes. Add the red wine and cook for 5 minutes, or until reduced by half.

3. Add the stock and bring to a boil. Reduce heat so that the soup simmers, return the pork to the pan, cover, and cook for 20 minutes. Add the apples and cook for 15 minutes. Once the pork, apples, and potatoes are tender, season with salt and pepper and serve in warm bowls.

CHOCOLATE AND WALNUT FUDGE

Makes 4 to 6 Servings   Active Time: 15 Minutes
Total Time: 2½ Hours

Vegetable oil spray

1 cup walnuts, coarsely chopped

¾ pound quality bittersweet chocolate, chopped

2 oz. unsweetened chocolate, chopped

8 tablespoons (1 stick) butter

2 cups granulated sugar

1 (12 oz.) can of evaporated milk

1 teaspoon pure vanilla extract

1. Preheat the oven to 350°F and line a 9 x 9–inch baking dish with heavy-duty aluminum foil so that the foil extends over the sides. Spray the foil with the vegetable oil spray.

2. Place the walnuts on a baking sheet, place them in the oven, and toast for 5 to 7 minutes, until lightly browned. Remove from the oven and set the walnuts aside.

3. Place the chocolates and the butter in a mixing bowl and set aside. Combine the sugar and evaporated milk in a deep saucepan, and cook over medium heat until the sugar has dissolved and the mixture is boiling. Continue to cook, while stirring constantly, until the mixture reaches 236°F. Pour this mixture over the chocolate and butter in the mixing bowl. Whisk until smooth, and then stir in the walnuts and the vanilla.

4. Spread the mixture in an even layer in the prepared baking dish. Refrigerate for 1 to 2 hours, until the fudge is set. Use the foil to lift the fudge out of the pan and cut into squares.

Thanksgiving

Your focus will be on the feast to come, as it should be. But that doesn't mean that people won't be ready to do some serious eating first thing in the morning. The festive combination of flavors in the Liquid Apple Pie is certain to get everyone excited for the main event, while the Roasted Barley and Carrots with Pasilla Peppers opens up a whole new vista. Toss a few eggs beside it, and you're sure to shepherd everyone through the first leg of the holiday season successfully.

Liquid Apple Pie

Popovers

Roasted Barley and Carrots with Pasilla Peppers

Cast-Iron Carrot Cake

LIQUID APPLE PIE

1 part vanilla vodka

Dash of brown sugar

3 parts apple cider, warmed

Dash of cinnamon

1 cinnamon stick, for garnish

1 star anise, for garnish

1. Add the vanilla vodka and brown sugar to your glass and stir them together.

2. Pour the apple cider over the top and then add the dusting of cinnamon. Garnish with a cinnamon stick and a star anise.

POPOVERS

Makes 12 Popovers   Active Time: 15 Minutes   Total Time: 1 Hour

---

3 eggs

1½ cups milk

1½ cups all-purpose flour

½ teaspoon salt

2 tablespoons butter, melted

1 teaspoon sugar

1. Preheat the oven to 450°F. Place the eggs and milk in a medium bowl, and whisk briskly until the mixture is foamy and you cannot see any sign of egg yolk. Whisk in the flour and salt, making sure that the large lumps are all worked out. Stir in the melted butter and the sugar.

2. Put a popover pan in the oven for 2 minutes. After 2 minutes, remove the pan and fill the cups three-quarters of the way with the batter. Place in the oven and cook for 20 minutes. Reduce heat to 350°F and bake for another 20 minutes, checking to make sure they don't get too brown on top. If the popovers start to get too dark, place your popover pan on a sheet pan and move to a lower rack. When the popovers are golden brown, remove from heat, immediately turn them out of the pan, and serve.

Tip: Popovers are so delicious all that they require is a bit of softened butter and your favorite preserve.

ROASTED BARLEY AND CARROTS WITH PASILLA PEPPERS

Makes 4 to 6 Servings   Active Time: 10 Minutes   Total Time: 2 Hours

---

5 carrots, cut lengthwise into 3-inch pieces

Extra virgin olive oil, to taste

Salt and pepper, to taste

6 dried Pasilla peppers

2¼ cups water

1 cup pearl barley

1 cup red onion, minced

2 tablespoons adobo seasoning

1 tablespoon sugar

1 tablespoon chili powder

¼ cup dried oregano

1. Preheat the oven to 375°F. Place the carrots in a 9 x 13–inch baking pan, drizzle with the olive oil, and season with salt and pepper. Place the pan in the oven and roast for 45 to 50 minutes, or until the carrots are slightly soft to the touch.

2. While the carrots are cooking, open the Pasilla peppers and remove the seeds and stems. Place the peppers in a bowl. Place the water in a saucepan and bring to a boil. Pour the boiling water over the peppers and cover the bowl with plastic wrap.

3. When the carrots are done, remove the baking pan from the oven, add the remaining ingredients, and pour the soaking liquid from the peppers into the pan. Chop the reconstituted peppers, add to the pan, and stir so that the liquid is covering the barley. Cover the pan tightly with aluminum foil and put it back in oven for another 45 minutes, or until the barley becomes tender. Fluff with a fork and serve.

CAST-IRON CARROT CAKE

Makes 8 Servings   Active Time: 20 Minutes
Total Time: 1 Hour

8 tablespoons (1 stick) butter

1 cup carrots, minced

1 cup canned pineapple chunks, drained

1 (15.25 oz.) box of carrot cake mix

¾ cup water

⅔ cup vegetable oil

¾ cup unsweetened applesauce

4 eggs

1 cup unsweetened coconut flakes

1. Preheat the oven to 350°F. Place the butter in a cast-iron skillet and melt over medium heat. When it's melted, add the carrots, reduce the heat to medium-low, and simmer until the butter is bubbling. Add the pineapple chunks, reduce the heat to low, and simmer.

2. Place the cake mix, water, oil, applesauce, eggs, and coconut in a large bowl and stir to combine.

3. Turn off the heat and pour the batter over the carrot-and-pineapple mixture. Place the skillet in the oven and bake for 35 to 40 minutes, until a toothpick inserted into the center comes out clean. Remove and let cool for 10 minutes. Put a large serving plate on the counter and, working quickly and deliberately, flip the skillet so the cake is inverted onto the plate.

Week 48

The weekend following Thanksgiving is the perfect time to unwind. Only your favorite relatives remain, and all those leftovers mean you can keep away from the kitchen for a few days. To maximize the last bit of this glorious weekend, start with a glass of the Fall Fruit Fiesta sangria. Then use up the last bit of your leftovers on the Mashed Potato Blini, Chickpea Chili with Leftover Turkey, and Pumpkin Pie.

Fall Fruit Fiesta

Apple Chai Spritzer

Mashed Potato Blini

Chickpea Chili
with Leftover Turkey

Pumpkin Pie

FALL FRUIT FIESTA

Makes 4 to 6 Servings

1 (750 ml) bottle of dry white wine

1 Red Delicious or Empire apple, cored and cut into bite-sized pieces

1 cup seedless green grapes, halved

1 cup pomegranate juice

Juice of 1 lime

¼ cup brandy

1 (12 oz.) can of lemon-lime soda

Pomegranate seeds, for garnish

Orange slices, for garnish

1. Combine all of the sangria ingredients, except for the soda, in a large pitcher or container. Cover and refrigerate for 4 or more hours.

2. After removing the sangria from the refrigerator, add ice and the soda. Stir, garnish with the pomegranate seeds and orange slices, and serve.

APPLE CHAI SPRITZER

Makes 8 Servings

1 large apple, cored and thinly sliced

2 cardamom pods, cracked

1 cinnamon stick

2 whole cloves

1 bay leaf

3 to 4 whole black peppercorns

1-inch piece of ginger, peeled and smashed

8 cups seltzer water

1. Place the fruit and aromatics in a half-gallon pitcher or jar and cover with the seltzer water.

2. Refrigerate for 2 to 4 hours, strain, and serve chilled.

MASHED POTATO BLINI

Makes 12 Blini   Active Time: 30 Minutes   Total Time: 1 Hour

---

2 cups mashed potatoes

3 oz. goat cheese

2 tablespoons chives, minced

2 eggs, beaten

2 tablespoons all-purpose flour

Salt and freshly ground black pepper, to taste

3 tablespoons butter

1. Preheat the oven to 200°F. In a large bowl, combine the mashed potatoes with the goat cheese and chives. Add the eggs, stir to combine, and then add the flour 1 tablespoon at a time until the dough is the consistency of thick pancake batter. Season with salt and pepper.

2. Place the butter in a cast-iron skillet and melt over medium-high heat. Place 4 small spoonfuls of batter in the skillet, making sure to leave room in between them. Cook until browned on one side, about 2 minutes. Flip over and cook until the other side is brown.

3. Place the cooked blini on a plate, cover with foil, and put in the oven to keep warm until all are cooked.

Note: Blini can facilitate a number of toppings. Here are some of our favorite combinations: sour cream and caviar, sour cream and smoked salmon, smoked salmon and caviar, chunky applesauce, scrambled eggs with chopped bacon, fried eggs and salsa, avocado and salsa, and avocado and smoked salmon.

CHICKPEA CHILI WITH LEFTOVER TURKEY

Makes 6 to 8 Servings   Active Time: 35 Minutes   Total Time: 2 Hours and 35 Minutes

1 tablespoon olive oil

1 onion, diced

5 garlic cloves, minced

1 tablespoon fresh oregano, chopped

Black pepper, to taste

1 tablespoon cumin

2 teaspoons chili powder

2 cups Chicken Stock (see page 24)

8 oz. tomatoes (canned or fresh)

3 dried New Mexico chilies

1 red bell pepper, seeded and diced

Pinch of salt

1 (14 oz.) can of chickpeas

1 pound leftover turkey

2 cups cheddar cheese, shredded (optional)

1 cup sour cream (optional)

Lime wedges, for serving

1. Place the olive oil in a Dutch oven and warm over medium-high heat. Add the onion, garlic, oregano, black pepper, cumin, and chili powder. Cook for 5 minutes, while stirring often.

2. Add the stock, tomatoes, New Mexico chilies, bell pepper, salt, chickpeas, and turkey. Stir the mixture, cover, and reduce the heat to low. Cook for 2 hours, while stirring occasionally.

3. Scoop the chili into bowls, top with cheese and sour cream, if desired, and serve with lime wedges.

PUMPKIN PIE

Makes 6 to 8 Servings   Active Time: 30 Minutes   Total Time: 1½ Hours

---

1 (14 oz.) can of pumpkin puree (not pumpkin pie filling)

1 (12 oz.) can of evaporated milk

2 eggs, lightly beaten

½ cup sugar

½ teaspoon salt

1 teaspoon cinnamon

¼ teaspoon ground ginger

¼ teaspoon ground nutmeg

1 tablespoon butter

1 tablespoon light brown sugar

1 Flaky Pastry Crust (see page 28)

Whipped cream, for serving

1. Preheat the oven to 400°F. In a large bowl, combine the pumpkin puree, evaporated milk, eggs, sugar, salt, cinnamon, ginger, and nutmeg. Stir to combine thoroughly.

2. Grease a 9" pie plate with the butter, and then sprinkle the brown sugar on top. Place the crust in the pie plate and fill it with the pumpkin mixture. Put the pie in the oven and bake for 15 minutes. Reduce the heat to 325°F and bake for an additional 30 to 45 minutes, until the filling is firm and a toothpick inserted in the middle comes out clean. Remove the pie from the oven and allow to cool before serving with whipped cream.

Week 49

There are very few decadent dishes that are easier to prepare than Baked Brie. We provided you with two options so you can tailor it to your guests' tastes, and once you put some slices of crusty bread, crackers, and dried figs beside it, your only concern will be getting in there before it's all gone. Serving some scrambled eggs that you've tossed some vegetables into is a lovely partner for the Chicken-Quinoa Casserole, which can be taken in a number of directions with the simple addition of soy sauce, barbecue sauce, or hot sauce.

Apple & Spice

Baked Brie Two Ways

Chicken-Quinoa Casserole

Sweet Potato Pie

APPLE & SPICE

Makes 4 to 6 Servings

1 Granny Smith apple, cored, seeded, peeled, and cut into bite-sized pieces

1 Empire apple, cored, seeded, peeled, and cut into bite-sized pieces

½ cup fresh cranberries

¼ cup cranberry juice

¼ cup apple cider

¼ cup apple vodka

Dash of nutmeg

1 (750 ml) bottle of sparkling wine, very cold

1. In a bowl, combine the apple pieces and cranberries. Pour the cranberry juice, apple cider, and apple vodka over the fruits. Add the dash of nutmeg and stir to combine. Cover and refrigerate for at least 2 hours, and up to 6 hours. Then remove from refrigerator and strain the liquid into a measuring cup.

2. In 4 to 6 glasses, ladle 2 spoonfuls of the fruit. Pour equal amounts of the juice-and-vodka combination into each glass and top with sparkling wine.

BAKED BRIE TWO WAYS

Makes 4 to 6 Servings   Active Time: 10 Minutes
Total Time: 25 Minutes

---

8 oz. Brie or Camembert

1 baguette, sliced

For Savory Topping

¼ cup roasted tomatoes, chopped

¼ cup artichokes, chopped

2 tablespoons olives, pitted and chopped

1 tablespoon capers

Pinch of black pepper

For Sweet Topping

¼ cup pecans, chopped

¼ cup dried apricots, chopped

⅓ cup Divina fig spread

¼ cup dried cherries

Pinch of ground cinnamon

1. Place all of the ingredients for your chosen topping in a medium bowl and stir to combine.

2. Preheat oven to 350°F. Place your cheese in a ceramic Brie baker and top it with your mixture of choice.

3. Place in the oven and bake for 15 minutes, or until cheese is gooey. Remove from oven and serve with the slices of baguette.

CHICKEN-QUINOA CASSEROLE

Makes 4 to 6 Servings   Active Time: 45 Minutes   Total Time: 1½ Hours

1 tablespoon olive oil

½ onion, diced

2 garlic cloves, minced

1 pound boneless, skinless chicken breasts, cut into 1-inch pieces

½ cup frozen vegetables (peas, beans, carrots, corn)

1 teaspoon turmeric

½ teaspoon salt

½ teaspoon black pepper

1½ cups crushed tomatoes in puree

1 cup water

1 cup quinoa

¼ cup parsley, chopped

½ cup feta cheese, crumbled

1. Heat a cast-iron skillet over medium-high heat. Add the olive oil, onion, and garlic and cook for 2 minutes, or until the onion is translucent. Add the chicken pieces and frozen vegetables and continue to cook, while stirring, until the chicken pieces are browned, about 8 minutes. Stir in the turmeric and season with salt and pepper.

2. Add the tomatoes and water, and bring to a boil. Stir in the quinoa, reduce the heat to medium, and cook for 15 to 20 minutes, until quinoa is tender and most of the liquid has evaporated. Stir in the parsley, sprinkle with feta cheese, and serve.

SWEET POTATO PIE

Makes 6 to 8 Servings   Active Time: 30 Minutes
Total Time: 1½ Hours

2 cups sweet potatoes, mashed

1 (12 oz.) can of evaporated milk

2 eggs, lightly beaten

½ cup sugar

½ teaspoon salt

1 teaspoon cinnamon

¼ teaspoon ground ginger

¼ teaspoon ground nutmeg

8 tablespoons (1 stick) butter

1 cup light brown sugar

1 Flaky Pastry Crust (see page 28)

1. Preheat the oven to 400°F. In a large bowl, add the sweet potatoes, evaporated milk, eggs, sugar, salt, cinnamon, ginger, and nutmeg and stir until combined.

2. Place a cast-iron skillet over medium heat and melt the butter in it. Add the brown sugar and cook, while stirring constantly, until the sugar is dissolved. Remove pan from heat.

3. Pour the butter-and-brown sugar into a 9" pie plate. Roll out the crust and gently place it over the butter-and-brown sugar mixture. Fill with the sweet potato mixture, place the pie in the oven, and bake for 15 minutes. Reduce the heat to 325°F and bake for an additional 30 to 45 minutes until the filling is firm and a toothpick inserted in the middle comes out clean. Remove the pie from the oven and allow to cool before serving.

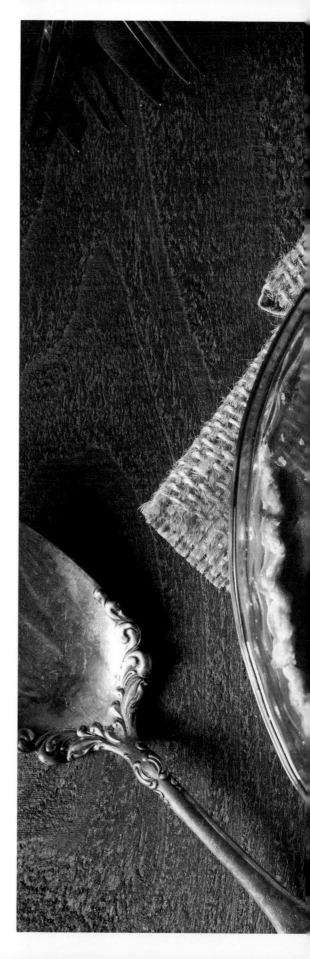

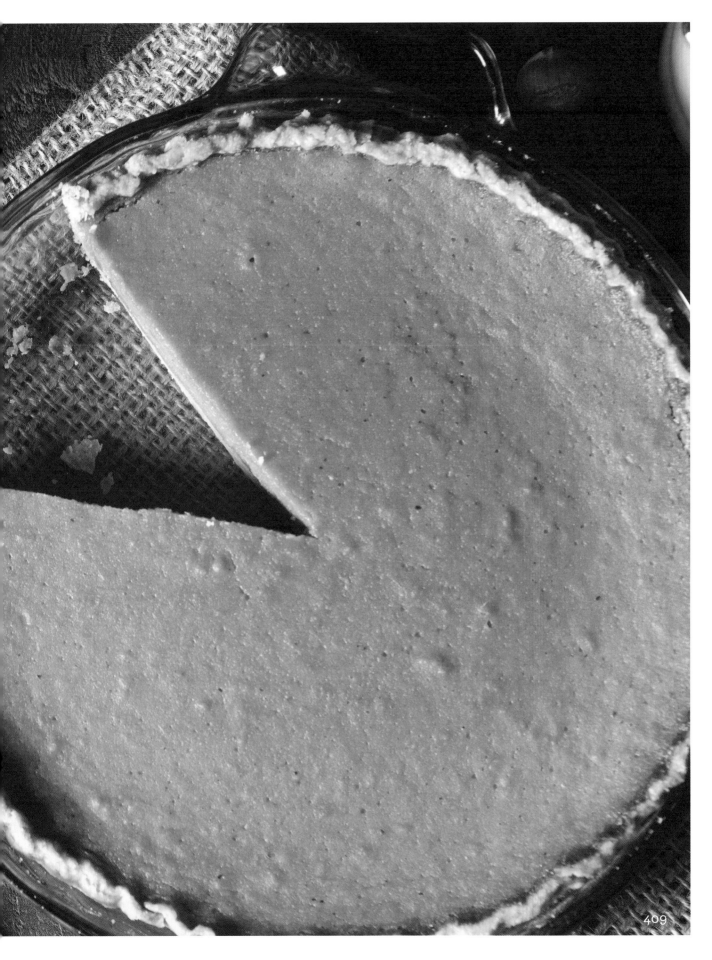

Week 50

With the days getting colder and shorter, we're betting that you're in need of some comfort. That's where the Cheesy Grits and the savory Sausage and Feta Quiche come in. The sudden return of warmth and calm just may bring a tear to your eye. The Puerto Rican Rice and Beans will spice things up a little bit, but in a healthy way. Follow it up with some traditional Polish Chrusciki, and suddenly those gray skies and early sunsets won't weigh so heavily on you.

Maple Margarita

Orange-Ginger Spritzer

Cheesy Grits

Sausage and Feta Quiche

Puerto Rican Rice and Beans

Chrusciki

MAPLE MARGARITA

1½ oz. tequila

½ oz. orange liqueur

¼ oz. mezcal

1¼ oz. pure maple syrup

1 oz. fresh lime juice

Sea salt, for the rim

1 lime or orange twist, for garnish

1. Fill a cocktail shaker with ice. Add all of the ingredients except for the sea salt and citrus twist and shake until well combined.

2. Wet the rim of a rocks glass and dip it into the salt. Strain the cocktail into the glass, add ice, and garnish with the twist of lime or orange.

ORANGE-GINGER SPRITZER

Makes 8 Servings

1 orange, thinly sliced

2-inch piece of ginger, peeled and smashed

8 cups seltzer water

1. Place the orange slices and ginger in a pitcher or jar and cover with the seltzer water.

2. Refrigerate for 2 to 4 hours and serve chilled.

CHEESY GRITS

Makes 4 to 6 Servings   Active Time: 20 Minutes   Total Time: 40 Minutes

2 cups whole milk

2 cups water

1 cup grits

1 teaspoon salt

1 teaspoon pepper

2 cups cheddar cheese, grated

1. Preheat the broiler to high. Place the milk and water in a saucepan and bring to a boil. Add the grits and cook, while stirring constantly, until the mixture has thickened and is cooked through, about 15 minutes. Add the salt, pepper, and 1 cup of the cheese. Stir to combine.

2. Pour the grits into a greased baking dish and sprinkle the remaining cheese on top. Put the grits in the oven and broil for about 2 minutes. Remove and serve immediately.

Tip: *If you want spicier grits, substitute 1 cup of Pepper Jack cheese for half of the cheddar.*

SAUSAGE AND FETA QUICHE

Makes 6 to 8 Servings   Active Time: 45 Minutes   Total Time: 1½ Hours

1 Baked Crust (see page 27)

2 tablespoons olive oil

½ pound Italian sausage

¼ cup red onion, diced

1 small tomato, concasse
(see page 21) and diced

¼ cup Kalamata olives, pitted
and halved

1 cup spinach

2 cups whole milk

1 teaspoon salt

1 teaspoon black pepper

4 eggs, beaten

½ cup feta cheese, crumbled

1. Preheat the oven to 350°F and place the crust into a greased 9" pie plate. In a skillet, heat the olive oil over medium heat and then add the sausage meat. Cook while pressing down to break up the meat into crumbles. When it is no longer pink throughout, transfer the sausage to a paper towel–lined plate.

2. Place the onion in the skillet and cook, while stirring, for about 3 minutes. Return the sausage to the pan, add the tomato, olives, and spinach, and stir to combine. Remove the skillet from heat and allow to cool slightly.

3. Whisk the milk, salt, and pepper into the beaten eggs. Fill the crust with the sausage-and-vegetable mixture. Sprinkle the crumbled feta evenly over the mixture. Pour the egg mixture over the other ingredients and shake gently to distribute evenly.

4. Put the quiche in the oven and bake for 30 to 40 minutes, or until it is puffy and golden brown. A knife inserted in the center should come out clean. Remove the quiche from the oven and allow to sit for 20 minutes before slicing and serving.

PUERTO RICAN RICE AND BEANS

Makes 6 Servings   Active Time: 25 Minutes   Total Time: 16 Hours

1 cup kidney beans, soaked
overnight and drained

½ cup vegetable oil

4 boneless, skinless chicken thighs

½ cup salt pork, minced

2 cups tomato sauce

2 cups white rice

3 to 3½ cups Chicken Stock
(see page 24)

2 packets Sazón with achiote

2 tablespoons dried oregano

1 cup Spanish olives with
the brine

Adobo seasoning, to taste

1. Place the beans in a Dutch oven and cover with water. Bring to a boil, reduce heat to medium-low, and cover the pot. Cook for 45 minutes to 1 hour, until the beans are tender. Drain and set the beans aside.

2. Place the pot back on the stove and add half of the oil. Add the chicken and cook over medium-high heat for 5 minutes on each side. Remove the chicken from the Dutch oven, cut it into 12 pieces, and set aside.

3. Add the salt pork and the remaining oil to the pot and cook until some of the salt pork's fat has rendered, about 5 minutes. Add the tomato sauce and cook for 5 minutes while stirring constantly. Add the rice to the pot, stir, and cook for 5 minutes.

4. Add the remaining ingredients and return the chicken to the pot. Reduce heat to medium and cook for 10 minutes. Cover the Dutch oven and cook for another 20 to 30 minutes, or until the liquid has been absorbed and the rice is tender.

5. Uncover the pot and add the beans. Stir to combine and serve.

CHRUSCIKI

Makes 20 Cookies   Active Time: 25 Minutes   Total Time: 1½ Hours

---

3 large eggs, at room temperature

¼ cup whole milk

¾ cup granulated sugar

8 tablespoons (1 stick) butter

1 teaspoon baking soda

1 teaspoon vanilla extract

½ teaspoon salt

½ teaspoon nutmeg, grated

3½ cups all-purpose flour, plus more for dusting

Vegetable oil, for frying

1 cup confectioners' sugar, for dusting

1. Combine the eggs, milk, granulated sugar, and butter in a mixing bowl and whisk until well combined. Whisk in the baking soda, vanilla, salt, and nutmeg, and then add the flour. Mix until a soft dough forms, cover the bowl tightly, and chill in the refrigerator for 1 hour. The dough will keep in the refrigerator for up to 3 days.

2. Dust a work surface and a rolling pin with flour. Roll out the dough to an even thickness of ¼ inch. Cut dough into 1-inch-wide strips. Cut strips on a diagonal at 3-inch intervals to form diamond-shaped cookies.

3. Pour 1½ inches of oil in a deep Dutch oven. Heat to 375°F and add the cookies a few at a time, using a slotted spoon to turn them as they brown. When cookies are browned all over, remove, set to drain on paper towels, and sprinkle with confectioners' sugar. Serve immediately.

Week 51

Christmas and the New Year are on the horizon, and you're still standing! Celebrate with a Dark Wings, a unique, sweet-and-spicy cocktail comprised of tequila, blackberry liqueur, and ginger beer. Roasted Root Vegetables and Pork Fried Rice will help keep you grounded, and the Maple-Bacon Sticky Buns will have you thinking differently about a season that seems to bring nothing but complications.

Dark Wings

Roasted Root Vegetables

Pork Fried Rice

Maple-Bacon Sticky Buns

DARK WINGS

1 part silver tequila

1 part blackberry liqueur

Juice of 1 lime

2 parts ginger beer

1 handful of blackberries, for garnish

1. Place the tequila, blackberry liqueur, and lime juice in a cocktail shaker filled with ice. Shake well.

2. Strain the resulting mixture into a highball glass filled with ice. Top with ginger beer and garnish with a handful of blackberries.

ROASTED ROOT VEGETABLES

Makes 4 to 6 Servings   Active Time: 20 Minutes
Total Time: 1 Hour

---

2 small parsnips, trimmed and scrubbed clean

1 turnip, trimmed and scrubbed clean

4 small beets, trimmed and scrubbed clean

4 medium carrots, trimmed and scrubbed clean

½ onion, sliced

1 small fennel bulb, trimmed and cut into slivers

¼ cup olive oil

Salt and black pepper, to taste

2 teaspoons dried rosemary

1. Preheat the oven to 400°F. Cut the vegetables into strips, place them in a large bowl with the olive oil, season with salt and pepper, and toss to combine.

2. Put the vegetables in a baking dish and sprinkle with the rosemary. Place in the oven and bake for about 40 minutes, turning the vegetables over halfway through .

PORK FRIED RICE

Makes 8 Servings   Active Time: 25 Minutes   Total Time: 35 Minutes

---

¼ cup canola oil

1 tablespoon fresh ginger, minced

1 tablespoon fresh garlic, minced

1 pound pork tenderloin, cooked and diced

3 to 4 large eggs

2 cups carrots, minced

4 cups white rice, cooked (day-old rice is preferred)

4 scallions, chopped

1 cup fresh or frozen peas

2 tablespoons light soy sauce

1 tablespoon rice vinegar

1 tablespoon fish sauce

1 tablespoon sesame oil

1. Place the canola oil in a cast-iron skillet and cook over medium-high heat until the oil just starts to shimmer. Add the ginger and garlic and cook for about 2 minutes, or until they start to brown.

2. Raise the heat to high and add the pork. Cook for 5 minutes, or until the pork starts to form a light crust. Push the meat to one side of the pan and add the eggs. Scramble with a fork until the eggs are cooked through, roughly 2 minutes.

3. Add the carrots, rice, scallions, and peas and stir to incorporate. Add the soy sauce, rice vinegar, fish sauce, and sesame oil and cook for 5 minutes while stirring constantly.

Tip: Fish sauce has been gaining in popularity over the past several years, and for good reason. If you've been searching for that perfect umami flavor, fish sauce is akin to striking gold. Just be careful not to overdo it. A good rule of thumb: add just enough fish sauce that you can vaguely smell it.

Variation:

If you'd prefer your eggs on top of the fried rice, rather than within it, simply skip that step and top each serving with poached or fried eggs.

MAPLE-BACON STICKY BUNS

Makes 6 Servings   Active Time: 25 Minutes   Total Time: 1½ Hours

---

All-purpose flour, for dusting

1 (26.4 oz.) package of frozen biscuits

4 tablespoons butter, softened

¼ cup maple syrup

¾ cup light brown sugar, firmly packed

¼ pound bacon, cooked and chopped

Confectioners' sugar, for serving

1. Preheat the oven to 375°F. Lightly dust a work surface with flour and spread the frozen biscuit dough out in rows of 4 biscuits each. Cover with a dishcloth and let sit for about 30 minutes until the dough is thawed but still cool.

2. Sprinkle flour over the top of the biscuit dough, fold the dough in half, and then press it out to form a large rectangle (approximately 10 x 12 inches). Spread the softened butter over the dough.

3. In a bowl, combine the maple syrup with the brown sugar. Spread the mixture on the over the buttered dough and then sprinkle the bacon on top.

4. Starting with a long end, roll the dough up and cut into 1-inch slices. Line a Bundt pan with parchment paper and place the slices along the bottom of the pan, making sure that the sides with the swirl are facing up. Place in the oven and bake for about 35 minutes, until the rolls are cooked through. Remove from the oven and allow to cool before dusting with confectioners' sugar and serving.

Christmas

Christmas is a time to take a step back and reflect on the bountiful gifts and wonderful people one has in his or her life. Such a perspective is easily accessed after a glass of the Get Figgy With It. A light, colorful, flavorful spread of Cashew Milk and Mung Bean Porridge and Beet and Goat Cheese Quiche will have all that warmth in your heart ready to boil over, while also keeping you from getting too full to enjoy the evening's feast. Once you get through this, pop in your favorite holiday movie and enjoy a slice of Orange Cake while you wait for the roast in the oven to be ready.

Get Figgy With It

Virgin Mimosa

Cashew Milk and
Mung Bean Porridge

Beet and Goat Cheese Quiche

Orange Cake

GET FIGGY WITH IT

Makes 4 to 6 Servings

1 (750 ml) bottle of dry red wine

1 cup fresh raspberries

2 or 3 figs, cut into bite-sized pieces and frozen

1 cup fig juice

½ cup pomegranate juice

1 cup seltzer

Sprigs of thyme, for garnish

1. Combine all ingredients, except the seltzer, in a large pitcher. Cover and refrigerate for at least 4 hours.

2. Add ice and seltzer. Stir and garnish each glass with a sprig of thyme before serving.

VIRGIN MIMOSA

1 part orange juice

1 part Sprite

1 orange slice, for garnish

Fill your champagne flute halfway with orange juice. Top off with Sprite, stir, and garnish with the slice of orange.

Variation:

Sprite not your thing? Try it with ginger ale instead!

CASHEW MILK AND MUNG BEAN PORRIDGE

Makes 6 Servings   Active Time: 15 Minutes
Total Time: 5½ Hours

1 cup mung beans, washed

5 cups cashew milk, plus more as needed

1 cinnamon stick

3-inch piece of ginger, peeled and smashed

1 cup light brown sugar

Pinch of salt

½ cup white rice

Black vinegar infused with dried red plums

Cashews, crushed, for garnish

1. Place the mung beans, cashew milk, cinnamon stick, ginger, brown sugar, and salt in a slow cooker. Cover and cook on high for 4½ hours.

2. Add the rice, reduce heat to low, and cook until soft, about 1 hour. If the porridge starts to look dry, stir in an additional cup of cashew milk.

3. Discard the cinnamon stick and the ginger. Ladle the porridge into bowls and add more cashew milk if needed. Drizzle infused vinegar on top, garnish with cashews, and serve.

Note: *Dried red plums and black vinegar are specialty items that you might have to order online if you do not live near an Asian specialty market. To infuse vinegar, place 1 to 2 cups of black vinegar and 6 to 8 dried red plums in a jar with a tight-fitting lid. Place in the cabinet for a minimum of 2 days.*

For a quicker infusion process, place 3 cups of black vinegar and 6 to 8 dried red plums in a small saucepan and cook over the lowest available heat setting until the vinegar has reduced by a third. Transfer to the refrigerator and chill for 2 to 3 hours.

BEET AND GOAT CHEESE QUICHE

Makes 6 to 8 Servings   Active Time: 45 Minutes   Total Time: 2 Hours

1 Flaky Pastry Crust (see page 28)

4 or 5 red or golden beets (or a combination), peeled and thinly sliced

2 tablespoons yellow onions, minced

1 teaspoon olive oil

1½ cups whole milk

2 teaspoons dried thyme

2 garlic cloves, pressed

6 eggs, beaten

4 oz. goat cheese, chopped

1. Preheat the oven to 400°F and place the crust in a greased 9" pie plate.

2. Put the beets and onions in a pouch of aluminum foil. Drizzle with olive oil and close securely. Put the pouch in the oven and roast the beets and onions for about 20 minutes until soft, checking after 10 to 15 minutes. Remove pouch from oven and set aside while you prep the other ingredients.

3. Add the milk, thyme, and garlic to the beaten eggs and whisk to combine. Carefully open the pouch of beets and onions and distribute over the crust. Pour the egg mixture over this, and dot with pieces of the goat cheese.

4. Cover the quiche with foil and bake for 40 minutes. Remove foil and continue to bake for another 10 to 15 minutes or until the quiche is golden brown and the eggs are set. A knife inserted in the center should come out clean. Remove from oven and allow to sit for about 30 minutes before slicing and serving.

ORANGE CAKE

Makes 6 to 8 Servings   Active Time: 40 Minutes   Total Time: 1½ Hours

¾ cup sugar

Zest of 2 oranges

8 tablespoons (1 stick) butter, cut into small pieces

3 eggs

1½ cups all-purpose flour

1 teaspoon baking powder

½ cup fresh orange juice

1. Preheat the oven to 350°F and put a cast-iron skillet in the oven. In a large bowl, combine the sugar and orange zest. Add the butter and beat until the mixture is light and fluffy. Add the eggs one at a time, stirring to combine thoroughly after each addition.

2. Combine the flour and baking powder. Alternately add the flour mixture and the orange juice to the butter-and-sugar mixture and stir until thoroughly combined.

3. Remove the skillet from the oven using pot holders or oven mitts and pour the batter into it. Put the skillet in the oven and bake for about 30 to 35 minutes, until the top is golden, the cake springs to the touch, and a toothpick inserted in the center comes out clean. Remove from the oven, let cool, and cut into wedges.

Week 52

Make sure you get a jump-start on the Overnight Pomegranate Freekeh and Oats. It's easy, but the oats need 2 days in the refrigerator to become tender and soak up all the delicious flavor. Affogato is Italian for "drowned," and the level of deliciousness of this desert is certain to keep any negative thoughts below the surface.

Gin Pom Pom

Overnight Pomegranate Freekeh and Oats

Chicken and Artichoke Pot Pie

Affogato

GIN POM POM

6 mint leaves

1 part gin

1 part pomegranate juice

Juice of 1 lime wedge

1 lime wheel, for garnish

1. Tear the mint leaves in half and place them in a cocktail shaker filled with ice. Add the gin, pomegranate juice, and lime juice and shake well.

2. Strain the resulting mixture into a rocks glass filled with ice and garnish with a lime wheel.

OVERNIGHT POMEGRANATE FREEKEH AND OATS

Makes 4 to 6 Servings
Active Time: 5 Minutes
Total Time: 2 Days

1 cup freekeh

1 cup oats

2 cups pomegranate juice

½ cup unsweetened almond milk

½ cup nonfat Greek yogurt

¼ cup flaxseed

3 tablespoons honey

½ teaspoon kosher salt

1. Mix all of the ingredients together in a jar and place in the refrigerator.

2. After the first day, remove from the refrigerator and stir. Place back in refrigerator for 1 more day.

CHICKEN AND ARTICHOKE POT PIE

Makes 4 to 6 Servings   Active Time: 45 Minutes   Total Time: 1½ Hours

2 Flaky Pastry Crusts
(see page 28)

2 tablespoons olive oil from the jar
of artichoke hearts

½ yellow onion, diced

1 garlic clove, chopped

1 (6 oz.) jar of quartered,
marinated artichoke hearts,
drained and chopped

½ teaspoon oregano

½ teaspoon red pepper flakes
(optional)

2 tablespoons butter, cut into
small pieces

2 tablespoons flour

1¼ cups milk, at room
temperature

Salt and pepper, to taste

1½ cups cooked chicken, cut into
bite-sized pieces

1 cup frozen peas

1 tablespoon half-and-half

1. Preheat the oven to 350°F and place one of the crusts in a greased 9"
   pie plate. In a small skillet, heat the oil from the artichoke hearts. Add
   the onion and garlic and cook, while stirring, for about 2 minutes. Add
   the artichoke hearts, oregano, and, if desired, red pepper flakes. Reduce
   the heat to low, cover, and cook, while stirring occasionally, until the
   vegetables soften and caramelize, about 5 minutes. Pour the mixture
   into the crust in the pie plate and set aside.

2. In another skillet, melt the butter over medium heat. Sprinkle the flour
   over it and stir quickly yet gently to blend. Reduce the heat slightly so
   the butter doesn't burn. Stir until the butter and flour form a paste. Add
   just a little of the warm milk and stir constantly to blend it in. Add the
   rest of the milk in small increments, stirring after each addition. When
   all of the milk has been incorporated, season with salt and pepper and
   cook, while stirring, for 5 minutes, until the sauce thickens.

3. Pour the sauce over the filling in the crust. Add the chicken and peas,
   place the other crust on top, push down slightly to secure, and cut 3
   or 4 slits in the middle. Brush the crust with the half-and-half. Put the
   pot pie in the oven and bake for 30 to 40 minutes, until the crust is
   browned and the filling is bubbly. Allow to cool slightly before serving.

AFFOGATO

Makes 5 Servings   Active Time: 5 Minutes
Total Time: 5 Minutes

1 pint vanilla ice cream

5 tablespoons Frangelico, Kahlúa, or Sambuca

Nutmeg, grated

1½ cups brewed espresso or very strong coffee

Chocolate shavings, for garnish (optional)

Whipped cream, for topping (optional)

1. Scoop ice cream into five small glasses. Pour 1 tablespoon of preferred liqueur over each scoop. Dust each scoop with the grated nutmeg.

2. Pour the espresso or coffee over the ice cream. Top with chocolate shavings and whipped cream, if desired.

METRIC CONVERSION CHART

U.S. Measurement	Approximate Metric Liquid Measurement	Approximate Metric Dry Measurement
1 teaspoon	5 mL	—
1 tablespoon or ½ ounce	15 mL	14 g
1 ounce or ⅛ cup	30 mL	29 g
¼ cup or 2 ounces	60 mL	57 g
⅓ cup	80 mL	—
½ cup or 4 ounces	120 mL	113 g
⅔ cup	160 mL	—
¾ cup or 6 ounces	180 mL	—
1 cup or 8 ounces or ½ pint	240 mL	227 g
1½ cups or 12 ounces	350 mL	—
2 cups or 1 pint or 16 ounces	475 mL	454 g
3 cups or 1½ pints	700 mL	—
4 cups or 2 pints or 1 quart	950 mL	—

Indexes

Alcoholic Drinks

While the cocktail selections are tailored to fit both the season and the other dishes on the menu, we do understand that there will be times when you want to take a different tack. Should you find yourself wishing there was something else, either because of a hankering for, or an aversion to, a particular spirit, we've made it easy to find what you're looking for.

Gin

Alabama Slammer, 329

Bright Ruby, 293

Christmas Cocoa, 85

Gin Pom Pom, 429

Gin Waterfall, 149

Salty Mutt, 129

Off the Beaten Path

Black Velvet
(beer and Champagne), 361

Cider 75
(apple brandy and hard cider), 381

Classic Michelada (beer), 163

Lemon Cooler (beer), 123

Pumpkin Pie Tea Latte
(Irish cream), 345

Snowball (advocaat), 91

Stout 'N' Cider
(beer and hard cider), 115

Rum

Caribbean Cranberry Twist, 323

Cool Summer, 221

Cuban Coffee, 47

Hot Buttered Rum, 387

Roses for Alex, 169

Spice Cake, 109

Tequila

Bloody Maria Express, 367

Dark Wings, 417

Elderflower Margarita, 157

Lavender Margarita, 201

Maple Margarita, 411

Paloma Plus, 194

Tequila Sparkler, 275

Tequila Sunrise, 337

Watermelon Margarita, 251

Vodka

Bloody Mary, 229

Blue Fireflies, 207

Borrowed Thyme, 59

Capescrew, 237

Creamsicle, 299

Hairy Navel, 71

Liquid Apple Pie, 393

Mocha Mocha Mocha, 65

Peach Tree Iced Tea, 269

Sage Advice, 103

Screwdriver, 245

Sea Breeze, 257

Vineyard Splash, 187

Vodka Sunrise, 263

Whiskey

Bourbon Sweet Tea, 315

Brown Derby, 179

Ice Age, 143

Irish Coffee, 115

Irish Rose, 375

Maple Creamer, 53

Old Fashioned, 213

Whalen Smash, 287

Wine

Apple & Spice, 405

Blackened Pear, 355

Fall Fruit Fiesta, 399

French 75, 39

Get Figgy With It, 423

Kombucha Sangria, 149

Mimosa, 97

Mixed Bag, 195

Orange You Pretty, 169

Peachy Keen, 299

Plumdemonium, 77

Prosecco Soup, 39

Raspberry Fizz, 307

Stars & Stripes, 237

Sweet Peach, 281

Unlikely Allies, 137

30 Minutes or Fewer

We've done our best to make sure you can count on having plenty of delicious offerings on hand in every menu. But we also know what can happen to the best-laid plans. Maybe you take a misstep with one dish and you need to sub in something else, or a friend or a family member decides to bring someone along unannounced and you need something extra to ensure that everyone gets enough. If either instance occurs, you can whip up one of these delicious dishes and keep your reputation intact.

Salads, Sides, & Mains

Avocado and Goat Cheese Toast, 324

Bacon Deviled Eggs, 72

Baked Brie Two Ways, 406

Bananas Foster French Toast, 145

Bite-Sized Zucchini Pizzas, 324

Black Bean Hummus, 300

Breakfast Tacos, 283

Broccoli Salad, 222

Bruschetta, 131

Caprese Salad, 247

Chilled Honeydew Melon Soup with Crispy Prosciutto di Parma, 246

Corn Fritters, 316

Fast Pho, 310

Fennel Seed Yogurt, 317

Fontina Jalapeño Hush Puppies, 60

Goat Cheese and Brussels Sprouts Slaw, 239

Grilled Asparagus Spears, 172

Grilled Beets and Toasted Sunflower Seeds Salad, 158

Grilled Fruit and Feta Salad, 208

Grilled Mexican Street Corn, 165

Grilled Peach Salad, 288

Grilled Romaine Salad, 214

Grilled Zucchini Nachos, 270

Guacamole, 60

Herb-Roasted Almonds, 130

Huevos Rancheros, 63

Hummus, 347

Mint-Cilantro Chutney, 309

Peanut Butter and Bacon Oats, 93

Peanut Butter and Banana Yogurt Bowl, 231

Salmon with Chinese Eggplants, 81

Steak and Pearl Onion Frittata, 183

Strawberry-Mint Salad, 239

Tzatziki, 253

Watermelon and Goat Cheese Salad, 276

Desserts

Affogato, 433

Chilled Blueberry and Yogurt Soup, 266

Chocolate, Peanut Butter, and Banana Milkshake, 313

Cinnamon Twists with Caramel Dipping Sauce, 94

Classic Summer Fruit Salad, 255

Classic Vanilla Milkshake, 217

Honey-Roasted Figs, 89

Lemon Curd, 112

Light Strawberry-Blueberry Trifle, 243

Tropical Fruit Salad, 304

Index

Recipes featured in the Essential Recipes chapter and on the individual menus are in italics